WOOSIE

WOOSIE

MY AUTOBIOGRAPHY

IAN WOOSNAM
with EDWARD GRIFFITHS

CollinsWillow
An Imprint of HarperCollinsPublishers

To Glen, Daniel, Rebecca and Ami,
and to Mum and Dad.

First published in 2002 by CollinsWillow
an imprint of HarperCollins*Publishers*, London

First published in paperback in 2003

© Ian Woosnam 2002, 2003

1 3 5 7 9 8 6 4 2

A CIP catalogue record for this book is
available from the British Library

ISBN 0 00 714443 1

Typeset by Palimpsest Book Production Limited,
Polmont, Stirlingshire
Printed and bound in Great Britain by Clays Ltd, St Ives plc

The HarperCollins website address is
www.**fire**and**water**.com

Photographic acknowledgments

All photographs courtesy of Ian Woosnam with the exception
of the following: **Allsport** 5(tl & tr), 6(m & bl), 7(ml, mr & bl),
8(t), 10(bl), 11, 12(tl), 13(m & br), 14(tl), 15; **Colorsport** 3(bl),
6(br), 16(t & b); **Empics** 3(tl), 13(t), 14(tr, bl & br); **Empics/
Alpha** 3(br), 5(b); **Getty Images** 16(mr); **Matthew Harris**
4(m & b), 7(br), 8(b), 9, 12(tr, m & b); **Hobbs Golf Collection**
3(m), 6(t); **Phil Sheldon** 7(t), 16(ml); **Nick Walker** 13(bl).

Contents

Acknowledgments

So many people have helped me in so many ways over the past 44 years that I could fill another book with thanks.

It started with my parents, and the immense debt that I owe to them for the advice, help and love is one that I repay to my own children. Above all, my mother and father taught me the true value of hard work, being brave and never giving up.

Once I started playing golf, I was able to develop my game in the solid structure of junior golf in Shropshire, selflessly maintained by so many men motivated only by a love of the game. To all those people who ran competitions and organised the squads, particularly Bernard Thomas and Geoff Roberts, thank you.

On the professional tour, D J Russell and Peter Baker have been nothing less than constant friends through the years, and I am also grateful to my various coaches – Bob Torrance, Bill Ferguson, Gavin

Christie and Pete Cowen – for their efforts.

Phil Morbey, or just 'Wobbly', obviously played a huge role in my career, as my caddie and great friend for 14 years. We walked many miles together, and enjoyed many great times.

I am privileged to enjoy the support and companionship of many good friends, but it is virtually impossible to mention them all here. They know who they are, and I am thankful.

I have also been fortunate to have worked with so many top-quality people from the International Management Group, managing my business issues, arranging my schedule, booking all my travel and hotels, securing and managing endorsements and sponsorships, and generally enabling me to focus on the actual golf.

David Barlow became a close friend through seven years with me, and he remains someone whom I trust completely. It was a blow when he was transferred to South Africa, but Andrew Hampel stepped in and proved a lively, bright, gifted source of support.

Adrian Mitchell has managed my career effectively in the past few years, providing a steady hand to help me through some tough times and assisting me through my recent revival.

Jonathan Dudman and Donna Cooksley, my financial advisors at IMG, have always been totally professional and reliable.

In the IMG office, Tracey Chapman thrived for

many years as my secretary, managing to resolve all kinds of situations and always being friendly at the other end of a telephone. She became a friend of the family and helped me in literally thousands of ways. Recently, Bridget Dunn has filled this role with distinction.

In terms of preparing this book, I would like to thank Edward Griffiths for his help in finding the words, Adrian Mitchell for his help in the exhaustive checking and proof-reading process and the staff at publishers HarperCollins for their patience and assistance.

I am also extremely pleased, and flattered, that Gary Player agreed to write the Foreword. He has been an inspiration to me for as long as I can remember.

Finally, and above all, I would like to thank my wife, Glen, for her endless love and support, and my children, Daniel, Rebecca and Ami, for accepting my long absences and making me so proud.

This book reflects upon the first 25 years of my professional golf career, and I look forward to providing another volume in 2027!

Ian Woosnam
Jersey, May 2002

Foreword

by GARY PLAYER

Ian Woosnam and I obviously have something in common: we're both little guys playing a professional game that is increasingly dominated by big men. For this reason, above all, I was extremely pleased when Woosie asked me to write this foreword.

The fact is, we send a message of hope and encouragement to all those small of stature that you can make it if you work hard and dedicate yourself. Remember, the harder you practise, the luckier you get.

I think the fact that Woosie and I have faced, and overcome, many of the same challenges has created a strong mutual respect. As small guys in golf, it's important we stick together!

There is no doubt in my mind that, pound for pound, Ian has been one of the finest players ever to take up the game. I clearly recall the morning in 1987, a couple of days before the Million Dollar Challenge, played on the testing Gary Player Country Club at Sun

City, South Africa, when Ian gave a clinic. He started with his wedge and ran right through his bag to the driver, and every shot was struck with perfection.

Everyone watching was blown away by this exhibition, and it was no surprise that Woosie went on to win the title at the end of the week. He was not just long, but he was accurate; and he showed a great touch around the green. It gave me a huge thrill.

Four years later, I was standing with Mark McCormack behind the 18th green at Augusta National as the 1991 Masters came down to the wire. Ian was strongly in contention, and I recall telling Mark that Woosie would hit his drive way left, clearing all the trouble and taking an unusual but smart route to the green.

That's exactly what he did. It was intelligent golf, and I was delighted when he holed that putt on the 18th and won The Masters and a Major championship that his talent and dedication richly deserved.

And I still maintain that, if he had had 14 clubs in his bag on the last day of The Open Championship at Lytham in 2001, he might have gone on to win a second Major title. That was sadly not to be, but the sporting way he accepted his misfortune served to enhance his outstanding reputation in the professional game.

Over the past 26 years, Ian has given such great pleasure to literally millions of people all around the world. There are many pros who choose to stay on their home tour, whether it's in the United States or Europe, but I really appreciate the guys who are prepared to play all over the globe and act as ambassadors for the game.

They say dynamite comes in small packages; well, Woosie has been dynamite on golf courses around the world during the past two decades – and the game of golf will always be grateful.

Introduction

At the start, it was a journey into the unknown. I had no idea what to expect, no clue as to how it would affect my life. My mother and father were taking the family to a golf course for the first time to play our first ever round. My older brother and sister thought it was all very strange. Aged seven, I tagged along for the ride.

Golf?

Hardly anybody played golf in our Shropshire village which straddled the border between England and Wales. It was a middle-class sport, and we were dairy farmers, anything but middle class. None of this mattered to my father, who had decided we were all going to take up the game and, on a bright, bracing Wednesday in the spring of 1965, we piled into the car and set off.

Even now, years later, I can close my eyes and recall the occasion vividly. It was market day in Oswestry, and we spent most of the morning in the town, successfully selling a couple of calves. We were, therefore, in high spirits as we left the hustle and bustle and headed eagerly down the Welshpool road.

Harold Woosnam, my father, is not and never has been a man who says much when there is not much to say, but he was excited about this adventure and, as we drove, he happily shared his newfound enthusiasm for golf with all of us. He recalled how he had stopped playing amateur football for the local club at the age of 30, and how he had spent the next five years focusing all his energy on the farm.

However, he explained, he had missed his involvement in sport and, one day, he noticed an advertisement in the local newspaper promoting a special exhibition match to be played at the Oswestry Golf Club. Harry Weetman, the well-known 1951 Ryder Cup player, was playing against Ken Bousfield and Max Faulkner. My father decided he would go to the club and watch.

He spoke, we listened. 'I was standing beside the fairway at the first,' my father said, 'and I watched Weetman hit a drive that seemed to keep soaring higher and higher before disappearing over the rise. It was fantastic. There and then, I decided we should all play this game. The great thing about golf is that we can play as individuals, and we can also play together as a family.'

Fair enough, we thought. We would give it a go.

We travelled through the outskirts of Oswestry,

past neat rows of grey stone cottages and then followed the winding road through a deep green patchwork of fields. After 15 minutes or so, we arrived in the village of Pant, turned right at Briggs Lane and followed a steep and winding lane up the hill towards Llanymynech Golf Club.

Some of his former team-mates from the football club had suggested to my father that this unpretentious, and yet amazingly beautiful, golf club would be the most accommodating place for the Woosnam family to start learning the game.

We arrived at the top of the hill and found that we were looking at amazing views all around us. There was a small car park beside the simple clubhouse; and, just after two o'clock on a Wednesday afternoon, the place was almost deserted.

I remember getting out of the car and looking around, sucking the gusting wind deep into my lungs and gazing across the Vale of Shropshire away to the south and the mist-clad, brooding mountains that stretched westwards into mid-Wales.

Llanymynech's fairways crowned the highest point for miles around and the golf course appeared at once part of this world and yet somehow removed from it. Every now and then, the sound of a cow mooing, or a car driving past, or even a raised voice would rise from below, but nothing ever really disturbed the calm.

So there we were, this enthusiastic family of five

sharing a set of second-hand clubs, heading towards the first tee.

I don't recall much of what happened next. My father led the way round the 18 holes, telling us how to stand and where to hit. My mother struck the ball surprisingly well. According to my parents, their seven-year-old son saw every drive as an opportunity to whack the cover off the ball. Not much has changed since then.

After playing our tee-shots at the par-four fourth, we strolled across the border from Wales, and then completed the fourth and played the fifth and sixth holes on English soil. We only crossed back into Wales as we approached the seventh tee. Llanymynech famously includes three holes in England, and 15 in Wales, but the club is affiliated to the English Golf Union because, according to the locals, the subscription to the EGU is cheaper than that required by the Welsh Golf Union.

The course was far from easy, challenging us to play from all sorts of stances in an ever-changing wind, but our experience was constantly enriched by the views. And, during this first round, I am sure we would have paused on the 12th tee and peered over Offa's Dyke, a cliff-like 30-foot drop that was once part of the wall built by the 8th century Anglo-Saxon king to repel the Welsh. It is said that, on a clear day, no fewer than seven of the old Shire counties can be seen from the tee at the 12th.

When we were done, we made our way to the clubhouse and found a table for five in the bar. I was given a packet of crisps and a glass of lemonade, and sat quietly, looking out of the window every once in a while, across the fields, across my heartland.

That was then, and this is now.

Thirty-seven years have passed and, although the glass of lemonade has probably become a pint of bitter, not much else has changed. At least, I hope not too much has changed. Llanymynech still represents something very important in my life.

The clubhouse has been enlarged and developed, the car park is now twice the size and Andy Griffiths, one of my close friends and a regular playing partner in my youth, is now the club professional. And yet the wind still gets up most days, the view from the 12th tee is still as magnificent as ever, and life goes gently on.

Our family has established a strong association with the club since that first tentative round back in 1965. My mother was Lady Captain in 1971, and my father became Club Captain in 1973: both their photographs now hang in the clubhouse. The name 'Woosnam' can be found here and there on the honours boards that record winners of various competitions held down the years and, for my part, I am proud to hold the course record: a 65 carded during the club's 50th anniversary celebrations in 1983.

Whenever I get the chance to visit the Llanymynech

Golf Club now, it feels the same as it has always felt. It doesn't seem to matter how many golf tournaments I have won or how much money I have earned, or how many Ryder Cups I have played or that I won the US Masters; and it doesn't make any difference that my present car eases up the hill more smoothly than our old car did back in 1965. Hopefully, nothing is changed by the fact that my photograph now hangs in the dining room, alongside a plaque with an inscription reading 'We are proud of Ian.'

I would like to think that, to all intents and purposes, I'm still just a local lad popping in for a drink, the same individual who first arrived at the club as an excited seven-year-old. So I have made a living by playing golf around the world. That doesn't change the way I was fetched up, and doesn't affect me as a person.

I was small for my age back then, and I am still short for my age now, standing just over 5'4" tall. Being short made me feel an underdog when I was a boy, and I still have a sense that I need to work twice as hard to beat the odds and succeed.

Then as now, I tend to be straightforward by nature, telling it as I see it, taking people as I find them, getting into a spot of trouble every once in a while, sometimes letting my emotions get the better of me, occasionally losing my temper but generally taking life as it comes. I have always enjoyed a drink with my friends, and I am almost always up for a party and a good time.

What I do know is that I was happy as a boy, and I am happy now, but much has happened in the 37 years since I took up golf. This book tells the story of those 37 years, recalling how a farmer's boy grew up to become the No.1 golfer in the world.

This is the account of a journey that began that bright spring day at Llanymynech Golf Club, a journey that has taken me around the world more times than I can recall, a journey that has made my wildest dreams come true. It is a journey through many happy days in golf, and a few sad days, in the company of selfless parents, a loving wife, three fine children and many great friends.

And it is a journey that will also end at Llanymynech Golf Club because, in spirit at least, I have never been away.

CHAPTER ONE

Out of the Cowshed

'So when can we go back, Dad?'

'Maybe Sunday, maybe next month, we'll see.'

Not for the first time, I stared out of the car window and wished the golf club was not so far from our home, and wondered why there was always so much work to be done on the farm. Our first family trip to Llanymynech had been a complete success. I had enjoyed myself, and was desperate to play again.

My father had taken to the game as well, but he seemed satisfied to play only once a month, typically a matchplay contest against my mother with a cup of tea for the winner.

We lived in New House Farm, on the outskirts of St Martins, a village six miles north of Oswestry. The Lightwoods were the only other family in the village who showed any remote interest in golf, a fact that meant the rest of our community reacted to news of our new hobby as though the Woosnams had taken up ballet.

9

Golf was something new in our lives, but I loved it. From the beginning, I enjoyed nothing more than whacking a golf ball straight down the fairway. There was something magical about the noise and the feeling of impact through the club. In fact, I even got some pleasure on the frequent occasions when I hooked a ball into the bushes or sliced it onto the next fairway. Aside from one stale period during the late 1990s, that thrill has never left me. There are few sweeter sensations than standing on the tee and hitting the ball perfectly.

'So when can we go back, Dad?'

I nagged and nagged and, within a few months, had cajoled my parents into a steady routine. Each Sunday morning, we would milk the cows on our farm as quickly as possible, and drive 14 miles cross country to play a full round at Llanymynech. And there would often be a bonus during the long summer holidays, when we could finish our chores on the farm by half past five on a Wednesday afternoon and, with a bit of luck, arrive at the club in time to race through 18 holes before sunset.

Most Sunday afternoons and the odd Wednesday evening in summer: this was the sum of my opportunities to play golf during my early years. It didn't seem very much to an impatient youngster, but it still represented a considerable sacrifice for my parents. Through to my mid-teens, golf was never easily accessible for me but, with hindsight, this was perhaps not such a bad thing. It meant I never took the game for granted. Any chance to get on the course always felt like a treat, always felt special.

Initially we all played from one set of second-hand, hickory shafted clubs that my father had bought in town, but it was not long before I was presented with a club of my very own. On my eighth birthday, I became the proud owner of a fine weathered old three-wood, cut down at the grip to my size. Club selection was not a problem. I used my wood off the tee, from the fairways or in the rough, and I used it for chipping out of bunkers and, of course, for putting on the greens.

Life became more complicated a couple of years later when my parents introduced me to irons, buying me a three, five, seven and nine, all second-hand and cut down to size. By the time I was given a putter of my own, I felt as if I was Gary Player!

The 'cack-handed' grip I used was common among young golfers at the time and, although it may have looked awkward, I always felt reasonably comfortable playing with my left hand gripping the club below my right hand. It seemed to make my swing feel more solid and compact, and it forced me to turn my wrists on the backswing, which was important, even if such technical considerations meant absolutely nothing to me at the time. I was just another mischievous lad having fun, just another face hanging around the first tee at a rural

11

golf club, trying to steer clear of the members, trying
to keep out of trouble. And the extent of my young
ambition was not to achieve the perfect swing . . .
no, it was simply to drive the ball further than my
brother Keith, who was four years older and four
years stronger.

To me, distance was always important. Chipping
and putting was fine, but powering the ball out of
sight off the tee or from the fairway gave me by far
the most pleasure. I tended to measure my achievements in yards rather than strokes.

This approach to the game was reflected in the fact
that the long par-five ninth hole at Llanymynech soon
began to assume a huge significance. There was a 15-
yard hollow stretching across the fairway around 200
yards from the yellow tee, and it became my single
greatest ambition, in fact my obsession, to drive the
ball past this hollow and on to the open fairway
beyond. School work, the moon landings, England's
painful 3–2 defeat against West Germany in the 1970
World Cup: nothing mattered as much as hitting my
drive past the hollow at the ninth.

When I was ten, then when I was eleven, for round
after round, I would wind myself up on the ninth tee
and hit the ball as hard as I could, only for my drive
to end up in the hollow. This hazard started to seem
like nothing less than the threshold of adulthood.

'Come on, Woosie! You can do it! Come on!'

'OK, Woos, it's your hole.'

'Big one, Woosie!'

In those days, my mates and I played amid a never-ending exchange of banter, and friends like Andy Griffiths and his brother, Basil, and Peter Martin would take merciless delight in winding me up whenever we approached the ninth tee. I obliged by becoming increasingly uptight until, one glorious afternoon in the autumn of 1970, my drive finally sailed over the hollow.

My father had drummed into me from an early age that the only way to being the best at anything is to work much harder than anyone else. There were no short cuts. And he would not tolerate any moaning or whining in his house. If I couldn't get something right, whether it was homework or driving past the hollow at the ninth, he would tell me: 'Just get out there and get on with it, Ian.' That was that.

There was equally no point complaining about not being able to play golf at Llanymynech as often as I wanted, so I learned to improvise and devise various forms of practice around the farm. At least I had plenty of land at my disposal; it would have been much worse if we lived in town with a small garden.

I used to take my clubs out into those fields that looked so green and beautiful from a distance, but were invariably wet and muddy; and I happily hacked up and down the hills, bashing my ball from one sodden, clogging lump of Shropshire soil onto the next sodden, clogging lump of Shropshire soil. This mild discomfort experienced during my youth would prove valuable later in life. I have never been scared of hitting the ball out of deep rough, perhaps because the 'rough' in the fields around our farm was far more daunting than anything manufactured on any tricked-up course hosting a major tournament.

When the weather was bad, and the England-Wales border is hardly the Riviera, I was forced indoors and a basic, round vanity mirror became my most valuable piece of equipment. I used to concentrate particularly on keeping my head perfectly still throughout my swing, so I devised a straightforward drill where I would assume the address position and place the vanity mirror on the floor just beyond the club head. As I practised my swing, I would be able to watch my head in the mirror. It was simple, but it worked and I was allowed to practise in my bedroom, in the living room, anywhere in the house where I could swing the club without knocking a chunk out of the wall.

The third area of my home-made practice facilities was one of the cowsheds, tucked away among the outbuildings adjacent to my parents' farmhouse. With a concrete floor and a few railings to the left, it was the most basic of sheds but it offered shelter from poor weather and it became my indoor driving range. Once he had been persuaded this space was not vital to the smooth running of the farm, my father helped me by putting a coconut mat inside the entrance. We then cobbled together a net by stitching some sacks together with baling twine, and we hung this at the far end of the shed. I was ready to start hitting.

After a while I decided I needed a specific target, so I suspended a piece of rope from the ceiling of the shed and then found the lid of an old biscuit tin, perhaps a foot square. I attached this to the rope and, by pulling up or lowering the rope, was able to adjust the height of the hanging tin lid. I hoisted it high when I was using a nine-iron, and set it much lower when I was hitting the driver. In my youth, the recognisable sound of perfection became the satisfying clunk of a golf ball striking a biscuit tin.

The reward for these long hours of target shooting in the cowshed has been a deep-seated confidence of being able to hit the ball through the narrowest of gaps. There have been many key moments in professional tournaments when I have been stuck among trees or considering a tight line between hazards, and I have blurred my eyes, visualising the old biscuit tin hanging in the cowshed and have managed to hit the target.

It was usually pretty cold and damp in that shed and, most of the time, it didn't smell too wonderful either, especially if the cows had just been in there, but I was brought up in Shropshire – and, in those days, youngsters in Shropshire learned to make the best of their circumstances. They understood they wouldn't get far in their lives without a bit of guts and graft. The county was frontier country, on the border between Wales and England, and Shropshire people always seemed full of spirit and enthusiasm, hard working and straight to the point. People had come to Shropshire from northern England, from Wales, from all corners of the country, and they brought a firm will to stake their claim for prosperity, a determination to achieve their goals and say their piece, and a willingness to be brash, even a bit forceful, whenever it was necessary.

That was life. In this county on the edge of England, there was always an element of living on the edge. Lads were not slow to have a pint or laugh out loud, or to raise their fists.

St Martins was a typical Shropshire village, established along a main road with a primary school, a secondary school, a working-men's club, a surgery, a church and a few shops. It had developed as a lively, unpretentious, sociable village of farmers and miners, at least until the Ifton mine was closed in 1972.

That was a difficult period for many people in the community, not least my friends, the Pugh family. As a teenager, I told a mate I was going to marry Glendryth Pugh; and I did.

First Terry Pugh, her father and my future father-in-law, was made redundant at the mine; then, when what seemed the entire village gathered to watch the spectacle of the cooling towers being brought to the ground by controlled explosions, a single brick flew out from the smoky rubble and struck Glen's brother Gareth in the thigh. He was rushed to hospital by ambulance.

The Pughs' final twist of fate was that Terry subsequently took a job as a foreman with a construction company and found himself included in the team given the task of levelling the site of the old mine. That left a hole in the landscape, and a hole in our village.

Many families were forced to leave our area, most of them travelling north to Wrexham in search of new jobs and a fresh start. We were generally unaffected in the farming sector, but there was a strange atmosphere of uncertainty and upheaval, a mood of hardship in the village that I still vividly recall.

My own childhood horizons hardly ever stretched beyond St Martins. The market town of Oswestry was barely ten minutes down the road, but we only went there for a special reason, like shopping in the high street or selling livestock. As for London, it may as well have been in a different world, and I didn't travel abroad until I was an 18-year-old starting out on the pro golf tour.

Even so, I never felt deprived. Quite apart from the powerful, comforting sense of community where you knew everybody in your village and everybody knew you, St Martins offered all the essential facilities and a few more enticing locations as well.

My friends and I used to walk past the Cross Keys

pub every day on the way to school, peering at the windows and wondering what kind of excitement had unfolded inside the night before, looking forward ever more eagerly to the day when we would be able to stroll up to the bar and place our orders with the barmaid.

Further up the road, the Ifton Miners Institute appeared as nothing less than a top-class entertainment complex, separated into three sections. The first was the dance hall, venue of the teenagers' disco where I first set eyes upon Glen; the middle section was the working-men's club barred to youngsters; and there was a snooker hall where, from the age of 11 onwards, I regularly played a frame or three with Pat Williams, and his brother Peter.

I was born on 2 March 1958 in a house called The Beeches. It stood two hundred yards from the River Dee, the border between England and Wales, so it is no exaggeration to say that Wales was barely a well struck two-iron away. That said, I was born on English soil. The fact of geography cannot be denied.

Both my older brother and sister had been born in hospital at the nearby village of Chirk but my mother wanted me to be born at home and, with the help of a mid-wife, I duly arrived, feet first, a breech birth. As my mother says, I 'hit the ground running.'

My hard-working parents combined the task of raising three children with the job of running the farm, almost with unfortunate consequences when I was only three months old. Although my recollection of the drama is not entirely clear, I am told that, one afternoon I was gurgling contentedly in my Silver Cross pram while my mother was helping my father on the farm. It started to rain and my mother thoughtfully pushed the pram under cover, setting it to rest just inside one of the cowsheds.

All seemed well, until the cows arrived. Scarcely two minutes later, my mother glanced back in horror to discover the pram on its side and her infant son lying in the mud, somewhere amid the feet of a restless and impatient herd, ready for milking. According to my mother, I survived because I happened to fall beside the quietest, calmest cow on the farm. At any rate, when I had been rescued, wiped down, cleaned up and placed back in the pram, my relieved parents simply got back to work.

It seemed to me my mother and father were always working hard, making the most of every hour in the day. I have never seen anyone work like them. I took it completely for granted back then, but now I look back in wonder and admiration.

Joan Woosnam, my mother, was a saint. She stacked bales of hay in the field, she herded the pedigree cows, she milked the cows, she cleaned the house, she put meals on the table, she took care of the three of us, and my brother Gareth, who was born ten years after me, and I just don't remember her resting.

My father, Harold Woosnam, also worked tirelessly, showing a meticulous attention to detail in everything he did. The easier option for dairy farmers was to keep a commercial herd but my father took enormous pride in his 40 pedigree cows, even though it meant each animal had to be looked after individually. We used to 'walk' them on a lead, and nurture them into prime condition and, when they were ready, we would then take them to agricultural shows in places like Crewe. I would often be given the task of leading a cow around the ring, and would share my father's pleasure when we managed to win a rosette.

Short in stature, determined by nature, my father was a fine boxer in his youth and once dreamed of turning professional. He got as far as appointing a manager, but his parents firmly disapproved of this career, and young Harold remained a farmer. In his disappointment, he made a promise that, if any of his children ever had ambitions to pursue a sporting career, he would be as supportive and totally positive as possible; and I am in a position to confirm he has proved as good as his word.

Both my parents considered themselves emphatically Welsh and, although we may have lived on the English side of the border, and even if I did support the England football team, there was never any doubt we were a Welsh family in Shropshire. My mother's parents came from Welshpool, where my grandfather served in the Welsh Guards before going to work on the railways, and my father's father farmed in the Newtown district, in mid-Wales, before joining the eastward migration in search of fertile land.

The Woosnam's purchased 77 acres at New House Farm, three miles outside the village of St Martins. My father worked for his own father on the farm and, in 1952, he married my mother and purchased an adjoining smallholding called The Beaches. In 1961, when I was three, it was agreed that my grandparents would retire and move to a small house nearby and that Harold, Joan and their three young kids – Keith, Julie and Ian – would move into New House Farm.

The pros and cons of living on a farm were clear. On the one hand, there was the space, the fresh air, working with animals and a general sense of wholesome, healthy living. I remember how there always seemed to be a tank of fresh milk standing just inside the house and how I used to drink gallons of the stuff, straight from the scoop. And the farm work gave us all healthy appetites: I would eat six Weetabix and a pint of milk for breakfast and, if I was at home, that would be followed by a cooked dinner at noon and another cooked dinner at five. Then there would be porridge or toast before bed, at nine in the evening. My mother says the family ate 21 loaves of bread each week, and five pounds of potatoes every meal.

Of course, in those days, most farmhouses didn't

have central heating. If you wanted a bath, you probably had to fetch some logs, put them on the open fire and heat the water to fill the tub; and if you were cold, you just went and sat by the Aga in the kitchen.

We all slept under mountains of blankets. I remember waking up in the morning and running my finger through the frost that had patterned the *inside* of my bedroom window. This was the life at the New House Farm, a happy and hearty life.

On the other hand, there were the endless hours of hard work and, on our farm, every member of the family was expected to play their part in getting the chores done, without complaint.

As children, we were occasionally asked to do something before we went to school in the morning, and were almost always given some kind of job when we got home. We would clean, and we would stack but most of the time we simply had to clean out the cowshed. Summer brought the most work: making bales of hay, carrying and stacking the bales, driving the tractor until sunset. It was a grind. A bale weighed 60lbs, and it required a major effort to spear one of them on the end of a large pitchfork and then propel it up to the top of the loft; and, of course, there was not just one bale to be stacked . . . in summer, there were often 5,000.

I didn't start milking cows until I was 13, but the tough part of that chore was not the actual milking. It was the non-negotiable, unremitting obligation of having to milk the cows at the same time of day, every day. There was no alternative. Someone always piped up and said there wasn't time to do that, or go there, or play golf, because we had to get home and milk the cows.

It was hard, and yet the never-ending lifting and carrying on the farm did mean I developed a level of upper body strength that I have managed to maintain ever since and that has unquestionably helped my golf. There are many conflicting views about what makes one player hit the ball further than the next, but I believe it is my strong shoulders and forearms that have helped me generate fast club head speed and consequently hit the ball long distances.

And I was desperately keen to be strong. If I had to be one of the smallest boys in the village (and there was not much I could do about that), I was determined not to be the weakest.

As time passed, certain incidents became enshrined in our family history, repeated with pride and relish, and these only served to enhance my prized reputation as a 'mighty mite'. For example, it was said that one day my father asked me to place a water trough on the tractor and drive it around to the next field. The story goes that I simply picked up the cast-iron trough and threw it into the field, over a six-foot hedge. It was probably a bit of an exaggeration, but it's a good story!

I suppose I should reflect upon the long hours

spent farming as a positive experience, an important dimension of my formative years, and, looking back, I appreciate the benefits. However, the truth is that, in those days, I hated the work. Every hour only increased my resolve that I would not get stuck in farming.

In a sense, professional golf became my escape route from a lifetime of having to milk the cows twice a day. I have huge respect for farmers, but it was not what I wanted to be. My brothers generally felt the same. Keith left the family farm when he was 16 and he still works as a central heating specialist in Wrexham; Gareth, ten years younger than me, has shared my great passion for golf. He has been a low-handicap player for many years and works as a green keeper at Oswestry Golf Club. Julie, my sister, also pursued a golf-related career, heading up the catering side at the Mile End Golf Club, just down the A5 from Oswestry. John Janicki, her son and my nephew, has grown up to be an excellent golfer, playing off a handicap of one or two.

In the end, with no children eager to work the land, my father decided to retire, and he sold the farm in 1989. I don't think he was disappointed. He and my mother brought us up firmly, teaching us not to ask but to wait and be offered, not to speak but to be asked, and they smothered us with love and support.

My formal education began at the Ifton Heath Primary School in St Martins, and my first day ended with a ripped blazer. Someone said something stupid and I reacted. We finished up in a brawl, and the general tone of my schooldays was established.

In due course, I progressed to St Martins Secondary Modern School, now called Rhyn Park School, and, as I recall, the first-year students were divided into three classes. There was 1A and 1B, and the rest of us were in 1R. I don't know why we weren't called 1C. It would have seemed more logical. I didn't think we were that thick, but we were known as 1R. My teachers might say 1R would be an accurate summary of my academic performance at school, and they might well be right. I was always far more interested in playing football and making sure I would not be pushed around in the playground.

A lad called Paul Sudelow became one of my closest friends. We were in the same class, we went fishing and we played in the same football team, and yet Paul and I ended up fighting each other what seemed like every day for five years. We brawled relentlessly: when we arrived at school, during breaks and on the way home, often with other schoolboys gathered around in a feverish circle, chanting our names. It was foolish but, from my point of view, there was no alternative. Other boys teased me because I was small and the only way to stop them was to show them that, although I was short, I was also tough.

Hard boys were respected in St Martins. I remember one day when a woman teacher was showing us foreign money in class, and somebody pocketed the notes while they were being passed around the desks. She got angry and demanded the culprit own up. We all knew exactly who had stolen the notes but this particular boy was a rough fighter, so nobody said anything. The result of this silence was that every boy in the class was caned, and every girl in the class was smacked with a slipper. There were a few mass beatings during my time at the secondary modern, but the lessons were obvious to me: tough guys were feared, tough guys did not get teased, tough guys survived.

Most of the boys got into scraps now and then, but I did start to earn a reputation as a fighter and, whenever someone wound me up, I almost felt obliged to take them on. That was how we grew up in Shropshire. When challenged, you fought back.

I scrapped my way through school, always sitting at the back of the class and invariably misbehaving. There was one day when I took my golf clubs to school because I was going to play a round at Llanymynech in the evening and my mates were going on and on at me to show them how to hit the ball. We were in an English lesson, and the teacher was battling to keep control when he made the fatal error of leaving a textbook in the staff room. He optimistically asked us to carry on with our work while he left the classroom for a few minutes.

'Come on, Woos, show us some golf.'

I looked up and smiled.

'Yeah, come on, Woosie! Man or mouse?'

I looked towards a window that opened on to the games field, and thought we couldn't possibly do that – no, not in the middle of a lesson. We were bad, but surely not that bad.

'Go on, Woos!'

I grinned broadly. Why not? What the hell!

In a mad moment , I grabbed my clubs and climbed out of the window, followed by the rest of my classmates. When the teacher returned, he found us hitting golf balls around the field. The bell went soon afterwards and that was that.

In the light of such carefree behaviour, I don't think anybody was particularly surprised when I failed all my examinations, always neglected my homework and eventually left school aged 16 without much credit and with no qualifications whatsoever.

One teacher did show some concern, calling me to one side towards the end of my last term at school.

'So, Ian,' he asked, 'what are you going to do?'

'I'm going to be a professional golfer,' I replied.

The teacher smiled as though he had heard that one before, before adding in solemn tones: 'OK, well, if you want my advice, I would get yourself along to the Farming Institute instead.'

My parents did not appear terribly concerned by the situation. In the first place, they knew nobody needed 'O' levels to work hard on the farm and, moreover, they had long recognised it was sport, not textbooks, that stirred my real commitment.

Golf and football were always important to me, but there were times when nothing mattered quite as much as boxing. Through the early 1970s, the undisputed highlight of our annual family holidays to the Butlins holiday camp in Pwllheli, north Wales was the chance to pull on gloves and step into the square ring.

We would arrive in what seemed this vast complex, full of the famous Butlins Redcoats, the camp organisers, and my father would take us straight down to the boxing hall where we would put our names on the entry list for age-group tournaments: under-14, under-12 etc.

I loved every minute of every bout. My mother would dress me in a white vest with white shorts, and I would throw myself into action against much taller boys, wheeling overhead right hooks at my opponents, head-down, bash, bash, bash.

The atmosphere was intense, and I was eager to win because the first prize in each tournament was free entry to Butlins the next time. I started to believe I had to win to make sure we would come back to the holiday camp, so there was no lack of motivation. One time, I was punching this lad, and he started crying, and his mother was crying and then my mother was crying as well. It wasn't my fault. I wanted to win, and I enjoyed winning.

On a few occasions, the crowd started throwing penny coins in the ring while I was fighting. It may have been Pwllheli, and not Las Vegas, but boxing made me feel on top of the world. Before long, the problem was that there were no kids in my age-group prepared to fight against me, so the instructor would get down on his knees and take me on. His name was Danny Doyle, but I found a way of getting in close and hitting him too. Mr Doyle liked me. One time, I heard him say I was 'ferocious'.

Butlins made me feel ten feet tall. Apart from the boxing, we also played table tennis and snooker. There was always something to do, some sport to play. It was the perfect holiday.

One morning, I was casually swimming in the main pool, and using a rubber ring for safety. After a while, I saw some of the Redcoats preparing to hold a series of races. Always keen to join in any form of competition, I hovered around hopefully.

'Come on, hurry up, boy. Get ready!'

The Redcoat was obviously talking to me, so I did what I was told and stood in line at the end of the pool. As the starter prepared to blow his whistle, I suddenly realised I had left the rubber ring at the side of the pool. Everything had happened so fast and there was now no time to tell anyone I couldn't swim. There was no turning back. Just as the other boys crouched in a starting position, so did I. The race started and I jumped into the water, took a deep breath fractionally before the splash, surfaced and steadied, closed my eyes, held my breath and started whirling my arms and kicking my legs for dear life.

Thirty seconds later, I bumped my head against the opposite side of the pool and opened my eyes to find the blurred image of a Redcoat standing over me, applauding and grinning.

'Well done,' he shouted. 'You won the race!'

Won?

I ran home to tell my family what had happened, but neither of my parents believed me until we saw one of the Redcoats later in the day, and he confirmed I had indeed won a swimming race. Even at a young age, I was starting to realise that, with a bit of guts and determination, almost anything was possible.

Back home in Shropshire, football was by far the most popular sport among my friends and I emerged as a spirited, hard-tackling, ball-winning midfielder in the mould of Billy Bremner. If it moved, I was not afraid to kick it, and I managed to win a place in the school team. We had a decent side, playing against rival schools as far as 15 miles away and winning far more than we lost.

One year we reached a regional final to be played at the local 'Wembley', the home ground of Oswestry Town FC where the town team was being coached by none other than the father of Alan Ball, one of England's 1966 World Cup winning heroes. The link with the greatest moment in English football history may have been tenuous, but it served to enhance the impression in our excited minds that this game was our World Cup final. We tried everything, but were eventually beaten 3–1. I was terribly disappointed, not remotely consoled by the fact that I had opened the scoring with a speculative lob.

Several weeks later, another important football match fell on the same Saturday as a junior golf event, and I had to make a choice. Football or golf? After a brief discussion with my father, when he expressed the fear that, sooner or later, my fervour for getting stuck in was going to cause a serious injury, I decided to put away my football boots and went to get my clubs ready.

My father saw I was prepared to make a real commitment to my golf and it was not long after my 13th birthday when he realised that, despite the fact I still seemed small for my age, I did have genuine potential to succeed in the game.

The *Daily Telegraph* sponsored schoolboy golf competitions in those days and still does. Once, I was playing in an event at Wrexham. Dad had come along to watch, and I could see he was pleased as I put together what was looking like a decent round. Then, on the 18th, I drove into the rough on the left and was left with just under 200 yards to the green.

'What are you going to do, Ian?'

I took a Junior Dunlop Blue Flash four-wood and said I would drift it out to the right and let the wind bring it round towards the green. Even then, I was confident of putting a natural draw on my long shots.

'That's a bit risky, don't you think?'

'Why?'

'Well, why don't you wedge it out on to fairway, give yourself a clear approach and a putt for par? You've got a good score going here. Don't take a risk now and throw it all away.'

'Dad, I want to use the wood.'

'OK, it's your shot. Do whatever you want.'

Feeling a little more pressure than usual, I addressed the ball and struck it just as I wanted. The ball soared right and drew round on the wind, coming to rest six feet from the pin.

I glanced across at my father and he smiled. 'Ian, I'm telling you, Jack Nicklaus couldn't have hit that shot better.'

As we walked up that fairway at Wrexham together, we both knew my future lay in golf. We both knew it would be tough and we both knew that, with a bit of guts, anything was possible.

CHAPTER TWO

The Low Road

One of golf's many advantages is that you can so easily measure your progress in the game. The handicap system is a visible, undeniable indicator and a clear ladder to climb.

When I was 12 years old and getting serious about my golf, my handicap was 13. I worked hard through the next year, playing in as many tournaments as possible at Llanymynech, always taking care to hand in my card after the monthly medal and, by the time I turned 13, my handicap had come down to six.

This success encouraged me to practise harder, so I hit more balls around the fields of New House Farm and spent more time aiming at the biscuit tin lid in the cowshed. Yet, my handicap stayed stuck at six for a while. It was starting to drive me nuts.

However, the knowledge that any improvement in my game was going to be reflected in my handicap motivated me to keep plugging away. So I kept putting across the living room carpet while my parents watched TV, kept squeezing the gun of the water hosepipe until tears welled in my eyes because I wanted to make my hands stronger, and kept swinging in front of a mirror on the wall. This effort paid off and, in due course, something clicked in my game. My scores improved and the number beside my name on the handicapping lists in the clubhouse dropped to 1. That was more like it: I was 15, and playing off one.

Next stop, the Open! Or so it seemed. All my goals in the game appeared to be within touching distance.

I began watching golf on the small, black-and-white television in the corner of our living room, studying the great players of the day. Jack Nicklaus was impressive as the big, strong champion but, for obvious reasons, I was most inspired by Gary Player, the feisty, brave little guy with plenty of guts. The South African dressed in black epitomised everything I ever wanted to be on the golf course. He marched through 18 holes with purpose and determination; he never gave up and never knew when he was beaten. Most important, he was only 5'7", a short man succeeding in what seemed to be a tall-man's game.

If Gary Player could win three Open Championships, three US Masters, two PGA Championships and one US Open in a celebrated professional career, then so could I. It didn't matter if people said I was too small to succeed. Player proved otherwise.

I can remember my excitement when he staged

his celebrated fightback against Tony Lema in the semi-final of the 1965 World Match Play Championship.

At seven down with 17 holes to play, Player was standing on the second tee when he overheard someone in the crowd saying he had no chance of winning the match. This remark prompted one of the greatest comebacks in the history of golf.

I remember reading and re-reading every account of how he made birdie after birdie and eventually squared the match by holing a long putt at the 18th. When he won the first play-off hole, he sank to his knees on the edge of the green, and wept.

Fantastic! Unbelievable! That was the kind of golf I wanted to play. On more than one occasion, the farmer's son at Llanymynech would crouch over a putt and mutter to himself: 'Now, it's going to be Gary Player, putting for another incredible win.'

Unfortunately, if there was any remote similarity between the legend and me in my youth, it did not extend to my conduct on the course. While Player was the model of discipline and self-control, I regularly hurled clubs and lost my temper. I know it's no excuse but I was only copying the tendency among junior golfers in our area. When I began playing with older boys, I soon assumed it was acceptable to throw your putter across the green whenever you happened to three-putt. We behaved badly. On one occasion, a formidable lady member at Llanymynech stormed across a fairway towards me, declaring: 'You are a naughty little boy, Ian Woosnam.' She had apparently seen me hurl my driver some 15 yards or so into a bush after hooking a ball out of bounds. My mates thought it was hilarious.

It reached the point where my own mother was embarrassed to play 18 holes with me. She would beg me to be more patient on the golf course, but her pleas usually fell on deaf ears. I didn't want to disappoint her, but I found it so frustrating to make a mistake when I knew I had the ability to play so much better.

On-course conduct didn't seem quite so important when I was playing with my friends because we were all as bad tempered as each other. In those wild days, it was not unusual for someone to hurl a club into a tree and then have to climb up and scramble in the branches to fetch it.

My temper was even worse if I lost. There was one occasion when I was playing against my older brother Keith in a junior club event at Llanymynech. We were all square on the 18th tee, but I stupidly went for death or glory, hit my drive into the rough and Keith beat me with a solid par at the last. I went ballistic. I always hated losing and generally went off to sulk for a few hours before rejoining the human race but, on this occasion, I sat in the car stubbornly refusing to join the rest of the group in the clubhouse for the prize-giving.

'Come on, Ian, it's only a game.'

The benign Club Steward was tapping calmly on the window. I tried to look the other way, pretending not to see him.

'Ian, everybody is waiting for you.'

As he spoke, he raised his right hand and showed me a couple of Mars bars and a packet of crisps. I opened the door.

'Oh, all right,' I said calmly, accepting the goodies. 'I was just on my way. Is that the time already?'

The Steward smiled. I had gradually become aware that most people around the club were prepared to give me the benefit of the doubt, with the result that I got away with more than I should have done. My father once said the members could see I had talent, and they excused the odd outburst. Small for my age and trying hard: maybe I did cut a sympathetic figure. If so, I was lucky.

I knew my father was always on my side. He often explained how losing my temper on the course was a waste of energy. 'Don't get too upset,' he would implore me, implying it was acceptable for a competitive sportsman to get a bit upset. 'Work harder and make sure you don't make the same mistake again.'

Dad matched these words with actions, arranging for me to be coached by a retired professional golfer who happened to live in the village of Pant, down the hill from Llanymynech. Cyril Hughes was a small man into his 80s when I cautiously knocked on the front door of his cottage. I knew he had been the club professional at Royal Liverpool, and I was aware of his close association with Henry Cotton, three times winner of the Open and one of England's greatest ever golfers. He answered the door and quickly set me at ease, inviting me through to a tiered piece of land behind his house, hard against the hill, where he had created three 50-yard holes.

I only visited Mr Hughes four times, for an hour's coaching on each occasion, but his profound knowledge and gentle manner left an impression on my approach to the game that remains clear and vivid in my mind more than three decades later. He taught me the basics of the swing: grip, stance, position of the ball, right elbow tucked in, eyes fixed on the back of the ball; and he gave me confidence when he said I had the strong arms, stocky build and talent to succeed.

As a junior golfer, I felt no pressing need for supervision and guidance – ever since I first picked up a wood at the age of seven, the game had seemed so natural to me. Having said that, there is no doubt that Cyril Hughes' wise guidance was hugely valuable. In essence, he pointed me in the right direction.

This is only part of my debt. Even if I was largely oblivious to the fact at the time, my early golfing career owed everything to willing club members who freely gave their time and commitment to running junior golf in Shropshire. Organising tournaments, selecting teams, arranging transport and prizes: there was usually no limit to their dedication, all for the pleasure of enabling a bunch of generally ungrateful, wild youngsters to realise their potential.

Among such gentlemen, Bernard Thomas stood apart. As the chairman of our junior golf section, he shouldered responsibility for ensuring the structure functioned but his contribution to his young players always extended far beyond logistics. Mr Thomas always took a special interest, offering guidance and support, endlessly encouraging us to work harder and get our handicaps down. At one stage, he noticed a group of us had begun to play on Wednesday evenings, so he organised a regular weekly tournament for us. He didn't have to do that. Nobody asked him to do that, but he was committed, and he cared. He also assisted the Shropshire and Herefordshire Junior Colts side and would take us on trips to play our counterparts in other Midlands counties. Hour after hour, week after week, year on year, Bernard Thomas remained a model of selfless dedication.

As a result, the club maintained a strong junior section, with youngsters such as Basil and Andy Griffiths and me, who all eventually turned professional, and many other talented players who decided to remain amateur.

I was grateful to reap the benefits of such a solid upbringing in the game, winning the Shropshire Junior Championships at The Wrekin when I was 13, getting a place in the Shropshire senior side at the age of 15 and winning various junior events like the *Daily Telegraph* competitions in 1972 and 1973.

The structure was so strong. Each year brought a new goal, and every level offered a new challenge.

Junior golf not only sustained my progress, but the various outings to play matches also exposed me to the big, bad world. On one trip with the Shropshire and Herefordshire Junior Colts, when I was just 13 years old, I was drawn to play in the foursomes with a much older boy. I didn't play badly but we were beaten four and three, and headed to the clubhouse for lunch.

'OK, Woosie, what do you want to drink?'

The older boy was standing at the bar of the Worcestershire Golf Club, and I asked for a shandy, because that is what I was allowed. A minute or so later, he placed a pint of bitter in front of me.

'Sorry, lad, there's no lemonade.'

I could hardly turn him down. So, feeling obliged, I drank the pint, and another, and another, and then a fourth before it was time for me to tee off in the afternoon singles. By that time, I was not in a fit state to do anything, let alone play golf!

There seemed to be three balls on the tee when I addressed my drive at the first, so I took a wild swipe and ended up losing the match by the resounding margin of seven and six.

Through my middle teens, I did manage to play

better when I didn't have a drink at lunchtime, winning the Shropshire and Herefordshire Amateur title, the *Hereford Times* Cup and the Griffiths Price Cup, and becoming the junior champion of Shropshire and Herefordshire.

International honours loomed, and it soon became clear that I was eligible to play for either England or Wales. It didn't take me long to choose. At heart, I had always felt part of a strong, proud Welsh family, so I wanted to represent Wales. On a practical level, I knew it would be tougher to win selection for England.

So what if I was born on English soil? I felt every bit as Welsh as David Lloyd George, born in Manchester.

More matches, more trips, more honours followed. I played for North Wales boys, and later captained the Welsh Boys team. I also reached the quarter-finals of the British Boys Championship. In 1976, aged 18, I played for the senior Welsh amateur team in an international against France at Royal Porthcawl, but later had to withdraw from the Wales team for the Home Internationals with glandular fever.

This was an exciting and frenetic period: rushing around the English Midlands and Wales, playing for this team and that side, all the time practising harder, focusing on the game, keeping out of trouble, being committed and sometimes winning.

The junior golf season ran through summer and, amidst the breathless blur of challenges and opportunities, of car journeys and pub lunches, of circulars and official notices, one face had begun to come ever more sharply into focus.

I had first heard his name several years earlier, but I only got to know him when we played in the same Shropshire and Herefordshire Colts team. Our paths had then crossed in stroke-play tournaments around the county. He was only 20 days older than me, but he was blonder than me, taller than me, a more consistent golfer than me and widely regarded as a better prospect than me.

Sandy Lyle grew up at the Hawkstone Park Golf Club, outside Shrewsbury, only 20 miles from our house in St Martins. His father Alex was the club professional, so Sandy learned golf with a putting green and driving range on his doorstep, literally.

Everything people said was true. Tall, strong, talented, he was a phenomenal junior player, so impressive to watch. I used to stand in the background and admire the way he struck the ball. It looked so smooth. That was how I wanted to play.

I remember feeling particularly flattered when I overheard an agitated, adamant organiser insisting that, under no circumstances, would he allow Woosnam and Lyle to play as a pair because, as he put it, 'then nobody else would have a chance'.

Beating Sandy became my goal. I would strive to match his number of strokes per round, his achievements and his reputation. In a positive way, he became my target. I reckoned that if I played like him, I would achieve all my ambitions in golf.

On one occasion, the two of us were battling head-to-head over the last nine holes of a Junior County Championship at Market Drayton and, once again, Sandy emerged as the winner.

A prize-giving ceremony had been arranged, and Colonel Arthur Jones, the respected organiser, gently ushered Sandy and me into position. At such moments, it was the colonel's custom to assist the new champion with his speech, and he duly gave Sandy a note with some appropriate, hand-written remarks. When everything was ready, Sandy stepped forward to accept the trophy and read out the colonel's words. People applauded, all seemed well and I was ready to go home. Then, to my great alarm, the MC suddenly invited 'the runner-up' to speak. I genuinely loathed public speaking and, even worse, nobody had given me any notes, but there was no escape. I edged forward nervously, and eventually blurted out: 'Ladies and gentlemen, I just want to say that one day I will beat Sandy Lyle.'

That was it. Amid a tiny ripple of applause and some laughter, I crept back to stand beside Sandy, who leaned over and muttered in my ear: 'You'll have to grow a bit first, Woos.'

Sandy turned professional in 1977, a year after me and, while I was struggling to make a cut, he won the European Order of Merit in his second and third years on Tour. He followed this unprecedented achievement by recording Major victories at the Open Championship in 1985 and at the US Masters three years later.

We have played together many, many times during the past quarter of a century, in tournaments around the world, but, strange though it seems, we have never properly sat down and talked about the good old days of junior golf in Shropshire. Said or unsaid, I'm sure both of us remain deeply proud of the fact that that happy, motivated Shropshire and Herefordshire Junior Colts team run by Bernard Thomas, Colonel Arthur Jones and all the other organisers, all those years ago, has somehow managed to produce not one, but two US Masters champions.

So I left school at the age of 16, and set out to become a professional golfer. I was not in the least bothered by the fact that my lack of academic qualifications meant I had few career options, if any, beyond farming and golf simply because there was never any uncertainty in my mind. I was fortunate in knowing exactly what I wanted to do; as a result, nothing else mattered.

I worked hard on the farm through the summer of 1974 but, by September, was starting to wonder how I could get into golf and make a decent living as well. I had won a few amateur events, but nobody was knocking on the door. I needed a break.

One evening, while my father and I took a break after milking the cows, the telephone started ringing.

'Hello?'

'Hello. Is that Ian?'

'Speaking.'

'It's Albert Minshall here, Tony's dad.'

I had met Tony Minshall through junior golf, and I was aware that his father was developing a new golf course at Hill Valley, near Whitchurch, no more than 35 minutes up the road from our home. I had also heard people talking about Albert Minshall as someone who was keen to support ambitious young golfers.

'Ian, I have a proposal for you.'

'Yes?'

'We're looking for an assistant in the pro shop at Hill Valley. Do you think you might be interested? There are a few youngsters around here now, and you'll be able to play the course. If you need somewhere to stay, we can sort that out as well.'

'That would be fantastic.'

I was so eager to accept the offer I forgot to ask Mr Minshall about the salary; this turned out to be £10 per week, half of which would go straight to pay the rent for my digs, a small room at the back of the clubhouse. That didn't leave much after I had bought food, but I was not complaining. On the contrary, I was delighted. I was not only going to be living in a golfing environment but I was also earning my keep. As my parents wished me the best of luck, I packed my suitcase and set out on my own, 20 miles north to Hill Valley.

John Anderson was the club professional, and he showed me the ropes in the pro shop as I moved in behind the counter, ready to spend my days selling tee-pegs and golf balls.

Only a few days later, I was asking Mr Minshall if there was anything else I could do at Hill Valley. I knew I was being impatient, and probably a bit of a nuisance, but working all day in the shop left me no time to get on the course and play golf. Mr Minshall was sensitive to my frustration and asked if I would like to join the green-keeping staff, and this proved the perfect solution. I would start work at 7.30 in the morning and always be finished by one, leaving the afternoons free to play golf and the evenings free to enjoy myself.

When anyone has asked me whether I regretted not going to university, I have always replied that, to all intents and purposes I did. If you define university as a place where you receive advanced tuition in your chosen trade and where you have an opportunity to do the things students do, then I consider myself fortunate to have been admitted to the University of Hill Valley. And, naturally, the course suited me down to the ground: no text-books, no essays, no lectures, no examinations . . . just 18 mown tees, lush fairways, a few bunkers and 18 greens.

Another hopeful youngster, David Parry from Llangollen Golf Club, arrived at Hill Valley soon afterwards, and we got along so well that, nine years later, he agreed to be best man at my wedding. In fact, I recall the exact moment when I realised I would get along with David: it was when he said his father would give him the use of a caravan, where he was going to stay during his time at the club.

It was soon agreed I could leave my room to the beer barrels and would join David in his caravan, which was going to be parked out of sight down beside the nine-hole course.

Life was now complete. Every morning I would work on the course, understanding different conditions, learning how to prepare fairways and greens, deciding where to place the pins; and almost every afternoon, we would play a round ourselves. Practice on the putting green or driving range is fine, but I have always believed the best form of practice is to play the course.

Our social lives also improved when the club started staging discos in the clubhouse. Free entrance, a friend behind the bar and less than 50 metres to stagger home afterwards: it was difficult to imagine a more convenient set of circumstances.

We were usually short of money, of course, and it did not take long for us to realise some of the Hill Valley members enjoyed a bit of a flutter out on the course. So David, Tony Minshall and I started spending time in the members' bar, having a few pints and sometimes challenging the guys to play against us for a fiver the next day. With a grin and some excellent golf when required, we were generally able to keep ourselves in beer money.

The course at Hill Valley had been built and designed by Dave Thomas and Peter Alliss, the BBC TV golf commentator, and, when the new clubhouse and facilities had settled down, plans were laid for a golf day to mark the official opening of the course.

I was asked to caddie for Peter Alliss, and I remember feeling nervous when I met him. He had this enormous bag of clubs and, although I reckoned I was strong for a 16-year-old, the first nine holes proved such a trial that, once he had finished the ninth, I ran across to the clubhouse and fetched a trolley to use on the back nine.

There have been many opportunities for Peter to remind me of this particular occasion during the intervening years, and he has gleefully taken advantage of almost every one. He is the true voice of golf, and we have always had a laugh together. In my view, Peter remains by some distance the finest golf commentator in the world. He is invariably informed, amusing and he speaks his mind. Some professionals have got upset when he is critical, but I think Peter is only saying what anyone who knows the game would say around the bar in the clubhouse. If someone plays a bad shot, he's entitled to say it's a bad shot.

Amid all the fun and drinking, and laughing and

golf, I came close to being killed at the Hill Valley Golf Club. I had already been fortunate enough to survive one tragic accident in my youth – it had been arranged that I should sleep in a caravan at the golf club but, for some reason, I decided to go home instead. Herbie, the old club steward at Llanymynech Golf Club and a close school friend of mine did spend the night in that ill-fated caravan, and both were killed by a gas leak.

A similar course of events unfolded at Hill Valley. There was some construction work in progress on the new clubhouse, and the Minshalls were concerned about hooligans breaking in. Since David had gone home for the weekend, I volunteered to sleep in the new building and check everything was secure. There was a massive storm that night and, being a very light sleeper, I lay awake listening to the lashing rain and high winds. In the end, I managed to get some sleep before rising at seven and wandering back down towards our caravan to get changed.

Something was wrong. I stood still.

'Where the hell is the caravan?'

This didn't make sense. I hadn't been drinking the previous night, but I squinted my eyes and looked again towards the empty parking space. Yes, our 'home' had disappeared.

'Where the hell is the caravan?' I asked aloud again.

The mystery deepened as I walked on along the

path, until I peered nervously down towards the bottom of the hill and saw what looked like the wreckage of a small aircraft. In fact, the debris of twisted white metal, clothing and personal items scattered across the grass was all that remained of our caravan. It subsequently emerged that the caravan had been uprooted during the storm and sent catapulting down the hill before crashing against a wooden fence. As I surveyed the shattered structure, my mind was full of the knowledge that, on any normal night, that was where David and I would have been sleeping.

The consensus in the clubhouse over the next few weeks was that we would both have slept for a very long time.

There was a rarely a dull moment for me at Hill Valley. Late one evening, not long after passing my driving test, I smashed Tony Minshall's car into a wall while driving without insurance. I ran back to the club and phoned home in a desperate panic, breaking down in tears as I explained to my father what had happened. I didn't cry often. Shropshire youngsters were generally not the crying type and Dad says I was always 'as tough as nails,' but, this particular night, I really thought I would go to prison.

At a time when he had every reason to be angry, my father responded calmly and practically. He drove up to see me at the club and wrote out a cheque to pay for the repair of Tony's car. By that stage, I had revisited the scene of the accident in daylight and seen a manhole cover in the road that prompted me to swerve into the wall. I had obviously been driving too fast.

During these two years at Hill Valley, I continued competing in amateur tournaments around the country, performing reasonably well, trying to make progress in the game; and I grew to rely more and more heavily on the incredible support of my father and a close friend of mine from Oswestry, Geoff Roberts.

In 1975, my father announced he was going to change New House Farm from a dairy farm to an arable farm. He would grow corn in the fields and sold his cherished pedigree cows. I remember how he explained to us that the price of corn had jumped from £26 per ton to £53 per ton, and that we could make a living. This decision dramatically altered the pattern of our family's life. Cereal farms tend to be frenetically busy when they sow in the spring and when they harvest at the end of the summer, but there are nothing like as many regular obligations as on a dairy farm. In short, nobody had to get home to milk the cows.

And yet, this was not the whole story. What I didn't entirely appreciate at the time, but understand more clearly now, was that my father's decision to change the farm was substantially motivated by his determination to support my ambitions in golf.

In the first place, the switch to cereals massively reduced my obligation to work on the farm: I would still help during the sowing and harvesting, but I was essentially free to play golf. Second, it soon became clear that, with a lighter workload at home, it would often be possible for my father to travel with me.

My first reaction to this news was great excitement. Life was going to be much easier with my father driving me to tournaments, staying with me in the caravan that we towed to golf events, helping me on the practice ground and caddying for me. I needed support, and I was delighted he could be with me when I was playing in events like the English Amateur, the Welsh Amateur, the British Amateur, the Welsh Boys Championship and the British Boys Championship.

However, father-son relationships are rarely that simple. There tends to be a thin line between what is meant by one as assistance and what can feel to the other like interference; and it's easy for the purest, most noble of intentions to become resented. Of course, there is always an underlying bond of love, but our experience leads me to the conclusion that fathers should not caddie for their sons. Unfortunately, it's a recipe for conflict.

If I look back now, I know exactly what Dad was trying to do and I recognise that his sense of commitment to me was incredible, but it is also true that youngsters have to lose for themselves, and make their own mistakes and learn from their mistakes.

These are harsh realities. Perhaps the seed of the conflict lies in the simple nature of the roles, father and caddie.

On a golf course, it is the player who must decide what club to take, what line to hit, what shot to play; the caddie is often asked for his view, but it is the player who decides. Yet, in most families, and certainly in our house, children are brought up to accept what their father says, to be respectful and obedient. Problems arise when, as a young golfer, you want to ignore your caddie's advice (as you have every right to do), but if the caddie is also your father, you instinctively feel you must obey.

It gets worse. If you do bite the bullet and ignore the advice, and your ball ends up buried in the rough, it is almost impossible not to turn to your caddie and see a look on his face that yells: 'What do you expect if you ignore your father's advice?' Tempers are lost, and you play badly, and everyone gets upset and blames each other, and you can't turn to the person who you instinctively want to turn to when things go wrong because he has become the person who you are fighting against.

It just doesn't work. It certainly wasn't my father's fault, and I hope it wasn't my fault. The situation was wrong.

In any case, I'm not sure it was much fun being my caddie in those days. I tended to play what we used to call 'army golf': I used to hit the ball left, then right, left, right, left, right . . . and when I say the ball went right, I don't mean a bit right, I am talking about 100 yards right. My father always said he was the fittest caddie in the tournament because he had to walk further than anyone else when he carried my bag. Every now and then, I was erratic off the tee!

Having said all this, the plain fact is that my father was there and, whether he was caddying or not, I desperately wanted him to be around. We may have argued now and then, but his enthusiasm for my golf has been a huge factor in my career.

It's a terrible cliché, and it sounds completely inadequate, but I would not have achieved what I have managed to achieve without my father's help. The debt I owe is the kind of debt I can never repay to him, but which I will hopefully pass on to my kids.

Geoff Roberts also played a crucial role during these formative years. A shrewd salesman from Cheshire, he and his wife moved to settle in Shropshire, and we met when I was starting to play more regularly at Oswestry Golf Club, where he was clearly a committed member, another one who gave his time and enthusiasm to help the junior section. We got along very well from the start and have played many, many rounds over the years.

There are no spots on Geoff. He says what he thinks, and I have always appreciated that quality in anyone. I like people to be blunt and frank, and Geoff was not lacking in this respect.

'Sorry I'm late, Geoff,' I said once, when I arrived at the club moments before we were due to tee off in a medal competition.

'Yes, and I'm not happy about it.'

'Sorry!'

'OK, you said that. Now, get on with it.'

And if I played a stupid shot, Geoff was certainly not the type to look nervously away, and avoid the issue. He would boom across the course: 'What the hell do you think you're doing?' I liked that too. I can't start to estimate the number of times Geoff would come and collect me from our house and take me to the course, or guess how often he told me what I needed to hear.

He also taught me to play bridge, and he has never been less than a tremendous source of support and friendship.

Through 1975 and into 1976, Hill Valley continued to seem like paradise for me. Golf in the day, discos at night, week after week: I could have stayed there for a very long time. However, by the end of that long, hot summer of 1976, I was beginning to think the time was right for me to turn professional and move on.

Maybe I was learning you can have too much of a good thing and, to be honest, I was probably drinking too much for somebody who hoped to make a career in professional sport. The decision was made. I was still having a great time but, I concluded, there was no point waiting to turn pro. I should get out there on the Tour and start earning real money.

In September 1976, at the age of 18 and with my handicap at one, I wrote a letter and properly registered my request to become a member of the European Tour. The next month, I was on my way to compete at the Qualifying School, which at that time was held at Foxhills Golf Club, near Chertsey, Surrey. The equation was clear and simple, merciless: 330 optimistic golfers converged on this course to compete for a set number of cards on the European Tour in 1977. A player's card entitled you to enter the pre-qualifying rounds of a Tour event, usually played on Mondays, from which the best 20 or 30 players would qualify for the tournament itself, starting on Thursday.

If you did manage to finish among the top 50 at Foxhills in October, you earned your Tour card for the following year and could start planning for life in the big time. If you finished 51st or worse, you went home. Goodbye. More often than not, you would start looking for a way of making a living, perhaps at a golf course, or in a pro shop, or behind the bar, in fact anywhere, just to keep you going until the next October when you would return to Foxhills and try again.

And you would keep trying, and trying, and trying, until you made it and lived out your dreams in the world of professional golf or until you gave up, and allowed your dream to die. That is what happened at Qualifying School. It was a tough place.

I thrived on the pressure in 1976 and, for once controlling my natural impatience, played solid golf at Foxhills, finished well up in the field and safely won my card. I was relieved. Failure would have sent me back to playing events on the local Midland region professional circuit; instead, success propelled me forward.

This was not, I must add, the end of my association with the nerve-racking shoot-out at Chertsey because my performances on the European Tour in 1977 and 1978 were not sufficiently strong for me to retain my card. At the end of each season, I was forced to join the fray at Foxhills and start all over again. Thankfully, fortunately, I managed to secure my card in each of three successive years at the Qualifying School.

News of my initial success in October 1976 was welcomed at Hill Valley as the perfect excuse for a party, but Peter Conliff, club manager at the time, realised this bash needed to yield something more useful than a few dozen hangovers.

The opening tournaments on the European Tour in 1977 had been scheduled to take place in Portugal and Spain, and Peter knew that, even if I did drive from Britain and sleep in a caravanette, the trip was going to cost me a reasonable sum of money.

In professional golf, the player is always liable for

his own expenses. So Peter began to organise 'Bertie's Party', a fund-raising event at Hill Valley intended to put some cash in my pocket and send me on my way. 'Bertie' was taken from the P.G. Wodehouse character, Bertie Wooster, but, as time has passed, only Peter Conliff and Peter Alliss have continued to use this nickname.

I was a bit embarrassed by the idea, but everyone seemed to enjoy the evening, and I was overwhelmed when Peter told me the next morning that more than £500 had been raised. I was amazed by the generosity of my mates and members of the golf club, and more determined than ever to play well and . . . well, not to let any of them down.

In the event, I was reasonably satisfied with my first venture on the pro tour. I successfully pre-qualified at both the Portuguese Open and the Spanish Open, but was maybe slightly overwhelmed by the big names in the tournament and missed both cuts.

It would be inaccurate to say that, as an 18-year-old rookie, I set the European Tour aflame with excitement. In fact, it would be a complete lie. The truth is that most people looked across at a small, self-conscious youngster standing beside a large bag of clubs and unthinkingly assumed he was a caddie.

In Spain, someone asked: 'So, whose bag are you carrying?'

I replied: 'What do you mean? I'm playing.'

Life seemed so much easier for those few, wonderfully gifted young players who, like Sandy Lyle a year later, arrived on Tour and took the high road to golfing fame and fortune. They instantly became competitive, their names soared onto leaderboards week after week, they were repeatedly featured in the television coverage and they were soon earning serious prize money; and, for them, success would breed success when sponsors and the media flocked to fuss over the new star.

The rest of us, in fact the overwhelming majority of us, found ourselves on the low road, discovering a different kind of existence on Tour. We would report at the course early on a Monday morning and struggle through pre-qualifying; and, if we did secure a place in a tournament, we would then battle to make the cut. Every pound of prize money, be it for tied-50th or even 62nd place, would be enthusiastically received because it would go to pay at least some of the mounting bills for the week.

It was my father, as ever, who put this daunting prospect into some kind of manageable, practical perspective.

'Look, Ian, you're learning a trade,' he told me bluntly. 'You can't expect to turn up and win every week. You must look at this period as your apprenticeship in the game. Try and learn from each round, work hard in practice and make progress.

'I think you should give yourself at least five years.

Whatever happens, you should spend five years on Tour. If you're not making a decent living in professional golf by 1982, then we'll have to find something else. But, for now, give yourself a chance.'

When he had finished, he pushed the keys of our Volkswagen Dormobile caravanette across the kitchen table towards me. He had bought the second-hand caravanette because it was perfect for travelling long distances to tournaments and sleeping numerous nights away from home, all at the absolute minimum cost.

I looked at the keys on the table, then up at him.

My father smiled broadly.

'Go on, Ian, it's yours,' he said.

This gesture signalled the start of an enduring, memorable association, for I began to live in that Dormobile week after week, going from tournament to tournament, not for one or maybe two years, and not even for two or three years. This vehicle not only transported me around the continent, from the north of Scotland to the south of Portugal (and everywhere else in between) but also provided a roof over my head for no fewer than five eventful years on the European Tour.

These were tough times, when I was struggling to make an impact or even a halfway cut, but the VW Dormobile grew to reflect my own identity and attitude. Yes, I was battling; yes, it was hard; but, damnit, we were going to get there in the end. It was the standard issue VW sleeper, long and rectangular in shape, with two upright seats in the front, two benches at the back that folded down into a small double bed and a concertina roof that could be pushed up to create room for another two bunks. It was all white when I started on Tour but, after a year or so, I took the caravanette into one of the cowsheds at home and tried to paint the lower section light blue. Maybe it's not surprising that I couldn't get that glossy sheen on the finish.

The vehicle lacked for nothing . . . well, not much: there was a sink with running water whose tank needed to be filled up every day, plenty of cupboards and locker space for storing clothes, food and golf clubs, and if you lifted up the passenger seat in the front, there was a gas cooking stove.

This essential piece of equipment was generally pressed into service every day on Tour, because it was cheaper to cook our own meals than to eat out. Sometimes, when we were running short of time to reach the golf course before an early tee-off, a friend of mine would be cooking breakfast while I was driving. Our menu was rich, healthy and varied: it was baked beans on toast, or baked beans on bread. There were baked beans with an egg or baked beans with a sausage; and of course there were baked beans on their own, neat with nothing added.

These were the late 1970s and early 1980s, an era when the great majority of pro golfers remained blissfully ignorant about the benefits of a balanced diet and physical conditioning. We ate what we wanted, and the nearest we came to going for a jog was when we had to sprint to reach the pub before closing time.

Washing was an issue. It was hard to find launderettes near Europe's leading golf courses, with the result that dirty clothes did tend to gather and, necessarily, had to be recycled.

This was our life. There were four or five of us following the Tour in caravanettes at this time. Joe Higgins, another gifted golfer from Nuneaton, often travelled with me, and my close friend, D.J. Russell, bought and kitted out his own van.

Most of the other players, those who could afford to fly from event to event and stay in hotels, understood our position and fully supported what we were trying to achieve but we were not always the most welcome guests at the golf clubs hosting the events.

First, as soon as we arrived, for obvious reasons, we wanted to park as close as possible to the clubhouse but this desire usually brought us into conflict with local officials. They appeared to believe that the appearance and tone of their club, and their event, would not be enhanced by our battered vans on their doorstep. Obviously, we all felt a deep sense of outrage when we were asked to park our vehicles elsewhere, usually anywhere out of sight and away from the public areas. In our minds, we were the stars of the future. In the club's eyes, we were an eyesore.

This unfavourable impression was generally sustained when, early each morning, wearing T-shirts and tracksuits and rubbing the sleep from our eyes, we would stagger out of our caravanettes and make our way to the clubhouse. At first, it was not much fun having to run the gauntlet of disapproving members on our way to shower, wash and shave in the locker room, but we soon grew accustomed to the routine. This was our life.

And we had fun, even in adversity. One year, it was so cold at the Northern Open in Nairn, Scotland, that Tony Minshall and I both slept in our waterproofs. Tony could have afforded to stay in a hotel but he had decided to keep me company in the van. At 6'4", he had taken the double bed, and I was up in the bunk.

'Eh, Woos, it's xxxxxxx freezing,' he exclaimed, waking up on the morning of the first round. We looked outside to find five inches of snow on the ground, and play was suspended. Confronted by a free day, with nothing else to do, most of the players decided to arrange a disco in the clubhouse. It began at ten o'clock in the morning, and we were all steaming by mid-afternoon. The party continued when one of the club's staff invited us back to his house. Well, it was one way of keeping warm.

At this point, I would like to reflect that, despite living out of a Dormobile and dressing from a locker full of dirty clothes, I began to play well and make my mark on the circuit. Sadly, fairy tales are as rare on the European Tour as anywhere else. After successfully reaching the tournament proper at the Portuguese Open and the Spanish Open in 1977, I failed to pre-qualify for another tournament in the whole season. Through my first year, I was hopeful every Monday, disappointed on Tuesday, then back on the road to the next tournament.

The next year was not much better, although I did manage to play through until Sunday at the Greater Manchester Open, producing rounds of 73-72-74-71 to finish tied for 60th place. My progress was painfully slow. I appeared to be going nowhere fast.

Invariably, erratic driving let me down. I often seemed to play a decent hole, and then, bursting with enthusiasm, I would get onto the next tee and hook my drive out of bounds. I wanted so badly to succeed, wanted to phone my parents and tell them how I had done this and that, but it wasn't happening for me.

As people began to suggest I was just too short to compete as a professional, I became increasingly desperate to get better, to make enough money to survive on Tour, most of all to save myself from having to go home and work on the farm. Every pound helped. In weeks when I couldn't afford to get to the Tour event, or when I failed to qualify for the tournament but was near enough to drive home by Tuesday, I entered tournaments on the Midlands circuit, and these kept me afloat. Winner's cheques could be worth as much as £1,000, enough to keep me going for a couple of months on Tour, but it was not just my bank balance that felt the benefit. The simple sight of my name on the leaderboard again and the pure thrill of winning renewed my confidence that, one day, I could win on Tour.

I was further encouraged when my name appeared on a list of six young players invited to take part in a five-day coaching course run by Tommy Horton and John Jacobs on the island of Jersey. Both were greatly respected in golf, and I was hopeful of them being able to help me become more consistent. D.J. Russell and another good friend of mine, John Hay, had also been included in the group. We were a close-knit bunch, so, at the very least, we were going to have a good time.

John Jacobs could not have been more positive. He looked at my swing for some time, and said he could see nothing wrong. 'You don't have to change anything,' he said. 'You've got a great swing, and I'm certain it's just a matter of time before you put everything together. Keep practising and it will come right.'

I stood and looked at him, almost disbelieving.

'I'm serious,' he repeated. 'That's a great swing.'

It's difficult to exaggerate the impact of his words. Suddenly, I felt strong and resolved. It is fantastic how a few well-chosen words from a respected source can transform a young mind. By the start of the 1979 season, I was raring to go again.

In compiling our tournament schedule, Joe Higgins and I had decided to enter the Northern Open, a PGA event, again, partially because we still had fond memories of the previous year. However, such indulgence carried a price because the next week, we were both obliged to play in the Italian Open, the first tour event of the year. Playing in both tournaments gave us no more than three days to drive from the distant north of Scotland to Milan. I asked Joe if it was possible, bearing in mind my Dormobile was not comfortable at speeds above 60mph. He said it would be a challenge.

We both played reasonably well at Nairn Golf Club, near Aberdeen, and managed to get away from the course when the tournament finished soon after four on the Thursday afternoon. By then, I had realised we would need to make a detour to Shropshire because I had left my wallet at Hill Valley. There was only £50 cash inside, but I needed that for the trip to Italy. So, I sat behind the wheel and drove deep into the night. It was past two o'clock in the morning when we reached Glasgow and pounded on towards Carlisle. I was shattered, and my eyelids were starting to feel heavy as we reached the M6.

'Joe, you're going to have to drive,' I said.

'I can't drive,' he replied, stirring from his snooze.

'You must have had some lessons?'

'No.'

There was no alternative. I was literally falling

asleep and, if we stopped for the night, we would never reach Milan in time. After some animated discussion, I drove into a service station, switched seats and gave Joe a quick lesson in changing gears.

'OK, Joe,' I said, 'just keep it in fourth gear. All you have to do is hold your foot on the accelerator so we go around 50, and keeping pointing the van in the right direction. Make sure you wake me up when you see the signs to Chester.' With those words, I immediately slumped asleep against the window.

I was eventually woken by the sound of *The Kiss* booming out from the radio/cassette player. Joe had turned up the music, but he was still driving and we were still alive. Everything seemed fine.

'Have we reached Chester yet, Joe?'

'No, Woos, not yet,' he replied.

Then I noticed a sign indicating we were six miles from Birmingham. We had driven at least 90 minutes past the turning for Chester. Without a word, I took over the driving again and doubled back. I collected my wallet from Hill Valley, grabbed another hour's sleep, and then headed south to Dover. Milan was still another thousand miles away.

The ferry crossing passed without incident, but it was already Friday evening when we reached the French *autoroute*. Aware that we were now behind schedule, we decided to pay the extra toll fees and drive on the motorway, but it soon became clear these were far too expensive and we returned to the *routes nationales*, winding our way through rural France towards Mont Blanc.

Joe was map reading; I was driving.

'We've been here once,' I exclaimed.

One part of countryside can look much like the next but, an hour or so earlier, I had noticed a bar beside the road, and now we were passing it again. I looked at the map, got us onto the right road and pressed on and on, driving through the night. We eventually reached the Alps by lunchtime on Saturday and Joe decided he wanted another go at driving. I was too exhausted to object, so I told him to take care and drive very slowly. Within 15 minutes, the engine had died completely, Joe was standing at the side of the road and I was under the bonnet. A few tugged cables mercifully revived the Dormobile, and we seemed to have reached the end of our adventure when we arrived in the outskirts of Milan late on Saturday night. All we needed to do was find the course for the pre-qualifying rounds.

Chug-chug-chug-sigh-silence.

The Dormobile had come to another full stop. Once again, I tugged at the cables but only succeeded in spurring the van to move forward at 10mph. Something was seriously wrong, and we needed to find a garage. We crawled towards the centre of town, but it was by now late at night, so we parked on a street in Milan, unfolded the beds and slept properly for the first time in 55 hours.

I woke early on Sunday morning, hopeful that somehow the engine would be fine. I turned the key . . . nothing, not even power to chug us forward at 10mph. I looked at the petrol gauge and cursed when I saw it was now flashing empty. How on earth was I going to find petrol in the middle of Milan on a Sunday?

This was not the glamorous world of professional golf that I had so often imagined in my youth. After standing in the middle of the road for some time, looking desperate and trying to signal that I needed help, I successfully stopped a man on a bicycle. He spoke some English, and said there was a can of petrol at his friend's house nearby, but that he would have to go back to his flat to fetch a funnel. This all sounded encouraging. Then he said I would have to come with him, back to his flat.

'Why?' I asked.

'To carry the funnel,' he replied blankly.

So, here I was: a 21-year-old Welsh golfer, holding a plastic funnel, perched on the handlebars while being bicycled through the deserted streets of Milan on a Sunday morning. We finally found the petrol, genuinely thanked the guy and, somehow, got the van chugging forward at 10mph again. Travelling at this speed in a major European city had long since ceased to be embarrassing; we were just happy to be moving.

It seemed sadly inevitable that we would struggle

to find the right golf course, but we eventually arrived at Monticello on Sunday evening, three days after leaving Nairn. In spite of everything, Joe and I both played pretty well on the Monday, passing through pre-qualifying with flying colours.

This meant that, on Tuesday, we needed to drive across Milan to the course where the tournament proper was going to start on the Thursday. The cara-vanette was still crawling along at 10mph, so we decided to try and find some help. We visited five garages, and encountered five bewildered Italian shrugs. I was beginning to fear we needed a new engine, which we couldn't afford.

My sense of humour was just starting to fade when we found a guy who told us to follow him to a Volkswagen garage. There, one of the mechanics opened the back, looked at the engine and, in about four seconds, saw a tiny tube had come loose from the carburettor. He pushed it back in place and the engine roared into life again!

Encouraged by this triumph, I played solid golf in the Italian Open, made the halfway cut and claimed the sum of £134.09 for finishing tied in 53rd place. Joe missed the halfway cut, but didn't appear too upset because it meant he would travel on his own to pre-qualify for the French Open, rather than chug along with me.

Fellow pro Ian Mosey bravely asked for a lift in my van and he may have regretted his decision when we got stuck in a snowdrift and had to spend the Sunday night somewhere in the Alps sleeping in a huge hall with about 20 other travellers. At least, trips with me were never boring.

The French Open was being played in Lyon and, by the time I arrived, Joe had failed to pre-qualify and gone home. I then played badly, missed the halfway cut and, with no-one needing a lift, faced the prospect of driving back to England on my own.

There were 200 French francs in my wallet when I drove away from Lyon, but the gauge was again veering towards empty. I spent all my money on petrol, and hoped it would be sufficient to get me all the way to Calais. Once over the Channel, I would be able to fill up with petrol in England using my cheque book.

I motored past Paris with scarcely a care in the world, but was soon starting to glance uneasily at the gauge. By the time I reached the turn-off for St Omer, still 20 miles from Calais, the red light had started to flash and I was running on empty.

'Don't stop, please. Don't stop.'

Every time the road sloped downhill, I slipped the gears into neutral and turned off the engine, frantically trying to conserve the few drops of petrol left in the tank. When I saw a signpost indicate one kilometre to the ferry, I breathed a sigh of relief.

Moments later, the van ground to a halt.

'No!'

It was not possible. I could actually see the ferry port no more than 800 yards ahead of me; I could even see the boat. I managed to coast to the side of the road and, there, like some kind of heroic, exhausted, faithful horse, my van stood, with its tank empty.

Now what? It was too far to push, although I did briefly think that might be the best option. I rummaged round in the van, finally emerging with a single pound note and the petrol can generously donated by the kind Italian with the bicycle in Milan. I started walking in search of petrol. The attendants in the first two garages barely concealed a grin as they told me it was not possible to buy French petrol with one English pound, but the man at the third garage smiled and gave me a gallon.

Not long afterwards, I had dozed on the ferry, filled up with petrol in Dover and was on the way home to Shropshire. After one day at home, Joe and I were on the road again, heading off to pre-qualify for the Martini International in Scotland. This was our life.

Through the remainder of 1979, my form improved to a point where I managed to pre-qualify for eight tournaments and I finished strongly with 46th place and £400 at the Dunlop Masters. These may have been small gains, but they kept me going.

I also won the *News of the World* Under-23 Match Play title at South Cliff Golf Club, near Scarborough, beating my friend John Hay 3 and 2 in the 36-hole final. My spirits soared again. Whenever I was struggling on the Tour, I always tried to sustain my self-confidence by making sure I won something somewhere . . . even if it was only a competitive money match against my mates in Oswestry.

By the end of 1979, my prize money for the year added up to the sum of £1,049 and, I had at last done enough to retain my Tour card without going to Qualifying School in October.

This progress resulted in my first sponsorship, when two local businessmen from Oswestry, Les Moss and Neville Tudor, effectively decided to take a large bet on my future. The deal was simple: their company, MTM Engineering, would give me £5,000 each year for a period of three years in return for 50% of my winnings. Based on my earnings for 1979, this seemed a great deal for me – and it was because it offered me some financial security at a time when it was urgently required – but Les and Neville had seen me play at Oswestry and were investing in my potential.

In 1980, recognising the need to introduce more control to my game, I began using a one-iron off the tee as much as possible. For the first time since I started smashing around Llanymynech, I made a decision to sacrifice power just to keep the ball in play.

The rewards were immediate: level par after four rounds and a respectable eighth place at the Italian Open. For the first time, the task of pre-qualifying was beginning to feel more like a formality. As the year wore on, I reached no fewer than 14 actual tournaments. Very few people on the Tour still assumed I was a caddie.

In these 14 European Tour events, I survived the halfway cut seven times, playing right through to Sunday in Italy, Spain, France, Jersey, Newcastle, Manchester and, with my parents present, at the Coral Welsh Classic. By the end of the year, my prize money added up to £3,481, leaving me 87th in the Order of Merit.

Life was getting better, but there were still moments of acute embarrassment. In the final round of one major tournament, I used my driver off the tee and hit the ball so far right that it ended up on the opposite side of the next fairway. I walked sheepishly across to hit my second, and was dismayed to find the infamously outspoken American, Hubert Green, striding down towards me. I stared resolutely at the ground, fearing some kind of rebuke but Hubert must have pitied me and said nothing.

And travelling from tournament to tournament still presented a significant challenge. On one occasion, DJ Russell and I drove to Italy in DJ's BMW, with fellow pros Martin Poxon and Mike English following behind in a Triumph Dolomite. I travelled home in the Triumph, and bounced for five hours when the shock absorbers packed up.

And we still scraped for every meal: playing in Nimes, France, we once parked in an orchard and thought we would save money by eating apples all week . . . except for the Friday evening when we ate ourselves stupid at the official barbecue.

After the marked improvement of 1980, I worked hard during the winter in preparation for what I honestly believed was going to be the long-awaited breakthrough in 1981. I had paid my dues, had learned a lot and now felt ready to compete.

Once again, it didn't happen. Maybe I was trying too hard but, by the middle of July, I had successfully qualified and reached the tournament seven times and survived only three halfway cuts. My driving seemed wayward again and the rest of my game collapsed like a house of cards.

The 1981 Open Championship was to be held at the Royal St George's Golf Club, Sandwich, and I drove down to Kent, hopeful of reviving my season by pre-qualifying for the tournament. Aside from my indifferent form, the omens were not good: at the time, I didn't particularly enjoy seaside links golf and, secondly, my previous efforts to make an impact at the Open offered little encouragement.

I had launched my first bid to pre-qualify for the Open when I was still an amateur, based at Hill Valley. It was obviously going to be a big occasion, and I even arranged to borrow a smart pair of shoes from the manager of the club at the time. My intentions were sound, even though the shoes were size nine and my feet were size seven. My hopes faded when

I scored nine, two, nine over an early par-five, par-three, par-five sequence of holes. Worse still, I suffered one of the bleeding noses that I used to get in those days, and I finished the round with a drenched red handkerchief stuck up one nostril. In the circumstances, I did well to miss pre-qualification by just a couple of shots.

Now, in my fifth season as a professional golfer, I planned an altogether more organised, effective Open bid. I was drawn to play in pre-qualifying at The Prince's Golf Club, next to Sandwich, and I started well, shooting 67 to lead the field after the first day.

Any kind of steady, solid performance on the Monday would probably have carried me safely through to the tournament, but my driving deteriorated and I was battling to stay in contention by the time I reached the turn in 37, one over par. A wayward tee-shot resulted in a double bogey at the 10th. My game had collapsed dramatically, and I didn't know whether to be angry or embarrassed as I pushed a peg into the ground at the 11th tee. I was using the driver, but hit it so badly the ball travelled no more than 20 yards, looped over a fence and finished out of bounds. Somehow it would not have seemed so bad if I sliced the ball high and right into some bushes, but this shot was the ultimate humiliation.

That was it. I had had enough.

I apologised to my playing partners, picked up my

clubs and marched 800 yards across the course to the car park.

'I.H. Woosnam – No Return'. The official entry in the records of the 1981 Open Championship pre-qualifying at Prince's neatly sums up probably the lowest point in my professional career. There was absolutely no media coverage of my furious with-drawal, no official censure and no repercussions. Nobody seemed to care.

Within 15 minutes, I was driving back to Oswestry, storming away from the Open and, I thought, my career in golf. My head was in a spin . . . 'What is the point in going on? My father told me to give myself five years. Well, five years has almost gone and I'm still playing like an idiot. I have to face it. I'm not good enough.'

It was almost midnight by the time I swung through the gates of New House Farm, still upset.

'It was a joke,' I told my parents. 'I've had enough. They are looking for an assistant professional at Oswestry, and I've decided I am going to apply. That's good enough for me.'

'Calm down,' they said. 'Don't do anything rash. Relax for a few days and see how you feel in a week or so.'

I didn't sleep much that night, staring instead at the ceiling of my bedroom and suffering the kind of silent, private agony known to anyone who has failed but who still believes, deep down where nobody else can see, that they can do so much better.

Potential: this was the word that began to dominate my mind as the days passed. I did have the
potential to do much better than I had played in that
second round at Prince's, and it was only necessary
to recall my efforts in the first round to prove that.
Before long, I was repeating to myself that my father
had told me to give it five years on the Tour, and
there were still six months of that period remaining.
I had fallen off the bicycle, but I needed to get back
in the saddle and start pedalling again. In the end, I
never did apply for that job at Oswestry.

My game marginally recovered in the remaining
events of the year on the European Tour, but I never
broke free from the group of pros who tended to pre-
qualify more often not, but then missed the cut more
often than they played the last two rounds. This was
evidently not good enough, and my time was fast
running out.

Early in January 1982, I set off to spend another
six weeks in central Africa, playing on the Safari Tour.
Since 1979, I had taken a handful of opportunities to
play abroad, travelling to tournaments in South Africa
and Australia, but the Safari Tour remained the most
enjoyable way of spending a couple of winter months.

A whole group of European professionals would
fly down each year and play five or six tournaments
while staying as lodgers in the homes of various expa-
triates. The cost was reasonable, the purses were

decent, the vibe was good and, above all, the top three on the Order of Merit earned exemption from having to pre-qualify for any tournament during that year's European Tour.

My early trips to Africa had been fun but, in my first year on the Safari Tour, I was pleased to have Tony Minshall as a travelling companion. Africa seemed about as foreign as you could get for two young lads from Shropshire and we had absolutely no idea of what to expect when we boarded the Nigerian Airways flight to Lagos. If somebody had warned us about lions roaming the fairways, we would have looked at each other and thought twice.

In any case, we arrived at the airport and were taken straight to the golf club where a woman seemed busy allocating lodgings to the European players. There appeared to be some kind of delay in settling Tony and me, so we found our way to the bar and enjoyed our first taste of a lager called Star Beer, served in huge bottles.

As we stood, glasses in hand, we gazed out across a nine-hole golf course like nothing we had ever seen before. The fairways were burned brown by the sun, with sporadic blades of grass appearing in baked earth; and the 'greens' were small round areas of sand mixed with oil and packed down to make an even putting surface. They were known as 'browns'.

Intrigued by this new world, Tony and I wandered outside to take a closer look at the 18th green. Every putt was obviously going to be dead straight, but it got even better than that: the actual hole was like a bucket, and this seemed to have the effect of making the sand around it sag down towards the hole.

As we soon discovered, one putt per green was the norm and chipping in from off the green was always on the cards. Of course, it made the scores lower, but conditions were the same for all players, so it didn't make the tournaments any easier to win.

After 45 minutes or so, the woman arranging accommodation found us in the bar and said she could lodge us both with a Welshman working on contract in Nigeria. He turned out to be a great guy and could not have been more friendly and helpful.

Neither of us played well that year, but those were carefree days when the game seemed fun and easy. The Safari Tour of 1982 seemed altogether more serious for me: these were the last events of my fifth full year, and I had to make progress.

It was fine having loads of potential – there are thousands of golfers up and down the country with great potential – but time was running out for me to prove I had the guts and resolve to transform ability into achievement on the professional Tour.

At last, I began to produce decent results: runner-up in the Nigerian Open after losing a play-off, runner-up in the Ivory Coast after the winner recorded a last round 64, fifth place in the Kenyan Open and then a tenth place in the Mufulira Open.

By the time the Tour reached the Zambian Open in Lusaka, I was lying second in the Order of Merit, on course to secure exempt status for the European Tour in 1982. I was playing nicely, showing control off the tee and fairway, and putting well. Checking my overall position whenever possible and taking very few risks, I remained solidly in the leading pack through four rounds under a punishing sun in Lusaka, but my 10th place finish proved sufficient to secure third place on the final Order of Merit.

I was thrilled, delighted by what felt like the first measurable achievement of my professional career. This was progress. Exempt status on the 1982 European Tour meant I would no longer need to report for pre-qualifying rounds early on Monday mornings because my name now passed straight into the tournament.

Prior to the 1982 Safari Tour, I was seriously considering my future on the Tour, wondering how I could justify another year with my costs far exceeding my prize money. By the time I arrived home in Shropshire, with my exempt status, I was buzzing.

In footballing terms, I suppose I had scored a winning goal in the last minute and advanced to the next round of the Cup.

The doubts evaporated, and confidence returned. From the point of exasperation, now I seemed permanently on the telephone, asking mates if they wanted to play a round at Oswestry. I wanted to play every day; I wanted to be ready for the European season. I convinced myself that 1982 would be my big year.

Yes, I did realise that, 12 months earlier, I had been saying exactly the same thing about 1981, but the key difference was that I was wrong then, and now I was right. I believed that. That's what I told myself, again and again. A massive part of being successful is being able to persuade yourself that success is possible.

I desperately wanted to believe.

CHAPTER THREE

Making a Living

It was just another day on the driving range: another stretch, another swift glance down the line to check who else was there, another bucket of balls – the same old routine.

As usual, I wanted to feel natural with my swing and to strike the ball straight and sweet; as usual, something didn't feel quite right, so, I started to swing; then I made a slight adjustment to that and swung again; I tried something else, swung, and that felt great.

I have sometimes been accused of incessantly tinkering with my swing, but every professional golfer spends week after week striving for the perfect swing that, deep down, we all know doesn't actually exist. But we keep trying.

And, in any case, playing golf has always been more fun than working for a living and, even at practice on this bright January day in Lagos, the capital of Nigeria, I was mindful that the sun was shining on my back while it was raining at home in Oswestry.

Gordon Brand senior had arrived to practise beside me, and I couldn't help but notice how he was hitting balls all over the place. Everyone hired local caddies on the Safari Tour and Gordon's guy was having a tough time gathering the balls. If I was spraying shots around like that, I thought to myself, I would be snapping clubs. Gordon just kept swinging.

For my part, I was feeling pretty pleased with myself because my swing felt solid. I had settled into a groove and appeared to be knocking long irons virtually into my caddie's pocket. He hardly had to move as each shot soared straight and true. This was fun. I was starting to feel confident about my game.

Hang on! My warm glow of well-being was abruptly shattered by the realisation that Gordon was nine strokes ahead of me after three rounds of the Nigerian Open. He had been shooting 67s and 68s while I was down the field on level par. It seemed so unfair. I was hitting the ball well, but he was scoring well.

So we kept swinging, and I kept thinking. Eventually, I said, 'Everything going all right, Gordon?'

'Yeah, not bad. You?'

'Well, I seem to be hitting the ball all right, but you wouldn't think so from the scores I'm shooting.'

'Golf isn't a beauty contest,' he replied. 'It's the strokes that count. There are no pictures on your scorecard.'

We chatted for a while, and I gradually began to understand the difference in our approach. Gordon didn't particularly mind how or where he hit the ball, so long as he completed the hole in as few strokes as possible. Nothing else bothered him.

By contrast, I was the eager perfectionist, who wanted to put every drive on the fairway, to find every green in regulation and to leave every long putt close enough for a tap-in.

If Gordon hit a drive into the rough and had to lay up short with his approach, he would focus his energies on chipping so close to the pin that he could hole his putt for par. In the same situation, I would curse my drive, panic about my swing, force my approach and more often than not drop a stroke or two. He was able to ride smoothly over bad shots, while I allowed myself to be upset when things went wrong. You might say he was travelling with first class suspension, while I didn't have any shock absorbers. No wonder I was having a bumpy ride.

Through the early months of 1982, principally inspired by my helpful chat with Gordon Brand Snr in Lagos, I started to develop a new mental attitude, a fresh strategy. The old joke about some football manager – that he thought tactics were a kind of mint – applied to me as a young golfer. At 23, I was getting serious.

Right, these were my thoughts: in an average round, I would be able to bank on making four birdies and hitting four poor shots. If the bad shots translated into bogeys, then I would end up around level par, and most probably be well down the field. However, if I could get down with a chip and putt from around the green, or maybe hole a long putt, and somehow scramble a par after each poor shot, then I could finish four under.

That was my new challenge: to change the way I reacted to a bad shot. Where I used to worry about what had gone wrong, now I needed to focus all my energy on saving par.

The first step in the process was to accept that bad shots are part of the game. I told myself there is no such thing as perfect golf but that bad shots will only ruin your card if you allow them to ruin your concentration, prompting you to throw clubs etc. I understood the principle because, as a youngster, I watched a lot of tennis on television and I remembered how Bjorn Borg had been transformed from a cursing racquet-thrower into the ice-cool No.1 player in the world. He simply learned to accept his bad shots. It was time for me to have the same attitude.

Secondly I estimated that I only spent 10% of practice time on my short game and putting, although these shots could account for as much as 65% of my shots in any one round. Recovery shots from hazards or bunkers did not frighten me at all, but I needed to be far more clinical from just off the green.

Now this may not have been rocket science, but I

did work most of it out for myself because I didn't have a coach in 1982. In fact, the sum total of professional guidance in my life added up to just four hours with Cyril Hughes, a few sessions with a top junior coach, Sid Collins, and five days with John Jacobs.

I learned to improvise and pick up tips along the way. If I had a specific problem, I would ask the opinions of good friends on the Tour like D.J. Russell, or I would seek out people who had watched me play for many years, such as my father and my old mates back in Shropshire, like Geoff Roberts and Andy Griffiths.

As the 1982 European Tour gathered momentum, I started to reap the rewards of staying calm and focusing on the course. Maybe the best way of describing this pivotal stage in my development as a golfer is to say my bad shots became much better.

This improvement in my game coincided with the first period in my professional career when I was not playing under the tyranny of having to pre-qualify for tournaments on the European Tour. The exempt status secured through the Safari Tour in Africa early in the year entirely changed the tone and pattern of my life.

I no longer needed to drive my caravanette through the night, hurtling down a motorway to make an early Monday morning tee-off time for the first round of pre-qualifying at a far-flung course. And I no longer needed to worry about failing to qualify and suffering the embarrassment of leaving town just as the big names were starting to arrive for the first round of the tournament on a Thursday.

Now in 1982 I was certainly not a big name, but exemption put me straight into the tournament and meant I could plan to arrive at the tournament on Tuesday, or maybe even Wednesday, settle down and fit in a practice round before starting the first round on Thursday. It was altogether more civilised.

As a pre-qualifier, I had felt like a mountaineer going around in circles among bleak foothills, going nowhere fast. When I became exempt, it was as if I had suddenly reached a point on the mountain where I could enjoy a clear view of the summit. Everything started to seem possible, achievable, within touching distance.

People often talk about the pressure and tension at the top of a professional sport, where the stakes are raised, the profile is high and only one can win. However, in my experience, the pressure and tension are greater at the bottom of the game, where guys fighting to pre-qualify are playing for their livelihoods, sometimes their next meal . . . rather than for thousands and their next car.

In any event, my precious exempt status earned on the Safari Tour was only valid for 1982, so the most important challenge was to earn enough prize money on the European Tour to make certain I retained exemption for 1983; and it was a phenomenal boost when I achieved this goal in only the third tournament.

Mark James had claimed victory in the Italian Open at Mores, in Sardinia, but nobody in the clubhouse was more overjoyed than me on that Sunday evening. I had tied for second with Bobby Clampett, the American, and claimed £4,274 in prize money.

The general consensus among pros in the clubhouse bar afterwards was that this amount would be more than enough to secure at least 60th place in the Order of Merit at the end of the year, and a top 60 finish was required to retain your player's card for the following year.

As I celebrated, I could literally feel the pressure melt away. I was now effectively exempt for the next 18 months. I felt liberated, exhilarated and eager to get out there and play.

My game remained solid and, as the weeks went by, I found I was collecting a cheque every Sunday: a joint 20th finish in the Martini International earned another £770 and fifth place at the Jersey Open put another £1,470 in my pocket.

By the time I travelled to Royal Troon to compete in the 111th Open Championship, I had missed only two cuts in 12 events on the European Tour. It suddenly seemed much longer than a year since I had stormed off the Prince's course, near Sandwich.

Sandy Lyle, my old rival, already twice a winner of the Order of Merit and on his way to a tremendous 15 top-10 finishes on Tour that year, was still playing in a different league, but more and more people seemed to have heard about the little Welshman who could drive the ball as far as anyone else. That was the label being hung around my neck, and I wasn't complaining. I began to relish the feeling of taking out the driver in a major event, and ripping it down the fairway, hitting the ball further than my playing partners and hearing that special 'Oooooh' ripple through the spectators gathered around the tee.

Distance has always excited me. It is only the method of measurement that has changed: aged 12, I wanted to pass a hollow in the ninth fairway at Llanymynech; as an established professional, I sought that gasp of admiration from the gallery. The sheer buzz of hitting the ball just right still thrilled me to the core.

Exempt for the next 18 months, earning regular money and starting to win a reputation: 1982 was turning out to be the kind of massive year I needed, but I still hadn't won a title.

Three rounds of 71 in tough conditions carried me strongly into contention at the Benson and Hedges International Open at Fulford, York, and I recall taking a deep breath when I realised I was going to be playing with Greg Norman in the last pair on the Sunday afternoon.

This was the 'Big Time', playing down the last nine with an icon like the Great White Shark, live on television, and I was determined to seize the opportunity and not be overwhelmed.

My initial nerves had largely subsided by the time we reached the second tee and I took out the driver with a persimmon wooden head bought during the Dutch Open two weeks earlier. With no messing about, I settled into position, swung full and hard and powered the ball over a rise, straight down what was almost a blind fairway.

Greg followed suit, and the two of us walked side by side until two balls came into view, one lying 20 yards beyond the other. Greg didn't even bother to look at the first ball and strode on towards the second. He assumed he would be longer off the tee. I walked on behind and allowed myself a discreet smile when I reached the first ball and discovered that it did, in truth, belong to the great Australian. I had outdriven him! At that moment, I looked up to watch my clearly embarrassed partner turn around and slowly walk back up the fairway to where the first ball lay.

As we passed each other, I heard Greg muttering to his caddie: 'Tell me how that little guy hits the ball further than me.'

I grinned broadly, delighted by this backhanded compliment from one of the longest hitters in the game, and I continued to play reasonably well into the afternoon. But Greg was also on top of his form and, when I narrowly missed a 10-foot putt on the 18th green to force a play-off, he claimed victory by a shot.

At the post-tournament press conference, the

Australian was kind enough to tell the assembled media: 'You must watch this little guy because he's going to be a superstar one day.'

It had been another highly successful week but, as I boarded a flight to Switzerland – my success meant that the Dormobile had been sent back home to Shropshire – I was still wondering when I would break through to win that elusive first title on the European Tour.

The 1982 Ebel Swiss Open was staged at the Crans-sur-Sierre course in Switzerland, and I managed to maintain my form by posting an opening 68, followed by another 68 on the Friday. After a third round 66, I led the field by four strokes. For the second week in succession, I had played my way into the last pairing on the Sunday afternoon, and I was firmly resolved to batten down the hatches and let nothing slip.

Perhaps I became a little too cautious because Bill Longmuir, the gifted Scot, emerged as a serious threat, cutting my advantage to three strokes, then two and then one. As the pressure mounted, Bill drew level and we moved into a play-off.

My mind was full of Borg and staying calm as we halved the first and second extra holes. I was holding my game together and, finally, Bill three-putted at the third extra hole. So, on 29 August, 1982, I clinched my first official European professional title.

It can happen that you spend so long looking forward to one particular achievement that, when it does take place, it can feel like an anti-climax. This was not the case in Crans.

After surviving the interviews, I called my parents at home in Oswestry and could hear the pleasure and pride in their voices. My first Tour victory had been a long time coming and I was relieved to start repaying them for their love and support.

And by happy coincidence, or good planning, D.J. Russell's wife had just given birth to a son, Christopher, so it was with a real sense of joy that our group launched a double celebration deep into a quiet, tranquil Sunday night in Switzerland. That was a party. We were drinking at altitude, so the alcohol went straight to our heads and most of us were rocking and rolling after three or four beers. But we were golfers not rugby players, so we were generally well disciplined and didn't upset anyone!

I didn't make any secret of the fact that I enjoyed a pint now and then, sometimes seven or eight pints. It wasn't an issue. It was usual for me to smoke five or six cigarettes during a round as well, and I still do. That was me. That was the way I was. I wasn't breaking a law. At this stage of life, when I was in my 20s and reasonably fit, my view was that it didn't matter how much I drank so long as I could get a full eight hours sleep afterwards. In fact, it was good for me. Going out and having a drink seemed to help me relax. It might not have worked for everyone, but it worked for me.

The winner of the 1982 Swiss Open took home £10,085 and, after the cheque had cleared my bank account, I headed to the Ford dealership to buy an RS2000, the hot car of the day. After so many years struggling, I felt I deserved the treat . . . yet success was never going to turn my head, not back in Shropshire.

I have always been fortunate to have family and friends who treat me the same whether I miss the cut or win the tournament. If I ever came home and tried to act a big deal, they'd quickly cut me back to size and bring me thudding down to earth.

So, thankfully, nothing changed. Crazy nights in the pub felt the same, and my mates and I would play regular games of golf at Oswestry, or Hill Valley or Llanymynech, that were never anything less than fiercely competitive and deadly serious. We would play for a pound on the front nine, a pound on the back nine and a pound on the match, but the humiliation of losing and the embarrassment of having to pay in the bar afterwards would not have been more painful if we had been playing for a few grand.

I used to enjoy these days of banter and needle when I was a youngster but, as time passed, they seemed to become even more precious and important. Within an increasingly exalted life on Tour, I started to appreciate my environment at home where I could revert to being just another ordinary guy on the course.

However far I travelled, however much I won, home was still home . . . although, in time, even this would change.

By any measure, 1982 had been a phenomenal year for me, exactly the kind of giant leap forward that I had spent so much of the previous winter convincing myself was possible. Golf is a sport easily drowned in statistics that prove everything and nothing, but these few numbers do illustrate my progress:

1981 – 104th in Order of Merit, £1,884 prize money

1982 – 8th in Order of Merit, £48,794 prize money.

Apart from winning at the Swiss Open, I had achieved top-five finishes in the Italian Open, the Jersey Open, the Dutch Open and the Spanish Open; and, at the end of the year, I rallied to win the Cacharel Under-25 championships at Nimes, France.

My transformation had taken place at astonishing speed. One moment, I was a struggling youngster, heating up baked beans in the Dormobile and a few weeks away from quitting the Tour; a few months later, I was a bright 24-year-old with promise. One day, you're down. The next day, you're up. The margins between success and failure in any sport are notoriously thin; there are many, many guys with talent, and there is usually an element of luck in who survives and who falls by the wayside.

Having said that, I did feel quietly proud of the fact that I had kept battling away when others would have quit. I had struggled for five years, not getting very far and not earning very much, but I had clung to a belief that I would win through in the end. I was fetched up that way. My parents told me anything was possible if you wanted it badly enough, and I wanted nothing more than to be a top professional golfer. That was what I wanted to do; that was all I could do, so that's what I did.

Determination, sheer bloody-mindedness, will-power, maybe a bit of talent: whatever it was that carried me into the top dozen on the European Order of Merit, it was probably the same qualities that enabled me to stay there for 14 of the next 15 years.

One satisfying consequence of my improved form in 1982 was that, in what was the final year of our three-year deal, I was able to deliver a decent return for MTM Engineering, the Oswestry company who had quietly been supporting me since 1980. Their annual investment of £5,000 as the stake for 50% of my total prize money had not looked too clever in 1980 and 1981 when I repaid them barely a thousand pounds, but I was pleased to write them a cheque for £30,840 at the end of 1982.

This amount represented half of my worldwide earnings, plus their share of the proceeds from the sale of the Range Rover I had won for a hole-in-one at the Zambian Open earlier in the year, and it brought a gratifying symmetry to the end of an arrangement that had worked out extremely well, for them and for me.

MTM Engineering had been battling in the tough economic climate of the early 1980s, and, just as they had helped me when I urgently needed financial assistance, I was pleased that my money helped them two years later.

Writing out such a large cheque did feel strange, but I didn't resent the payment because that was the deal; and, in any event, I also knew the fact that, without their sponsorship, which essentially enabled me to join the Safari Tour, it would have been much more difficult for me to make progress in my career.

I had established myself on the European Tour, and proved I could win. The next step, which many first-time winners had failed to take over the years, was to become consistently competitive with the top players in the world. I hated to think I would win once and disappear, sliding unnoticed back into the pack.

This was principally a mental challenge. In my mind, men like Tom Watson, Nick Faldo, Seve Ballesteros, Greg Norman and Sandy Lyle were heroes, idols, legends. I needed to respect them, but not to hold them in such esteem that I couldn't compete against them.

I remember returning home after the 1982 Open and telling how well Watson had played, how he had been so aggressive and determined, how he was always attacking the flags, how he swung the putter with real purpose, bashing in big putts.

'Excuse me,' my father asked, 'this Watson sounds amazing. Has he got three arms or four legs or something?'

I took the point and turned back to my plate of mince and mashed potato. Watson was only human, maybe.

In those days, that's how we were. Young players on the Tour hardly dared speak to the superstars. One year in Tunisia, I was in a large group of players who spent almost three hours together in a bus travelling from the airport to a hotel, and I didn't utter a single word. I was shy. Most of us youngsters were quiet and in awe of the more established players.

Everything changed in the 1990s, of course. Then, we would watch these wise, young lads, cocky as hell, arriving on the circuit, chirping, 'so, what do you think about that, Nick' or 'how were you playing today, Seve,' and we would wonder if we were perhaps too respectful. I don't think so. Deference is not a fault.

In May 1983 I was drawn to play with Seve for the first time in the first two rounds of the Car Care Plan International at Sand Moor, near Leeds. He had just won his second US Masters at Augusta and I was beside the practice green when I spotted him, this dark, brooding and magnificent presence. I decided it would be the right thing to walk up and introduce myself.

'Hello, I'm Ian Woosnam.'

'Oh, hello.'

He didn't seem enormously interested, and there was no good reason why he should have been, but I was excited and nervous to be playing beside him. I had once read in a newspaper that Seve goes after a golf course in the way a lion goes after a zebra, and that image left an impression on me. That was the way to play.

In the context of my golfing education, those two rounds at Sand Moor proved to be the most invigorating of the year. As bold and unbowed as his reputation had promised, Seve simply bounded onto the tee and unfurled this flamboyant and spectacular swing. It was breathtaking to watch, and the ball flew left at the first, curled right at the second and boomed straight at the third. I hit all three fairways in regulation but, as we walked to the fourth tee, he was two under and I was level.

I was bewildered. My first response was to think that, if this guy could win Majors playing here, there and everywhere, then I would certainly be able to win Majors one day.

Then I began to realise that Seve's ability to hit the ball out of trouble is probably unique in the history of the game. Certainly, he had the best short game of his generation.

By the end of that first round, I was thinking that if I could chip and putt like him, I could win many Major tournaments.

By the Friday evening, I had a clear understanding of why he would always be such an electric presence on the course. I had also learned there was no reason for me to tremble at his name because we were both three-under par after 36 holes.

I finished 12th at Sand Moor, and played with a brand new set of Dunlop clubs in the PGA Championship the next week at Royal St George's, Sandwich. Going into the final round, I lay just two shots behind the leader, Seve, and level with Sandy Lyle.

Seve won by two, with Sandy second and me fourth, but the important fact was that I had been in contention again, keeping up with the big boys. The auras were starting to fall away and, as far as I was concerned, the great household names were starting to be just first names.

A week later, I won again. In 1983, the Silk Cut Masters was held at the St Pierre Golf and Country Club, near Chepstow, and the pre-tournament publicity focused on me as an in-form, bold, young Welshman bidding to win an event on home soil.

For some reason I was slicing everything during the practice round, so, once again not hesitating to make a change, I went back to my old set of Dunlop clubs and this proved an inspired decision.

Some weeks, you feel fantastic and hole everything. With the local crowd becoming increasingly enthusiastic, this was just such a week for me; and the cheers became louder each time another putt rolled towards the hole and dropped out of sight.

Rounds of 68, 69 and 67 should have set me clear, but Bernard Gallacher was playing well at the time, and I needed to hole a series of long putts on the back nine of the final round to win by three shots. Someone gave me a Welsh flag at the prize-giving, to end a great day.

Tied in 61st place at the 1983 Silk Cut Masters, having missed the halfway cut, one of the greatest names in British golf had begun to focus on another issue. Tony Jacklin had been selected to captain Europe versus the United States in the Ryder Cup to be contested at Palm Beach Gardens, Florida, in September 1983. This buoyant and positive man was destined to emerge as the impetus behind the revival of this great sporting event but, for now, he was putting the final touches to his team and tactics.

With five top-10 finishes already in the year, I felt confident of being included in the European team, and I was pleased when I was told that Jacklin had appeared on television, explaining how people liked me because I was a 'wonderful, little guy who couldn't get to the ball fast enough'.

Everybody was aware of the history that America had retained the cup year after year since 1957, when Dai Rees' team triumphed at Lindrick Golf Club; and everyone knew the popularity of the event had faded with its boring predictability.

Then, in 1979, the Ryder Cup was reborn by the decision to expand the annually overwhelmed Britain and Ireland side into what would be a fully-fledged European team. Europe lost by emphatic margins in 1979 and 1981, but the announcement of Jacklin's team in the late summer of 1983 prompted a widespread belief that the perennial underdogs would mount a serious challenge to the Americans, even away from home.

Ballesteros, Faldo, Lyle, Langer, Gallacher, Canizares, Brand senior, Torrance, Brown, Gallacher, Way and me: it did look a strong team, and I was delighted to have been included, second only to Paul Way as the youngest member of the side.

This adventure was going to be my first ever trip to play in the United States, and I arranged for my mother and father to fly to Florida and bolster European support in the crowd.

Tony Jacklin stood at the heart of everything. He brought new energy to the role of captain, he planned and organised relentlessly, he pulled everyone around him, he cajoled every player to buy into our shared goals and, most important of all, he took 12 established professionals and blended them into a family.

This was no mean feat. Golf is an individual career played by its fair share of different, strong, self-minded people, yet Tony drew us together and established the magical kind of camaraderie that has remained a feature of every European team ever since. He knew when to crack a joke, and he knew when to impose discipline. He chaired the regular team meetings where we were all encouraged to discuss our strategy for the foursomes and fourball matches. He kept a close, almost paternal eye on every member of the team, and took enormous care in choosing his pairings for the first and second day of competition at Palm Beach Gardens.

In almost every way, Tony proved an extraordinary captain, setting the exceptional standards by which his successors have each been judged and which all will struggle to match.

As a team, we settled comfortably in Palm Beach Gardens and practised efficiently over the PGA National golf course, content to be cast as the underdogs with genuine potential.

Tony took me to one side on the Thursday afternoon and told me I wouldn't be playing in the morning foursomes on the first day, but that, if everything went according to plan, I would partner Sam Torrance in the fourballs later in the afternoon.

I was relieved. The captain had given me time to adjust to the atmosphere before having to get out there and play.

In most golf tournaments, the pressure builds up through four days and reaches a crescendo over the last nine holes on a Sunday afternoon. A Ryder Cup is different because that kind of gut-twisting pressure starts on the first tee on Day One and stays there until one team walks away with the small, gold trophy.

As I hovered around the edges, we managed to win two of the four morning foursomes and eat lunch at 2–2. By then, I knew Sam and I would be playing Ben Crenshaw and Calvin Peete in what was the final four-ball match of the afternoon.

Sam has always been a good friend and he certainly knew me well enough to notice I was incredibly tense on the first tee. In fact, at one stage, I thought I was going to be sick. I had always thought of myself as an easygoing type, but this kind of pressure was new.

'OK, Woosie, calm down now,' the Scot told me in his calmest, gentlest voice. 'Just take your time. I'll look after things for a few holes, just until you find your feet.'

'Thanks, I appreciate that.'

Sam sounded reassuring, and I was starting to feel better as he stepped onto the first tee. He placed his ball and proceeded to slice his drive way right. It landed out of bounds. He turned to look at me with an apologetic shrug of the shoulders and, in his broad Scottish accent, said: 'Welcome to the Ryder Cup, Woos.'

Pulling myself together somehow, I managed to keep my ball on the first fairway and eventually shared the hole with Crenshaw with birdie 3s. As the close battle wore on, Sam came more into his own and it was largely through his skill that we halved the match.

Meanwhile, our team-mates had managed to win two of the other fourballs, giving us an unlikely four and a half to three and a half lead by the end of the first day. Nobody was taking anything for granted, but we had made a promising start.

Tony said he was pleased with the way Sam and I had played, and he told us we would play another fourball match on the second morning. We were getting along extremely well, but it was then our luck to be drawn against Tom Watson, who had won his fifth Open Championship eight weeks before, and Bob Gilder.

We tried our best, of course, but our morning was summed up by events on the ninth green. Sam had secured a half in par with Gilder, and Watson had an almost impossible chip from the rough above and behind the green to seize an unlikely win.

As the American sized up the shot, I tugged Sam's sleeve and gibbered in his ear: 'Watch this, Sam, he's going to hole it. He's the best in the world at this kind of shot. It's like the US Open at Pebble Beach last year.' Sam replied with a thin smile, economically telling me to calm down, keep quiet and shut up.

Watson duly played the shot, which crashed against the flag and flew into the cup. 'America wins the hole in three,' chanted the scorer and, before long, we were beaten five and four.

Our hopes were sustained through Saturday by the

Faldo and Langer pairing who won in both the morning and afternoon, and by the Ballesteros and Way combination who halved their match in the morning and beat Watson and Gilder in the afternoon.

By Saturday night, the Americans knew they were involved in a dogfight. The teams were locked at 8–8, with the 12 singles to be played on the Sunday. Jacklin buzzed around the hotel, chatting to players here and there, keeping us all on the boil.

I tried to focus on my singles match, and was again slightly disappointed when the draw paired me against the formidable Craig Stadler, the 1982 US Masters champion, a powerful man at the top of his game, known worldwide as 'The Walrus'.

He played consistently well, while I too often strayed into the punishing rough. Several times, I found my ball lying at the bottom of grass that resembled wire wool. Since I had no clear idea of how to extricate myself, Stadler won the hole each time.

Trailing by three at the turn, I thought I had an opportunity to get back into the match when the Walrus seemed to have drifted off into the water at the 10th, but his ball stayed on dry land and, like the good pro that he is, he chipped and putted to get the half.

At the par-five 11th hole, my drive came to rest in a basket on a golf cart but, since the cart was ruled to be stationary at the time, I was awarded a free drop. I suppose they thought a moving cart might have carried the ball closer to the green!

This break didn't do me much good because Stadler continued to be too solid and strong, eventually winning three and two. I was bitterly disappointed and was left with a horrible sense of having let my team-mates down but all I could do was get back on the course and lend my vocal support to those guys still playing.

At one point during the extremely tense afternoon, the teams were locked at 12–12 with each side needing two and half points from the four singles matches still in progress; and it ultimately all came down to the match between Lanny Wadkins and Jose-Maria Canizares. The Spaniard led by one hole coming up to the last, but Wadkins then played a sublime wedge shot that finished less than a foot from the flag. I remember watching Jack Nicklaus, the US captain in 1983, walking across the fairway to kiss the divot from Wadkins' shot. The American got away with half a point, and the home team eventually ran out winners by 14 and a half to 13 and a half.

We were bitterly disappointed, of course, particularly those of us who had lost our singles matches. If just one of us had managed to win a point, the whole team would have made history as the first visiting side ever to win the Ryder Cup in America.

However, as Tony Jacklin said, our achievement was to prove beyond any doubt that the Ryder Cup was a contest again. For each member of our side,

1985 and the chance to meet those Americans on our home soil could not come soon enough.

I duly completed the 1983 season, finishing in ninth position on the European Order of Merit with total earnings of £48,164 and one tournament victory. Strangely, this was almost identical to my performance in 1982 and, in my mind, it represented an important consolidation among the leading players on the Tour.

By the afternoon of 12 November, 1983, I was confronted by an entirely different prospect – Glendryth Pugh at the altar.

CHAPTER FOUR

Living the Life

Sitting nervously in the front row of the church, all I wanted to do was turn round to see whether my bride had arrived. Amid the organ music, the flowers and the expectant family and friends, I needed to look back up the aisle and see if Glen was there.

She was.

In fact, Glen has always been there.

For as long as I can remember, Glen has always been there. Our families were friends in the village of St Martins, and I used to see her around and about school. I knew who she was, and she knew who I was; and I quite liked her then but, of course, that was not something I was going to tell anyone.

The years passed and, in 1978, I happened to notice Glen at a mutual friend's wedding in the village. I was only 20 and she was almost 17. The disco music was playing and the dance floor was lit by those old-fashioned fluorescent lights. I remember watching Glen dancing and all I could see were her blue eyes.

'Eh, Ronnie,' I muttered, elbowing my friend Ronnie Owen in the ribs. 'I'm going to marry that girl over there.'

We started seeing each other soon afterwards, and seemed to be what, back then, people called 'an item', but then she went off to be a nanny, I joined the Tour, and we drifted apart.

It was the summer of 1982, and I had just finished playing in a pro-am at Sunningdale when my mother passed me the message that Glen Pugh had called. She was now training as a nurse at one of the big London hospitals; she had left her number and said I should call some time, if I ever happened to be passing by.

Well, as luck would have it, and after changing a few commitments, I 'happened to be passing by' the very next evening.

We were duly married in Oswestry on 12 November, 1983, emerging from the church arm-in-arm and walking under an archway of golf clubs held aloft by our friends, five standing on each side of the path. David Parry was my best man.

Glen has been there ever since.

I haven't. The nature of my job has meant I have been away for between 30 and 35 weeks of each year. The world's highest-paid businessmen would refuse to spend that amount of time away from home, but this was, and is, the reality for professional golfers.

It's a reality that Glen has accepted ever since that

difficult moment when I told her we would not be able to go on honeymoon because I was already committed to playing a tournament starting in Indonesia on the Thursday after our wedding.

Glen understood then, and she understands now. She saw me grow up in St Martins and she knew what I wanted to achieve in my life. She knew I was going to play golf, she knew it was going to be tough at times; and, since we've been together, she has been right behind me, totally supportive every step of the way.

The key to our relationship is that we have always shared the same two basic goals: to live in a comfortable house and to give our three children a great education. So, if I had to be away playing golf to make this possible, then we could accept that.

Glen often travelled with me in the early years and, even after our son Daniel was born, she used to bring him along to the golf course; and he quickly became a hit with the photographers who, whenever I happened to win the tournament, would ask for Glen and me to pose with young Daniel sitting happily in the trophy.

We both agreed Glen would stay home when he was ready to start going to school and, as Rebecca and Ami have followed, that is where Glen has largely remained, with her opportunities to join me at tournaments restricted to the school holidays.

It has not been easy. I have suffered through not

having Glen with me, and she has suffered with me being away, and I recognise that, throughout these years, I have missed many, many important moments in the lives of our children; that hurts.

However, I have never had any doubts that I was correct in always wanting to be a golfer. I turned professional because, firstly, that was what I was good at, and, secondly, because I wanted to provide a high standard of living for my family.

Of course, I have frequently been disappointed to miss one of the children playing in a sports match at school, or singing in a concert or something because I was away, but the simple fact is they would not have been at that school if I didn't play golf for a living. And I have generally tried to compensate for the weeks away by ensuring I spend December and January at home. Guys working nine to five may go home every night, but they don't get that kind of extended break around Christmas and New Year.

In truth, golf has given us a fantastic lifestyle. We have made enormous sacrifices as a family, but it is also the case that we have enjoyed fantastic benefits as a family.

That's life, and I very much hope that, as they grow older, our children will look back and agree that Glen and I made the right choices. At the end of the day, everything was done for them.

As the 1984 season approached, I set myself the simple goal of maintaining my progress in the game.

I had won two tournaments, now I wanted to win again. I had twice finished in the top 10 of the European Order of Merit, now I wanted to finish in the top five. I needed to keep working hard, to keep improving and to keep earning.

I looked around for guidance, someone to provide a word of inspiration or suggest a change in my swing that would make all the difference, and I found a gentleman by the name of Gavin Christie, who happened to be assisting D.J. Russell at the time. Gavin knew the game inside out and, one morning at Kedlestone Park, D.J.'s home club, I got him to take a look at my swing for an hour or so.

'It's OK,' he said, in his gentle Scottish accent, 'but you'll get more control if you can keep your left wrist ahead of the clubhead at the moment of impact.'

I adjusted my swing accordingly, and it did feel better; another valuable hour spent with another wise man, and another step in the right direction. Gavin eventually became my official coach when he started to spend time on the Tour, and I always appreciated his time and valued his opinion.

As the season got under way, I was playing reasonably well, taking home something like a grand each week after a top 20 finish, but I wanted to do better and, during the two days of practice before the French Open in May, my game stepped up a gear.

Not for the first time in my career, and thankfully not for the last, I began to produce a fantastic run of form. Almost every drive seemed to soar down the fairway, almost every iron shot felt so solid and accurate, almost every chip went close and almost every putt disappeared into the hole.

I can't explain how or why this happened. All I know is that it felt instinctive and natural, almost as though I was doing everything right without focusing on anything in particular. In many ways, I felt like a surfer riding the crest of the perfect wave.

These sudden, intense bursts of form became a feature of my golfing career. Of course, they were fun while they lasted, but they also became a source of immense frustration because, when things didn't go so well, that form seemed so elusive.

'Just do what you were doing in May,' people would say.

'But I don't know what I was doing! I just did it.'

Confident, happy, assured; a first round 67 and 13th place at the French Open; chatting to playing partners, searching for Glen in the galleries; tied for eighth at the PGA Championship; stomping up and down the fairways, relishing each moment in the groove; equal fifth place at the Jersey Open; smiling, a chat in the bar; rounds of 69, 67, 66, 64, third place and six grand in the Benson & Hedges International at St Mellion.

Soon we were preparing to play the Scandinavian Enterprise Open, the tournament hosted by Sven Tumba, a former ice-hockey star, at his challenging

Ullna Golf Club, Stockholm. The people were friendly, the atmosphere was positive and I was enjoying myself on Tour: first tee, swing, smack, here we go again. I was six shots off the lead after the first round, four shots off the pace after the second, but I wasn't making too many errors and a third round 69 on a tough course put me in contention. With Craig Stadler heading the chase, I stayed steady on Sunday and posted a 70 to finish three strokes clear of a strong field.

My increasingly consistent performances had begun to attract the attention of the top marketing agents in golf, Mark McCormack's International Management Group, and it was in 1984 that IMG and I started what has become a long, successful association.

I had been aware of the need to maximise my marketing and sponsorship potential for some time and, before I even met IMG, I got involved in discussions with another prominent agent. This guy definitely looked the part, with his smart suits, bright ties and good manners, and he was soon promising me the world. Naïve youngster that I was, I was starting to get excited. His legal people drew up contracts, and I was invited to visit him at his large house in the country and agree the deal.

'Now, Ian,' he began, 'there's plenty of money to be made in personal appearances these days. Companies don't mind paying big name sportsmen to speak at their functions.'

'OK,' I said.

'I want to put you in touch with somebody who will help with your accent and public speaking, and we can run through the rules about cutlery and things later. That's no problem.'

The agent was grinning. My jaw was hanging open. Did I hear him right? Help with my accent? Rules about cutlery? I reckoned he must have been joking. He wasn't. I drove back home, and told my parents the whole story. They thought I had made it up. Next day, I called the agent and told him I wasn't interested.

There has often been an element of snobbery in British golf, as I suppose there is in anything, but I can't say I was bothered if anybody thought I was from the wrong side of the tracks. It was their problem. I took people just as I found them.

However, one thing was certain: if anyone wanted to market me to sponsors, they would have to market me as they found me, complete with a working-class Shropshire accent.

IMG have never tried to change me over the years, and I have generally been happy in a stable that included Faldo and Lyle in the early days and now manages Tiger Woods. The sheer size and scope of their organisation has proved that if you want to get big in golf, it's usually easier to get big with IMG.

As an example, the organisers of a tournament in Japan might have approached IMG in 1984, and said they want Faldo and Lyle in their field. With me on their books, IMG would use their influence and reply that Faldo and Lyle can play, but the organisers might want to take Woosnam as well. So, I would go, and get my chance. That's how the system worked.

They have the contacts and experience; they have the best players, the TV arm and the biggest clout. A golfer signing with IMG is like a promising footballer signing for Manchester United. All of a sudden, the world seems a bigger, richer place.

While never quite matching my purple patch in mid-summer, I was generally satisfied with my form towards the end of 1984. Year on year, every measure indicated I was making progress.

In terms of the European Order of Merit, I had finished 8th in 1982 and 9th in 1983; my position improved to 6th in 1984, rose to 4th in 1985, and then remained at 4th in 1986.

This upward trend was sustained in the annual money stakes: £48,794 in 1982, £48,164 in 1983 and a remarkable 40% increase to £68,126 in 1984. At least, I reckoned that was remarkable. Then, my earnings soared again to £153,605 in 1985.

Such sums were more than I ever imagined possible, but my basic approach remained the same. Playing golf was always fun for me. Playing against friends on Tour like Sam Torrance, D J Russell and Peter Baker was even more fun – we would often get together for practice rounds and, when Sam and I were playing, the stakes could get as high as £500. Playing with friends on Tour and earning exceptional prize money was a fantastic way of life.

Victory in the Zambian Open got 1985 off to a promising start but early optimism gave way to a creeping frustration when, week after week on the European Tour, I battled my way into contention but then lacked the killer touch to claim the title.

Second place in Jersey, third place at the Irish Open, fourth at the Glasgow Open: my prize money was going through the roof but I wanted to win. We were into August, and I still hadn't secured a title. I was just starting to get a little bit frustrated and grumpy.

My form was respectable during the first three rounds of the Benson and Hedges International Open at Fulford, but I didn't seem to have much chance of securing that elusive tournament win when I arrived at the course on the Sunday morning.

Rodger Davis, the Australian, led the field at nine-under par, with Des Smyth and Sam Torrance eight-under, and Sandy Lyle and Howard Clark a further two strokes back. I was on three-under par, apparently left to contest the minor placings.

'Excuse me, can I see your parking pass?'

'What?'

'Your parking pass, please.'

It was an official at Fulford. Pedigree Yorkshireman, he did not give a damn who I was – and he gave every indication that he knew exactly who I was. It didn't matter. If I didn't have a pass, he wasn't going to wave me through to the players' area. My pass should have been wedged just inside the windscreen, but it wasn't there, and it wasn't on the back seat, and it wasn't on the floor either.

'Look, I'm a player,' I said, pleading.

'If you don't have a pass, you'll have to pay,' he said bluntly, as a triumphant expression crossed his face.

'What?'

'That's five pounds, please!'

Furious, I scrabbled around to find a fiver in my wallet, and angrily handed it over. He was grinning broadly now.

'I'll show that bugger,' I muttered as I parked my car. If ever I needed motivation to play well, I had it now. I was so charged up I could feel my heart pounding on the first tee.

Four hectic hours later, I was reflecting upon one of the best, most satisfying rounds of my life. I had shot a course record 62 and become the first ever player to make eight consecutive birdies in a European Tour event. In my pent-up fury, I had fired every shot at every flag and rammed nearly every putt at the cup.

I had finished at 13-under par, and hurled down the challenge to those players still on the course. At one stage, I thought it would be enough to secure a dramatic victory but I was destined to finish second yet again. Fresh from winning the Open, Sandy Lyle started holing putts on the back nine, and my old friend got home with an outstanding 64 to beat me by a single stroke.

It had been a memorable day, and as I drove out of Fulford that Sunday evening, I looked around for the official, not sure whether I should tell him where to stuff his pass or to thank him for firing me up so effectively. In any case, he had gone home.

Without a win on Tour in 1985, I resolved to make amends in 1986 but the year began to follow a strangely familiar pattern. I started by winning again in Africa, at the Kenyan Open, but then in Europe took up where I seemed to have left off: playing well and earning well, but apparently unable to nail down a title.

I played myself into winning positions at the Madrid Open, at the PGA Championship and at the Irish Open and, even though each event yielded another large cheque, I always stumbled just short of taking the title.

The jokes were on me. At Turnberry for the Open, I produced some gutsy golf in a gruelling wind and actually led the tournament after the first round. Then, Greg Norman blew everyone away with a memorable 63 in the second round and, despite playing really well, I finished in third place, a bridesmaid once again.

'Well played, Woosie,' some joker shouted as I walked up the 18th. 'You've been playing three feet below the wind.'

It wasn't a bad gag, but I scarcely raised a smile. It was now almost two years since I had won on the European Tour and, even if the money was still rolling in, I was not satisfied.

Fifth place at the Benson and Hedges International, fifth place at the German Open: this was getting frustrating. I was starting to become superstitious. It was getting that bad.

'What's your favourite colour,' Glen asked one morning.

'Red,' I replied.

'And what's your unlucky colour?'

'Green,' I said, acting bored.

'So why are you driving a green car?'

That was it! It was a great car, a special BMW 635, but it was undeniably green and, we both agreed, it had to go.

Later that week, I was driving a white Ford when I arrived at The Belfry to compete in the Lawrence Batley Championship, hoping this change in vehicle would bring a change in luck. The evidence of the first two rounds was not especially encouraging: two 71s left me tucked in behind the leading pack, as usual.

Practising on the putting green before the start of my third round, I took a gamble and decided to change the method that I used to line up my putts. The results were instant and, in difficult conditions on the Saturday afternoon, I produced a solid round of 66, three shots better than anyone else managed that day.

The leaderboard beside the 18th green showed I would carry a three-stroke lead over Spain's Jose Rivero into the fourth round; so I took few risks on the Sunday, shot 69 and was massively relieved to win the tournament by seven clear shots from Ken Brown. It was 21 September, 1986, and my waiting was over.

A weight seemed to have been lifted from my shoulders, and I felt ready to move forward again, to the next level. I started looking around for someone who would help me get there.

Shortly after winning at the Belfry, I headed to St Andrews for the Dunhill Cup, and I had just finished a practice round on the Old Course when I noticed Sam Torrance and his father, Bob, standing perhaps 15 yards away, near the Royal and Ancient clubhouse.

Bob gestured towards me, and asked Sam: 'Isn't that the lad who was playing in front of you? Who is he?'

'That's Woosie,' Sam replied.

We were introduced to each other and, as we chatted, I began to realise why so many players rated Bob as one of the most astute and knowledgeable coaches on the Tour. The thought occurred to me that this friendly, animated and broad-accented man from Largs on the west coast of Scotland could take me to the next level.

'Bob, would you look at my swing?'

'Of course,' he said in his broad Scots accent.

I spent an increasing amount of time with Bob towards the end of 1986, and it was not long before I asked him to become my coach. He was obviously helping a few other players on Tour at the time, so he was already attending most of the tournaments, and he agreed to start guiding me on a regular basis.

In Bob's view, the effective transfer of your weight from the start of the backswing to the follow through was the vital element of any good swing. He liked to get your legs moving in the right way, and he suggested I should try to raise my left heel off the ground on the backswing. It felt strange at first, but we worked hard and I soon found the adjustment stopped me reverse pivoting. Without wishing to get bogged down in technical jargon, my weight transfer was therefore smoother and wider, and this made my swing feel that much more solid.

This progress was encouraging but, as usual, I had decided to take a complete break at home over the Christmas period, and golf was far from my mind when Glen and I invited some friends to a New Year's Eve party at our home in Oswestry.

It was a smart occasion but, midway through an increasingly festive evening, someone suggested that

I should get a club and drive a ball into the New Year. I was dressed in black tie, but there was no way I could back down from the challenge.

A driver was produced and a friend of ours, Mike Vaughan, crunched up some silver foil to serve as the golf ball. As midnight approached, I took the club and prepared to hit the 'ball' into 1987. Wearing smooth black shoes on frosty grass, I was worried about slipping and, as I swung the club, I took the precaution of keeping most of my weight for that split second longer on my right foot. The ball didn't go far, but everyone cheered and, as Big Ben chimed on the TV, we all toasted the New Year.

'Happy New Year!'

Glen was at my side, but I was now in another world. It was that swing; it had felt so good. We had only been messing around at a party, but something felt different, much better.

Next morning, not too early, I was on the driving range at Oswestry, hitting shot after shot and still keeping my weight on the right foot for that extra moment. This alteration seemed to have sorted out my tendency to hook the ball, and it also meant I was hitting the ball higher, which was perfect.

By lunchtime on 1 January, 1987, I was already starting to believe this was going to be a special year.

Eager to find some sun, Glen and I had decided to spend January and February on the Gold Coast in Queensland, Australia. We took Daniel and rented an apartment on the beach. The plan was that, using this flat as a base, I would enter a couple of tournaments in Australia and the Hong Kong Open. When Geoff Roberts, my good friend from Oswestry, said he could join us in Australia, I asked him if he would caddie for me. He agreed, and everything was set for an ideal start to the year.

I didn't play particularly well in either the Australian Masters or the Victorian Open, but my inconsistency in these tournaments was largely explained by my decision to use a new set of clubs, which I was still getting used to. I had collected the Dunlop DP30s in Japan towards the end of 1986 and, manufactured with a softer forged steel in the club head, they felt softer at impact and produced more spin.

By the time Geoff and I flew north to Hong Kong, I was happy with the clubs and feeling positive about my game. The tournament was played at the Fanling Golf Club, where the grass is so strange that it feels as though you're playing off a cabbage leaf, but I was soon hitting the ball well and getting into contention.

It doesn't always work to use friends as your caddie, but Geoff and I combined well in Hong Kong, even if his endless puffing on a succession of brown cigarillos meant I smoked 11 or 12 cigarettes in each round, more than twice as many as normal.

In fact, we worked so well that I emerged as the first British winner of the Hong Kong Open in 29 years, finishing four shots clear of David Feherty and my friend, Sam Torrance.

Notwithstanding a disastrous winner's speech, when I tried to thank the marshals but stumbled over my words and then forgot to say anything about Geoff, it had been a great start to the year and I flew home, via the Gold Coast, in high spirits.

Everything was falling into place. Bob Torrance was never far away, my hook seemed to be under control and the new clubs were working well. Confident, bright and enthusiastic, I just couldn't wait to get to the next tournament and challenge again . . .

22 March – It's hot but I finish three-under par and tied for fifth on a tough course at the Moroccan Open.

9 April – Amid much banter, D.J. Russell and I both shoot 68 to share the first round lead in the Jersey Open at the La Moye Golf Club. The prize money is not huge, but this island is a fun place and the pros rate this as one of the best weeks on Tour.

12 April – D.J. slips back, but a fourth round of level par is enough for me to remain a single stroke ahead of the chasing pack, and I've suddenly won a second title of the year.

17 April – After an indifferent first round, I catch fire on the second day of the Suze Open at the Mougins Golf Club, near Cannes, shooting 64 with no bogeys and almost no mistakes. Ballesteros is a couple back, with the rest of the field scattered.

19 April – Seve and I finish level at 13-under par, with third place eight shots back, but he makes a birdie on the first extra hole to win the play-off. That putt cost me nine grand.

23 April – It's Thursday, we are now in Spain, and I shoot an enjoyable 67 on the first day of the Cepsa Madrid Open at Puerta da Hierro Golf Club. Seve also posts a 67 before his elated home crowd, and we end up sharing the first round lead.

26 April – I carry a four-stroke lead into the final round but, playing in the last group with a pumped-up Seve, I need to be right at my best. I'm still not safe when we reach the 18th, a long par-five made for Seve. He powers his drive down the fairway but the crowd falls silent when my drive rolls 25 yards further. I drill my second to the heart of the green, and two-putt to win again . . .

In five weeks at the peak of my game, I had claimed another two titles on the European Tour, won nearly £70,000 in prize money and soared to the top of the Order of Merit. A relative calm followed in May, but the adrenalin was flowing again in June . . .

4 June – It's amazing how pumped up you get. I crunch one drive 295 yards in the first round of the British Masters at Woburn and, by sunset, I'm sharing the lead after a steady 67.

7 June – What is it with Mark McNulty? Whenever I play well, he seems to hit form as well. We start the fourth round, sharing the lead at nine-under par, and slug it out around Woburn. I shoot a 68, but it's not enough. Mark blitzes a 67 and wins by a stroke. Losing is not much fun, but losing to nice guys is not much pain.

20 June – I set the pace with a first round 66 in the Belgian Open at Royal Waterloo Golf Club and manage the same score in the second round but, when the tournament is reduced to three rounds, the scoring goes wild on the last day. Eamonn Darcy scorches 64 to win by a shot from me, Faldo and Ronan Rafferty.

5 July – A final round 67 leaves me tied for third in the Irish Open at Portmarnock Golf Club, Dublin, but the tournament belongs to Bernhard Langer, who leads from start to finish.

8 July – To Gleneagles, and I glide around the King's Course, shooting 65 to take a first round lead in the Scottish Open.

11 July – My driving is steady, my irons are accurate and the putts are dropping. Following another 65 on the Friday and a 66 on the Saturday, I finish with a rock-solid 68 to win the Scottish Open by seven shots from Seve, Couples, Faldo and the rest. Somebody says I'm now the new favourite to win the Open . . .

The world's top golfers gathered to contest the 116th Open Championship at Muirfield and, although I found my status as 'the favourite' difficult to accept, I spent a useful hour or so with Bob Torrance on the Tuesday and enthusiastically applied myself to the challenge of trying to win my first Major title.

It was a peculiar tournament in many ways, played out in persistently grey, cold and damp conditions. My steady performance from tee to green kept me on or around the leaderboard throughout but I simply didn't hole enough putts to put me in a position to challenge either Paul Azinger, who made so much of the running, or Nick Faldo, who held his cool to produce 18 straight pars in the final round and emerge as the Open champion.

I finished in joint eighth position, level par, five shots behind Faldo, and I was left with a genuine sense of frustration because I had played much better than this result suggested.

Nonetheless, I had competed well at a third successive Open and my mood remained bright as the rewards of my success began to emerge in the form of new marketing opportunities and an improved standard of living at home. We were living the life.

Sergio Tacchini, the clothes manufacturer, had come forward with an attractive offer for me to wear their product. Sergio, the man himself, was a friendly former Italian Davis Cup star and, even though I did give him a lesson after the pro-am at the Italian Open one year, it was obvious that he knew a great deal more about tennis than he did about professional golf. At one point, the company wanted me to wear shirts with the same design and colour every round for the entire year. That was to be my 'signature shirt'. I said that this was impossible.

'But it's not a problem for Pat Cash,' they insisted.

'He plays tennis!'

My friends on Tour would have had a field day if I turned up wearing the same shirt every day and, when I pointed out this was simply not practical in golf, Tacchini produced a decent variety of patterns. Although I say so myself, I reckon I looked quite presentable in the Tacchini shirts with their colourful, geometric patterns and their neatly checked trousers!

Other changes in my appearance were less successful. A full perm with blond highlights was the fashionable haircut at that time, and I impulsively gave in to the temptation. Glen was sensitive and kind when I asked what she thought, although I do look at the old photographs now and wonder what on earth I was doing.

We were living the life in Oswestry as well, having moved into a large five-bedroom house on the outskirts of town. It had its own snooker room, Jacuzzi and sauna and I bought a huge satellite dish so I could watch American golf tournaments on TV.

Meanwhile in the garage, I had a white Porsche with a number plate reading PRO IW, while Glen drove a Mercedes.

We were living well, enjoying the benefits of my success, yet we were still neighbours with our families and oldest friends and, I liked to think, we were still the same people.

My smooth progress during 1987 was rudely interrupted in August when I crossed the Atlantic to compete in the last Major of the year, the US PGA Championship, and missed the cut.

With the family, left, at Butlins: mum Joan, dad Harold, and elder siblings Julie and Keith; and below, boxing with the taller boys, in the presence of pro boxer Danny Doyle.

I developed in a strong junior golf structure through my teens, above: playing for the North Wales team, right, and those trousers were fashionable in the 1970s!

Successes, like this one, left, playing for North Wales against South Wales, encouraged my commitment to golf but there was still time to spend with Glendryth Pugh, below, who later became my wife.

I spent my winters playing on the Safari Tour in Africa. This Land Rover for my hole-in-one in Zambia had to be sold because 50% of my earnings were owed to my sponsor.

One of my earliest golfing memories is of Gary Player, below, staging a memorable comeback against Tony Lema, left, at the World Match Play Championship in 1965.

Tom Watson, five-times Open champion, below right, provided a model of decency off the course and controlled aggression on it for a young golfer such as myself, below.

Glen and I were married in Oswestry on 12 November 1983; and we lived in our home town until 1994, when we moved to Jersey.

Sandy Lyle, right, grew up 20 miles from me, and we played together many times; here, we are contesting the World Match Play final in 1987. I had managed to defeat Seve Ballesteros in the semi-final, below.

Kissing and hugging trophies, at the 1988 Irish Open, left, and the PGA Championship, right, in the same year.

Clubs at the ready – the 1985 European team before our Ryder Cup victory over USA at the Belfry.

All smiles – in 1987 we became the first European team to beat the USA on American soil.

The Ryder Cup has been a huge part of my career, through the captaincy of Bernard Gallacher, left, (1991, 1993, 1995), Tony Jacklin (1983, 1985, 1987, 1989) and Seve Ballesteros (1997).

Bob Torrance, above, on the left, and Bill Ferguson, left, are two coaches who have helped me during my career.

A moment's rest with Wobbly – Phil Morbey, friend and caddie for 14 years.

With current coach, Pete Cowan, right. It's hours of practice that leads to the great moments; leading the field, below, in the last round of The Masters, 1991.

The final putt drops at Augusta...and I have won The Masters.

Wobbly's victory hug lifted me off my feet, below right, and Nick Faldo, the 1990 champion, helped me into my green jacket.

The Good Life – with Glen, Daniel and Rebecca, after winning the Masters at Augusta 1991. Daniel anxiously asked his mother: 'Does Daddy have to wear that green jacket the whole time?' Below, jubilation and celebration after another Ryder Cup victory.

The humidity in West Palm Beach Gardens was stifling, and I struggled in the same 'wire wool' rough on the PGA National course that had troubled me at the 1983 Ryder Cup. If anyone knew how to get out of that stuff, they certainly hadn't told me.

I had played with Freddie Couples in the first round and felt embarrassed when I reached the clubhouse with a horrendous opening 86. At a time when I was shooting below 70 more often than not on the European Tour, this was hard to accept and my instant reaction was to withdraw from the tournament and catch the next flight home.

In fact, it was Renton Laidlaw, the respected golf writer and broadcaster, who told me I should stay, pointing out that I would get slaughtered in the press if I quit. He was right, so I played on the Friday, duly missed the cut and hurried back across the Atlantic that evening.

In an ideal world, I would have immediately redis-covered my form in Europe, but this nightmare at the PGA played on my mind and, even three weeks later, I was struggling to make an impact in the European Open at Walton Heath. Rounds of 73 and 71 left me off the pace, and confidence was draining away. There was not much improvement in the third round when I scarcely holed a putt longer than four feet, and the two-over par 74 left me well down the field. It was raining heavily when we walked off the 18th green, and my caddie, Phil Morbey, generally known as 'Wobbly', didn't look too thrilled when I told him I wanted to spend some time working on my putting at the practice green.

The year had started so brilliantly for me, I didn't want 1987 now to fade away in disappointment and mediocrity and, just as my father always said, only hard work would put things right.

So, despite the continuing downpour, I began putting while Wobbly stood holding an umbrella over me.

'You all right, Woosie?'

An Australian voice penetrated the gloom. I looked up and saw the familiar figure of Greg Norman, huddled under an umbrella. He had just completed his third round, and stood at four-under par, six shots better than me and one off the lead.

'Yeah,' I replied, 'I'm just battling with the putting.'

'What's the problem?'

For the next two and a half hours – that's right, two and a half hours – one of the top players in the world stood under an umbrella in the lashing rain and offered me advice. On a Saturday evening, when he had every right to be focusing on his own game, Greg was prepared to stand there, suggesting I should widen my stance, and maybe hold the face of my putter a bit squarer.

It was an amazing gesture from one pro to another, and the sincere thanks I offered when we eventually left the practice green at around quarter past eight hardly seemed adequate. We were the only players left at the course, and it was still raining.

'Thanks, Greg.'

'No worries, Woos.'

I returned to Walton Heath the following day, and produced a much improved round of 65 that cata-pulted me up the leaderboard and eventually proved enough to leave me on my own in fifth place. I had finished four shots behind the winner, Paul Way, and – to my embarrassment – a shot ahead of Greg Norman.

As the Irish would say, the wind was at my back again and I carried my best form into the Lancome Trophy in Paris. The St Nom La Bretêche Golf Club, near Paris, might not be the toughest course in Europe, but I wasn't going to hold anything back.

I was seven-under par in the first round and eight-under par in the second round. After a relatively quiet 69 on the Saturday, I produced a six-under par 66 in the final round to beat Mark McNulty by two strokes. My total of 264 left me fully 24 shots below par and secured the fifth title of what was now becoming a phenomenal year.

'You've holed everything this week, Ian,' said the interviewer, live on television straight after the prize-giving.

'Yes,' I replied, holding the trophy in my hands, 'and it was Greg Norman who helped me with the putting. The next time I see him, I'm going to buy him a few bottles of champagne.'

Affording that gift was not going to be a problem. First prize at the Lancome Trophy was £50,000, and this cheque took my prize money for the year past the £250,000-mark, more than any player had ever earned before on the European Tour.

It was already the middle of September but 1987 was going to get even better. Shortly after winning in Paris, I took my place in the first European team ever to retain the Ryder Cup on American soil, a contest covered in the next chapter.

This was the life. Every week brought a new tournament, and a new opportunity to win. Since my irons have generally been so reliable, the measure of my game has generally been my driving and my putting: if I'm hitting the fairways and holing the five-footers, then my game is right and I will usually be in contention.

As I arrived at Wentworth to compete at the World Match Play Championship, my driving and putting were both so solid that, looking back now, I may well have been playing the best golf of my life. That's more of a hunch than a verdict, and there have been other periods when I played better, but my performances in 1987 were natural and carefree in a way that was hard to repeat.

I worked hard at my game, but everything seemed so instinctive and straightforward. I marched onto the course, put the ball on the tee and smacked it down the fairway; I got the yardage, picked the iron and drilled it onto the green; and, all being well, I holed the putt.

Wentworth seemed green, overcast and damp during the third week of October 1987, but I wasn't troubled by the autumn weather and overcame Sam Randolph, an American, 5 and 4 in the first round, setting up a quarter-final against Nick Faldo. Various interruptions for rain reduced that match to 27 holes and there was never much between us but, having been all square coming down the last, I played a neat approach and was left with a five-foot putt on the 18th green to win by one hole.

I took my stance, glanced from putter head to the hole . . . smooth swing, firm impact, and it rolled, and fell, and I was through to a semi-final against Ballesteros.

My form remained strong through the next morning and into the afternoon and, at three up with six to play, I started to ponder the prospect of a place in the final, but the competitive flame was still burning within Seve.

He pulled one hole back at the 14th, holed a long putt at the 16th, and then produced a trademark up and down from the edge of the green to win the 17th. Just as in the quarterfinal, I reached the 18th hole, all square and one to play.

I remember glancing across at Seve on the tee. He looked so driven and inspired. Appearing to have seized the momentum, he pounded a wonderful drive down the fairway.

When I blocked my tee-shot into trees on the right, my initial reaction was that it was gone. In fact, I had been lucky: the ball had clipped a branch and landed on a wet, trampled area where spectators had been walking, entitling me to take a free drop. I played a decent second, but was still left with 135 yards to the flag.

Seve had taken control, and he only needed a solid second shot and a two-putt to win the match. However, nothing is ever straightforward when the pressure is mounting in matchplay and he carved his three-wood into the bushes on the right.

When I had punched a satisfying eight-iron to just five feet short of the pin, the contest was delayed for 20 minutes while Seve sought a ruling, and then a second opinion, on whether he could take a free drop. I took a seat on my golf bag, and waited patiently in the fairway.

With scarcely a whisper in the gallery, and eager faces pushed against every window in the hospitality grandstand, Seve chipped six feet past the flag and then prodded his putt past the right edge of the cup. As against Faldo, I was left with a five-foot putt to win.

While lining up my putt, I was distracted by Seve still prowling around at the back of the green, wondering how he had missed his putt.

This was hard, competitive golf at the highest level and I was not going to shrink from the moment. I glanced once from the putter to the hole, and then knocked the putt in, allowing myself a satisfied grin as I walked away knowing I was in the final.

When Sandy Lyle beat Mark McNulty in the other semi-final, the World Match Play Championship was assured of the first British winner in its 23-year history. The fates had generously decreed two Shropshire lads would contest the 36-hole final on the Monday, delayed a day by high storms earlier in the week.

My mother set the tone for a memorable occasion when she said, in all sincerity, she didn't really mind who won. 'We've known Sandy for years,' she said, 'and we've always liked him very much. I only hope they have a great final together and that the best man on the day comes out on top.'

In many ways, it was strange to be facing Sandy in such an important match. We had played so many times over the years, at Oswestry, or Hill Valley or Hawkstone Park, and it was always easy for one of us to pick up the phone and fix a round. Now we were rivals, and it was all I could do to stop myself chattering to him as though we were playing for a couple of quid back home, rather than competing for a prestigious title at Wentworth.

The stakes were high. Sandy had lost three World Match Play finals in the past eight years, and was clearly determined to win. He finished the morning round birdie, birdie, eagle to reach lunch with a one-hole lead, and he opened up a two-hole advantage early in the afternoon. But I holed a long putt at the 26th, and knocked in another birdie to pull all square with eight to play.

We were both playing exceptional golf, speeding around the Burma Road course, thrilling the crowds, egging each other on as we duelled down the home straight. It was fun.

When Sandy missed his approach and bogeyed the 33rd, it was the first shot either of us had dropped all afternoon. I made par and moved one hole ahead with three to play. We both faced birdie putts on the 34th green and, when he holed his and I pushed mine past the outside, we were all square all over again.

Our drives at the long par-five 35th landed side by side in the middle of the fairway. We both hit solid second shots and, when I had played a sweet 55-yard wedge to one foot from the flag, Sandy responded by knocking his approach to three feet.

As an increasingly excited gallery cheered our progress, we arrived at the green together. Sandy conceded my putt, and holed his three-footer to halve the hole with birdies. For the third time in three days, I was all square coming to the last.

Both drives finished safely on the 36th fairway and, with 232 yards to the pin, I struck a solid three-wood. 'Hook, darling, hook,' I said, eyes fixed on the ball. 'Come on baby, hook.'

Peter Alliss was commentating at the time and, as my ball drifted in to the centre of the green, he mused on air: 'There you are. You see, you only have to talk sweetly to them.'

Sandy hit a two-iron into a bunker on the right, and his bunker shot came up 18 feet short of the pin. My first putt swung across the face of the hole and hurried past, so when Sandy missed his putt, I found myself in exactly the same position that I had been in against Faldo and Ballesteros in the previous rounds.

This was amazing: for the third time in three days, I lined up a five-foot putt to claim victory on the 18th green. I made no mistake, and immediately walked across to shake Sandy by the hand. I was thrilled to have won, but I understood how disappointed he would be feeling to have lost a fourth final at Wentworth. His turn would come 12 months later.

It had been a tremendous week, not only for me but for my family as well. My father told me afterwards how, late on that last evening, he had been walking across a field to his parked car when he started to feel strange. 'I was so happy,' he said, laughing out loud. 'Ian, it felt as though I was walking on air.'

Victory at the World Match Play Championship ensured I would finish first in the 1987 European Order of Merit. I was delighted, not least because it meant I would receive an invitation to play in the Masters the following April, my first visit to Augusta National.

From being a decent professional nervously wondering where his next win was coming from at the end of 1986, I had developed in 12 months to a point where I was being recognised as one of the top players in the world. My lifestyle had been transformed; money was no longer an issue. I was living the life.

And 1987 was still not finished.

The World Cup was to be played at Kapalua in Hawaii. This team event, contested by two players from each qualifying country, had held an uncertain place on the world golfing calendar, sometimes failing to attract much public interest, but it was always on my schedule because it gave me a chance to play for Wales.

Pulling on a red sweater at an often obscure golf course may not stand comparison with the thrill of pulling on the red rugby jersey at the old Cardiff Arms Park, but it meant a great deal to me and I had been selected to represent Wales in every World Cup since 1980.

By 1987, the significance of my Welshness seemed somehow index-linked to my success in the game. The more I won, the more people seemed to know where I came from and, consequently, the more proud I felt to call myself a Welshman.

'So, Woosie, you're from Wales?' an American journalist had asked during a press conference earlier in the year.

'That's right,' I replied.

'So what part of Scotland is that?'

The room erupted in laughter, but the guy had been entirely serious! I shook my head, and took another question.

David Llewellyn had been selected as my teammate at the 1987 World Cup in Hawaii, and we scarcely figured among the pre-event favourites when we arrived at Kapalua.

However, we applied ourselves to the task in high winds and driving rain and, by the end of the first day, we realised we were in with a shout. The format of the event combined the 72-hole totals of both players to give one aggregate score for each country and, as I sustained my recent form and David, otherwise known as Lulu, played steady golf, Wales started to hover around the leaderboard

The wind and rain persisted throughout the second and third rounds and, while most scores soared, I kept holing putts and our dream started to look increasingly possible. Everyone was soaked and, while some players looked as though they wanted to go home, David and I were obviously relishing the challenge.

On the Sunday afternoon, with palm trees bent double in the gale, encouraging each other through the final round, we produced a competitive performance: David finished at 12-over par and I had managed to post what turned out to be the best individual score of the week, a combative 274, 14-under par. That was seven shots ahead of second-placed Sandy Lyle, who in turn finished seven shots clear of third place.

Our combined total of 574, two-under par, carried us into an all-Celt sudden death play-off against Scotland.

Sandy and I were both born in England but, just as I had chosen to follow my heritage and represent Wales, he had taken his parents' nationality and, as a professional, played for Scotland . . . so, on this sodden golf course in Hawaii, with a few hundred spectators braving the awful weather, we confronted the Scots, Sandy and Sam Torrance. And nobody was more exhilarated than me when it fell to my partner, David Llewellyn, to hole the winning putt from six feet on the second extra hole. We were drenched, but delighted.

Looking back, it still seems almost unbelievable that a small country with only four touring professional golfers, such as Wales in 1987, could emerge to win the World Cup, and I was flattered when David decided to celebrate our achievement by building an extension on his house and christening it 'Woosie's Room'.

I was not popular the next year when my schedule didn't enable me to defend our title in Melbourne, but I returned to play at successive World Cups through the 1990s and, although we never repeated our triumph in Hawaii, Phil Price and I finished second to Sweden in 1991. In these events and at the Dunhill Cup, it has never been less than an honour to play for Wales.

Dai and I returned home as national heroes, acclaimed in the papers, but the media were not so kind to me when it emerged that my last commitment in 1987 was to participate in the controversial Million Dollar Challenge at Sun City, South Africa.

Nelson Mandela was still in prison and almost all governments around the world discouraged sporting contact with the country that practised apartheid. I understood the boycott, but maintained it was my individual right to play golf wherever I wanted.

There was some negative comment in the British press, I was subsequently banned from competing in Kenya and my name was placed on some kind of black list, but I was not bothered by these political developments. People might say I was naïve in saying I just wanted to play golf, rather than get involved in any kind of political debate, but that's exactly how I felt at the time.

In pure golfing terms, Sun City presented a unique and exciting prospect. I had enjoyed the Gary Player Country Club since playing in the first tournament ever staged there back in 1979, and the fact that no more than a dozen top players were ever invited to play in the Million Dollar Challenge meant that, even if you finished stone last, the trip would still have been worthwhile.

There was an added attraction in 1987. Determined to keep the world's leading players coming to Sun City, the organisers took a dramatic and, at that time, unprecedented step: the Million Dollar Challenge was originally named after the total purse but, in 1987, the first prize, alone, was increased to US$1,000,000.

The prospect of earning a million dollars in four days lured a high quality field to this challenging course cradled in an extinct volcano crater west of Johannesburg and, towards the end of four hot days playing before large and excited galleries, the event boiled down to a contest between me and Nick Faldo.

Suffering from a severe attack of nerves, I was barely managing to hold my game together and led by just one stroke when we reached the 17th tee. Nick had driven down the middle of the fairway, but I pushed my drive into the light rough on the right.

With 154 yards to go, I took a seven-iron and proceeded to play an approach that landed softly six foot to the right of the pin, spun left, rolled towards the hole and dropped for an eagle two. The crowd around the green went berserk and, though I had seldom felt more nervous on a golf course, I had seldom felt more excited.

Nick eventually made a par, leaving me three ahead with only the 18th hole to play. Under normal circumstances, that would have been enough to calm my anxiety. However, to a farmer's son playing for a million dollars, nothing seemed enough.

Working hard to clear my mind, I made a solid par at the 18th and emerged as golf's first ever winner of a $1m cheque. We all flew back to London that same night, but I was quiet on the plane, struggling to get my head round the fact that I had just won such an immense amount of money for playing golf.

Within moments of landing at Heathrow airport, the thought occurred to me that a few other people could also find it hard to accept a professional sportsman could win so much money.

As I quietly pushed my luggage trolley towards the 'Nothing to Declare' green route, a customs officer evidently recognised my face and beckoned me over for an inspection.

'Anything to declare, sir?'

'No,' I replied.

'May we have a look at your luggage, sir?'

As he started running through my belongings, I felt relaxed because I could account for everything. Then, he held this silver Ebel watch up for inspection, and my heart sank. I had bought it as a gift for Glen, and I immediately realised I was in trouble.

All three of us – me, Glen and Daniel, aged two – were moved to a separate room, where we were eventually made to wait for five hours. I telephoned IMG, and I contacted lawyers because this was getting serious. You see, it was my second offence . . .

Four months earlier at the USPGA in Florida, I had happened to mention to Renton Laidlaw that Footjoy had given me a smart pair of crocodile shoes, and he included this as an aside in one of his newspaper articles. I thought nothing more about it.

Then, returning home, I had been pulled aside in the green channel at Heathrow and asked if I had anything to declare.

'No,' I had said, truthfully.

'What about the crocodile shoes?'

'They were a gift.'

'Where are they, sir?'

'On my feet!'

After some time, the customs officials confiscated the shoes, and said I would have to pay £450 in duty to get them back. I told them they might as well keep the damn things.

With this incident on my record, and the Ebel watch found in my luggage from South Africa, I was in trouble. We were eventually released to drive home to Oswestry, but the matter came to court a few months later and I was given a £5,000 fine.

These episodes were unpleasant and unnecessary, and, at first, I felt angry and indignant that I had been the victim of nothing more than small-minded envy. However, upon reflection, I realised I had to accept the pressures of being in the news. In truth, I had been careless and I resolved to be more cautious in future. Happily, I have not troubled any customs officials since.

And even these skirmishes failed to remove the

gloss from what had unfolded as a truly sensational year. I may not have won a Major, but 1987 has remained established in my own mind as the standard by which future years would be judged.

I had played consistently well, won no fewer than eight times, topped the European Order of Merit, brought honour to my country at the World Cup, and, with worldwide earnings in excess of £1.2m, guaranteed financial security for my family.

When I told the press that, so long as my putting was good, I believed I could win every week, some people thought I was being cocky. In fact, I was only being honest. When I was buzzing, driving the ball out of sight, playing fast, anything seemed possible.

This was my life.

And I was loving every minute.

CHAPTER FIVE

Against America

Nobody understood why an American was hanging around the foyer at the European team hotel; in any case, he wasn't particularly welcome. It was the eve of the 1985 Ryder Cup matches at The Belfry, and the tension was starting to show.

'So, you guys reckon you have a chance,' he drawled towards where I happened to be standing among a group of European players, who were starting to assemble for dinner.

'What?' I responded.

I wasn't in the mood to discuss our chances of regaining the Ryder Cup after 28 barren years.

He repeated: 'You guys really think you can win?'

'Sure.'

'Tell me,' he continued, 'is Steve playing?'

'Steve who?'

'That guy from Spain . . .'

'Who?'

'Er, Ballee-something.'

'Ballesteros?'

'Yeah, that's right . . . Steve Ballesteros. Is he playing?'

I turned and walked in to dinner. Some of these Americans were unbelievable.

Nothing infuriated the then four-time Major winner more than being called 'Steve', and nothing wound up the European team quite as effectively as an outspoken American . . . not that, in this particular week, we needed any extra motivation.

Every so often in sport, there is an event, a time and a place when an overwhelming sense of destiny seems to take control. The 1985 Ryder Cup at the Belfry was such an occasion.

As we settled down to dinner on the evening of Thursday 12 September 1985, there were fewer jokes than normal. I glanced around the table and started to wonder whether any group of golfers had ever been bonded together by such a bloody-minded determination to get the job done.

We all understood the equation. Nobody needed to be reminded how the Americans had lost only once in the past 50 years, or how Jack Nicklaus had proposed in 1979 that our team be extended to include players from all over Europe, or how we had been beaten by a single point two years before. Nine of us who had been so disappointed to lose at West Palm Beach in 1983 had retained our places in the 12-man team and were having dinner in Sutton

Coldfield, desperately wanting to believe that, this week, our time had come to end one of the most demoralising losing streaks in sport.

Tony Jacklin had been retained as captain and the room hushed as he stood to address his team. 'Each of us knows what we have to do over the next three days,' he said, speaking slowly, intently, 'and we all know it's going to be really tough, but I want to tell you two things this evening.

'First, something has changed from two years ago. Back then, the Americans were wondering how many points they would win by. This week, they've started to think about losing. For the first time since any of them can remember, it's a possibility, and they know it. The mindset has changed.

'Second, they may look impressive on paper, but we have a team full of passion and determination, and that's going to be the difference this week. We want this more, don't we?'

As he sat down, we started to applaud. Each of us recognised the captain's obvious commitment and his impeccable organisation. Our accommodation, clothing and the practice arrangements: everything was perfect and it all contributed to our confidence that we would seize this historic opportunity.

Every member of our team had bought in to the mission. Seve was our anchorman, proud and at the peak of his powers, resolved to prove it was not just Americans who can play golf. Sandy Lyle had just won the Open, Bernhard Langer was the reigning Masters Champion. Nick Faldo, Howard Clark, Sam Torrance, Manuel Pinero and Jose Maria Canizares all brought the experience of playing in the last two Ryder Cups. Paul Way, Jose Rivero, Ken Brown and I would not lack spirit.

'Woosie, do you have a moment?'

It was Tony Jacklin, ushering me away from the group as the meal ended. I had been wondering who he would pair me with, and this was the moment when all would be revealed. 'I want you to play with Paul,' he said, 'most probably in the afternoon four-balls rather than in the morning.'

Way-Way, as we called him, had been struggling with tonsillitis for some time, but he was the type of guy who liked to get stuck in, and I knew we would get along. Of course, I had hoped to play in the morning as well. Everyone wants to play as much as possible at the Ryder Cup, but four guys sit out during the morning and afternoon on the first two days, and you have to accept the captain's decision.

Day One dawned and more than 24,000 people, the largest crowd in Ryder Cup history, poured across the Brabazon course, creating a tangible mood of excitement and anticipation. I spent some time down at the driving range, trying to stay calm, trying to be supportive to the guys playing in the morning four-somes. Some of them looked nervous. After all the preparation, suddenly it was time to deliver.

That morning, only Ballesteros and Pinero delivered. Red, denoting the American team, dominated the scoreboard through most of the morning, and they had taken a 3–1 lead by lunchtime. I saw Tony hurry away, walkie-talkie in hand, evidently concerned, and I noticed Sandy looking agitated and unhappy. Everything was happening so quickly. Word spread through the team that Tony had decided to rest Sandy, the Open Champion. If nothing else, it was a brave decision. The chips were down. Then somebody said Paul and I would be playing Fuzzy Zoeller and Hubert Green in the afternoon fourballs. If ever there was a contest between youth and experience, this was it!

It did seem a tough draw but, even when we were three down after ten holes, we kept playing decent golf and the match began to turn. Into the afternoon, as bursts of applause began to erupt around the course, presumably signalling European successes, we started to claw our way back.

Once we had pulled level at the 17th, Way-Way seized the moment and struck a sensational two-iron at the last that came to rest 15 feet from the pin. He would have that putt to win the 18th, and the match.

'Just keep calm,' I told Paul, stating the obvious as we walked up the fairway. Just then a fantastic roar thundered across the course from back at the 17th green, and I heard a young voice from behind the ropes shout out that Ballesteros and Pinero had beaten North and Jacobsen.

Way-Way was known for rising to the big moments and he rolled his putt beautifully into the middle of the hole. I celebrated by thumping him on the back, maybe a bit too enthusiastically, but it had been a crucial point and Europe trailed only 4½ to 3½ at the end of the first day. We were still in the match.

The sheer intensity of the competition, the noise of the crowd and the constant pressure on every shot at every hole had taken us all by surprise, but I was enjoying every moment out there. Before our very eyes, the Ryder Cup was evolving from a one-sided folly that scarcely anyone noticed into the most hard-fought contest in the game of golf and one of the most exciting sporting events in the world.

When the team gathered that evening, Tony Jacklin said he was particularly pleased by the way Paul and I had hung in there and ground out our point and, afterwards, he indicated we would be required to play in the morning and the afternoon on the second day. I was thrilled, raring to go again.

The luck of the draw set us against Green and Zoeller for the second day in a row, and Way-Way and I dovetailed perfectly in our morning fourball, winning 4 and 3 on the 15th green. We were feeling pretty pleased with ourselves when we returned to the team room but this Ryder Cup was an event in which you had to experience the atmosphere in person, not watch on television, so I went back out on the course to give Sandy some moral support.

He was in trouble. When I joined the gallery beside the 17th green, Sandy and Bernhard Langer were two down with two to play against Craig Stadler and Curtis Strange. I knelt down on the grass beside Tony, inside the ropes. Being only 5'4½" tall has always given me an advantage at the Ryder Cup in that I can take my place virtually anywhere on the course, and nobody ever complains I'm obscuring their view!

'We need to win the last two holes,' the captain muttered grimly.

Heroics were required, and Sandy stepped forward. Stadler made a birdie at the par-five 17th, which he must have hoped would at least halve the hole and end the match, but Sandy rolled in an 18-foot putt to win the hole with an eagle. Another roar reverberated around the course, and this time my voice joined the chorus. Grinning, breathing deep, hoping, Tony and I elbowed our way down the last.

We probably needed someone to make a birdie at the tough 18th hole, but both Sandy and Bernhard left their second shots some distance from the pin, and both missed their putts.

That appeared to be that. Stadler had been rock solid, reaching the green in two and leaving himself a two-foot putt for par to halve the hole and win the match. The American glanced across at the two

Europeans on the edge of the green, perhaps suggesting his putt was short enough to be conceded, but our guys correctly stared straight ahead. In a friendly the putt would probably have been given, but this was to win a crucial point in the Ryder Cup, and he was going to have to putt.

To our amazement, Craig missed the putt. Europe won the hole in par, the match was halved and we had reached lunch on the second day with the scores now level at 6–6. It was hard on Craig, and some in the crowd did cheer when his putt lipped out, which was wrong, but this was a battle and I congratulated Sandy on what had been a gutsy half as we walked away to the sanctuary of the team room.

'What happened?' asked Sam Torrance as we arrived.

'We halved,' Sandy replied, smiling.

Scot shook hands with fellow Scot. We had spent so long telling ourselves we could win, and now that the Americans were missing two-footers at the 18th, we started to believe we really could win. Stadler's misfortune proved a turning point in the match, and we threw ourselves into the Saturday afternoon foursomes.

Paul and I saw our fairy-tale run of success come to an abrupt halt with a 4 and 2 defeat against Curtis Strange and Peter Jacobsen, but Europe began to seize the momentum when the four Spaniards stepped to the fore. Tony had taken special measures to integrate this quartet into the group, ensuring they never became a team within a team and taking care language never became a problem. In fact, as Canizares and Rivero demolished Calvin Peete and Tom Kite 7 and 5, and Ballesteros and Pinero closed out Stadler and Hal Sutton 5 and 4, language suddenly became an advantage: the guys started discussing tactics in Spanish, much to the irritation of the bewildered Americans.

The concluding match of an increasingly dramatic afternoon matched Bernhard Langer and Ken Brown, two of the slowest players on the European circuit, against Lanny Wadkins and Raymond Floyd, two guys who liked to play fast and keep moving. Minute by minute, hour by hour, the tortoises wore down the hares, eking out a 3 and 2 victory, and carrying Europe into a 9–7 lead on Saturday night.

Our task was now clear: we needed to win 5½ points from the 12 singles matches on Sunday to earn our place in history as the first team to beat the Americans since 1957. As we assembled in the team room that evening, our general mood was reflected in one buoyant Spaniard.

'Give me Lanny!'

Manuel Pinero was leaping around, begging Tony Jacklin to write his name at the top of our playing order for the Sunday singles. It seemed Lanny Wadkins was the most likely to appear first on the American list and, pumped up by winning three of his four matches so far, Manuel was desperate to take on the player who we admired as the most formidable matchplay opponent in the American team.

'Please, I want Wadkins.'

Our captain relented, placing Pinero first, with me second, Paul Way third and Seve fourth. 'They're two points behind,' Tony reasoned, 'so they're going to put some big guns up front to try and wipe out the deficit early in the afternoon. At least, that's what I would do in their position.'

Lee Trevino, the United States captain, was thinking along the same lines and, later in the evening, we received news of the Americans' team sheet: Wadkins was indeed first, followed by Craig Stadler, Ray Floyd and Tom Kite. Just as in 1983, I had drawn Stadler in the singles on Sunday.

Some players might have crumbled after missing the two-footer at the 18th on the previous day, but you only needed to take one look at Craig to realise he was not the type of man to crumble. He responded to the pressure by constructing a solid brick wall of steady pars and the occasional birdie and, although I was a couple of shots under par myself, I couldn't make any impression. Craig holed important birdie putts at the 15th and 16th, slammed the door and beat me 2 and 1.

Throughout my match, I took regular encouragement from events taking place ahead of me as Pinero duelled with Wadkins. I had watched from the tee when Manuel chipped in from 35 feet at the 10th, clenched my fist with delight when he holed a 15-footer to go three up at the 15th, and I was cheering from the fairway when he clinched the 3 and 1 win and he immediately rushed to embrace Jacklin beside the 17th green.

This warm, sunny Sunday afternoon in September was assuming a momentum all its own and, as soon as I had congratulated Stadler on his victory and thanked my caddie, I walked over to the vantage point beside the 17th green where Tony Jacklin and Manuel Pinero were already kneeling on the grass. My golf was over for the day, so I took my place as another face in the crowd, still daring to believe.

Within minutes, Way and Floyd came into view back down the fairway. Paul was one up with two to play, and he hit a long second that rolled onto the front of the green and brought us all to our feet. Two putts later, he had made birdie and beaten the formidable Floyd by two holes. Amid backslaps and cheers, Way-Way came and sat beside us; now we were four, waiting for Ballesteros to reach the 17th.

I had been monitoring Seve's progress on the scoreboards, and had almost given up hope when he fell three down with five to play against Tom Kite, but he won both the 14th and 15th with birdies and was now just one down as, in the distance, his familiar frame appeared on the dog-leg 17th.

'He's got to make the green in two,' Tony murmured. 'He's got to get a half.'

Seve duly pounded his second onto the green, two-putted for a birdie to win the hole and, amid growing delirium around us, strode confidently away to the 18th tee all square. We rushed after him, daring to think he could win the 18th and the match, but Kite held firm and the match was halved. It was good enough. We had now secured 11½ points, and were just three short of paradise.

Moments later, Tony, Manuel, Paul, Seve and I were standing together beside the 18th green, gazing up at the enormous scoreboard. Nobody said anything; words were not necessary. I glanced across at Tony and saw a tear welling in the corner of his eye. Was all this happening? Yes, it was.

Sandy was three up over Jacobsen, Bernhard was four up on Sutton and Sam Torrance was involved in a close match against Andy North. We all headed back out on the course and, as we walked, two tremendous explosions of noise boomed around The Belfry: the first came from the distant 14th green where Bernhard won 5 and 4, the second came from the 16th green when Sandy beat Jacobsen 3 and 2.

'Come on,' Seve urged, 'let's pick up Sam's match at the 16th.'

So, we all hurried behind the 17th tee, cut down along the 16th and found a grassy bank on the right of the fairway, inside the ropes; and as spectators recognised our red sweaters, our team uniform for the day, they started to cheer. Everyone seemed to be smiling, everyone seemed to be babbling with enthusiasm, everyone seemed just so thrilled to be at The Belfry on this day.

I soon spotted Sam on the tee. We had been close friends since the early days on the Safari Tour, possibly because we saw something of ourselves in each other. We both enjoyed an occasional drink and smoke, and we both liked to play hard on the course.

Sam is a player who goes for everything. Whether he's leading, missing the cut or playing to win the Ryder Cup, he doesn't hold back. His philosophy is that every shot is there to be hit. In fact, to a much greater degree than he realises, I have been influenced and encouraged by watching him play. Now, on this afternoon, fate conspired to shine the spotlight on these broad shoulders from Largs.

Along with many millions watching on television around the world, we followed him up the 16th and down the 17th, all the way to the 18th . . . where he eventually stood on the tee knowing that if he won the hole, and the match, he would go down in history as the man who clinched the Ryder Cup.

Equal to the moment, Sam hit a great drive at the 18th, long and over the corner, leaving no more than a solid nine-iron to the flag. Andy North then stepped up and hit his drive high and into the water. He was not the first American to land in the lake at the last and, not for the first time, unfortunately, the crowd cheered.

As Sam walked down from the tee, he glanced across to where we, his team-mates, were standing and I could see he was emotional. He smiled, but kept walking, trying to focus on playing just another approach to the green, rather than the winning putt for which so many people had waited so long.

I was standing directly behind Sam when he struck the most impeccable nine iron of his life, and I watched the ball draw in from the right and roll, finishing 18 feet from the hole. Instinctively, I ran forward to pat my friend on the back . . . however, at the precise moment that I reached him, he flung his arms upwards in celebration, and his right elbow whacked me in the eye.

As we followed Sam up the 18th fairway, it was the impact of that blow, not the occasion, that brought moisture to my eyes – at least, that was my story – and, blinking back the tears, I watched from just short of the green as Sam rolled in his birdie putt, and then stood with arms raised aloft.

We had won!

Tony was crying, Sam was crying, the wives and girlfriends were crying, people in the crowd were crying. Tony choked up with emotion during his interview on BBC television, and the sense of relief and triumph was so intense that Sam, eyes red with tears, could hardly utter a single word. It was fantastic and, amid this joy, the other matches were completed to leave a final score of Europe 16½–USA 11½.

And the celebrations began. Before long, we were staring up to see Concorde flying low over The Belfry to honour an historic achievement. And the champagne flowed . . .

It flowed in Tony Jacklin's hotel suite when we opened the crate of pink champagne that Dai Rees, Britain's winning Ryder Cup captain, had set aside in 1957, giving strict instructions that the bottles should only be opened by the next team to defeat the Americans. And it flowed on a low, flat roof of the hotel where we emerged later to celebrate our victory with the crowds gathered below.

'Eh, give us some champagne down here!'

'Who's that?'

Someone was shouting from below, but I couldn't get close enough to the edge to see who. However, the request seemed reasonable enough so I lay flat on the roof, stomach down, and wriggled towards the edge so I could pass a bottle into outstretched hands. As this guy grasped the bottle, I saw his face: it was a friend of mine from Hill Valley, John Williams! The coincidence was staggering.

Our celebrations continued into the early hours of the morning, and we were feted at endless banquets and awards functions in the months that followed. It soon became clear that, whatever happened in the future, the 1985 European Ryder Cup team had carved its own place in sporting history.

With sound planning and boundless passion, we

had achieved what for so long had seemed unthinkable and we had beaten opponents who for so long had seemed unbeatable. Tony Jacklin had rallied a gifted group of golfers to produce a victory that will be recalled as long as the game is played.

Lee Trevino and his team were cordial in defeat, and the wounded body of American golf was borne back across the Atlantic. It would be revived, and prepared to resume battle in 1987.

Everybody in sport knows that continuity is crucial to sustain any kind of success, and the crucial reappointment of Tony Jacklin to captain the European team in 1987 combined with the fact that he was able to retain nine of his 12 players from The Belfry, suggested we would perform well again.

As far as I was concerned, by late September 1987, I could hardly wait to get stuck into another Ryder Cup. I had just won the Lancome Trophy, my fifth title of the year, and was playing the best golf of my life. Nothing excited me more than the prospect of helping my European teammates revive memories of 1985 and become the first team ever to win the golden chalice on American soil.

'How's it going, Seve?'

'Nick, everything OK?'

'You feeling all right, Bernhard?'

The usual suspects gathered again. We competed against each other week in, week out, and generally got along well, but a Ryder Cup challenge seemed to transform amicable rivals into a family. That might sound like an empty cliché, but it was exactly this spirit and camaraderie that propelled this generation of European golfers to such success. We cared deeply about the Ryder Cup, and each other.

'Is this a circus or a sporting event?' one of my team-mates muttered as the brass bands played on and on during the 1987 Ryder Cup opening ceremony at Muirfield Village, near Dublin, Ohio.

Eager to regain the trophy, and restore their national pride at a time when their yachtsmen had lost the America's Cup, the Americans pinned their hopes on the elder statesman of our game, probably the greatest golfer of all time. It was announced that Jack Nicklaus would not only captain the United States team but that the matches would be played on the course he himself designed, Muirfield Village.

Jack was back, leading an impressive team that included only four survivors from two years before, and the green keeping staff at this superb woodland course had rallied to the cause by producing fast, bone-hard greens and tight, narrow fairways and, still, the Ohio State brass band played on.

We were not particularly concerned by any of these developments. First, Tony Jacklin had once again ensured our preparation was immaculate, even to the point of arranging for the team to fly across the Atlantic on Concorde; second, in what was fast becoming a contest between the European Tour and the PGA Tour, we had confidence in the ability within our team to withstand the pressure and opposition.

At the Belfry, we had arrived in hope; at Muirfield Village, we arrived in expectation. We had beaten them once and, wherever we played, we believed we could beat them again. I repeat, so much of doing something is the simple act of believing that something is possible; and, in 1987, we believed.

Our team meetings were once again positive and constructive and, on the Thursday evening, I was once again expecting to receive details of my role from Tony Jacklin.

'Woosie, do you have a moment?' It was the captain speaking.

'Sure.'

'I want you to partner Nick Faldo in the foursomes and fourballs.'

'No problem.'

'Thanks.'

I was surprised. There was no problem between Nick and me, but our personalities did seem so different that I wondered how we would come together as a pair. He was calm, methodical and focused while I tended to be more aggressive, impulsive and talkative. I assumed Nick was happy with Tony's decision.

My admiration for Nick Faldo as a golfer began in 1975 when we both played in an amateur tournament at Kedlestone Park. His long, smooth swing was impressive, his focus was total and his dedication to the game was simply amazing: that week, he won the event and I finished third. Our careers had been intertwined ever since, although I suppose we did take slightly different routes to the top of the game. Nick spent more time grooving his swing on the driving range, while I tended to take more detours to the bar for a drink with my mates. This was no big deal. We were different kinds of people, each with our own priorities and goals in life. Neither was right, neither was wrong.

Nick and I spent some time together that Thursday evening in Muirfield Village, talking about the way we wanted to play the foursomes and how our tactics would change in the afternoon fourballs, and we seemed to be communicating well. I was hopeful our combination would be successful.

Tony sent us out third on the Friday morning, drawn to play foursomes against the formidable American pair of Masters champion Larry Mize and the aggressive Lanny Wadkins, and our status as the European 'dream team' wasn't looking too clever when we were three down after only 10 holes. We weren't exactly panicking, but the captain was following our match and he wasn't looking too thrilled.

We arrived at the 11th tee, and I was preparing to drive when the usual calm was interrupted by a large, middle-aged, square-jawed, brightly clothed American sitting at the back of the tee.

'Oh my!' he exclaimed, loud enough for everyone to hear. 'He's only a boy!'

I sensed a barely suppressed snigger in the gallery, but I focused on the back of the ball and thumped a drive straight down the fairway, where it finished 40 yards past Mize's ball. 'Yes,' I declared as I bent to collect the tee peg, 'but think what I'll be like when I grow up and become a man.'

Nick laughed out loud, and the spark was struck. We won four of the next seven holes, turned the match on its head and were leading one up as we approached the last. By then, the Americans had won the first two foursomes of the morning, and Europe desperately needed our point.

Our second shot at the 18th rolled ominously into a greenside bunker, but Nick could not have been more animated and supportive as we walked, side by side, up the fairway. His unflappable calm gave me confidence under pressure. 'Come on, Woos, you can get this close,' he told me firmly. Wadkins was already on the green in two, so it looked as though we would need to get up and down in two. The bunker shot came out perfectly, as sweet as any in my career, and the ball landed softly and came to rest barely a foot from the hole. Nick led the applause, as the Europeans around the green cheered. Under pressure, the Americans three-putted, and we had won by two holes. Nick walked across and shook me warmly by the hand. Our point was secure, and our partnership was up and running.

Seve Ballesteros and Jose Maria Olazabal were

following up the 18th and, when they managed to hold off Larry Nelson and Payne Stewart to win by one hole, the European team was relieved to have escaped from a potentially disastrous morning with the match score level at 2–2. As someone mentioned, the Americans had burst off the blocks, but we had managed to match them stride for stride.

Nick and I particularly looked forward to the four-ball because we reckoned our games would complement each other: he would drill out the pars, enabling me to attack what was a difficult course and try to contribute a birdie every now and then. Hal Sutton and Dan Pohl proved strong opponents in the afternoon and, after halving the first 10 holes, we needed a stroke of luck to get ahead.

I blocked my approach to the 11th green, but the ball ricocheted off the trees and rebounded straight back on to the green. Having managed to hole the eagle putt from 12 feet, I was grinning sheepishly as we walked to the next tee, one up when we might so easily have been one down. Nick pressed home the advantage with a long putt for birdie at the 12th green, and we held on to win 2 and 1.

All our rivalries had been swept away by our shared desire to win and, by the end of that opening day Nick and I felt established as a solid, winning combination. Tony Jacklin's decision to throw us together had initially seemed intriguing, but now it was looking inspired.

In fact, the entire team was buzzing. Gordon Brand junior and Jose Rivero, Sandy Lyle and Bernhard Langer, Nick and me, Ballesteros and Olazabal: Jacklin had conceived these recipes for the afternoon four-balls, and what emerged from the oven of competition was a 4–0 sweep for Europe. No American team had suffered such a disastrous, literally pointless, afternoon in the entire history of the event.

Jack Nicklaus was concerned, not simply by our 6–2 lead but also the general mood on the course. We had expected to be playing in a star-spangled cauldron of American patriotism but, miraculously, it turned out that several hundred British miners had settled in this particular part of Ohio in the 1930s, and it seemed most of their descendants were now committed to supporting the European cause.

'U-S-A! U-S-A! U-S-A!'

We anticipated a backlash on the Saturday morning, and it arrived in the form of the American wives and girlfriends: 15 determined women dressed in red, white and blue, waving American flags as they rampaged over the course, chanting, 'U-S-A! U-S-A! U-S-A!' Glen and the other European wives wondered if they should have their own war cry. Mercifully, they kept quiet and watched the golf.

Working on the principle that if it wasn't broken, it didn't need fixing, Jacklin sent out the same four pairs who had triumphed on the Friday afternoon to resume the contest in the Saturday morning foursomes, and his faith was rewarded with another useful haul of 2½ points from the possible four.

Nick and I found ourselves embroiled in a painstaking struggle against Hal Sutton and Larry Mize, but we went one up at the 14th and seemed poised to close out the match when I hit a nine-iron to three feet from the flag at the 17th. But the Americans were desperate not to lose, and Mize holed a monster putt to salvage a half and send us to the last tee still defending a slender one-hole lead.

For once – in fact, for the only time in two days of intense competition – we cracked, failing to get up and down from around the green. Sutton holed a five-footer to win the hole and halve the match, leaving Nick and me feeling as though we had lost, rather than drawn. And yet, a half was still a half, and Europe had battled through a tense morning of four tight matches, and still led the match 8½–3½.

'Come on, Woosie, this is our chance to put things right,' Nick said when he saw the draw put us against the top-rated American pair, Tom Kite and Curtis Strange, in the afternoon fourball. We sat together for lunch, discussed our strategy and decided I would take an aggressive approach.

This was the Ryder Cup; this was America. There was no point in being cautious. We had to get out there and seize control. It was resolved Nick would get into his groove and roll out the pars, and I would attack Muirfield Village at every turn, taking every tiger line after tiger line, chasing every putt.

Tom and Curtis had won their past two matches and they expected to win again, but they were soon confronted by both Nick and me playing as well as we could play. This particular Saturday afternoon in Ohio unfolded as one of those golden afternoons, the memory of which will sustain me in old age.

We went for everything, and almost everything came off. Our driving was long and accurate, our irons felt so solid and reliable, and every putt seemed ready to drop. We were four up at the 13th and, as we waited just beside the 14th tee, I overheard Jack Nicklaus talking to an assistant.

'How can Curtis and Tom be four down?' the US captain asked.

'The Europeans are effectively ten-under-par at this stage, Jack.'

'What?'

'Yes, Jack. Ten-under-par.'

'Well, that's unbelievable golf. I suppose we're doing well to be only four down.'

Encouraging each other, advising each other and congratulating each other: Nick and I appeared almost unstoppable and we moved in for the kill. My approach finished ten feet from the pin, and the birdie putt left us skaking hands with the Americans on the 14th green. The outcome sent shockwaves around the course: Nick and I had defeated Strange and Kite by 5 and 4, a huge margin in a fourballs match. As a pair, we had taken 3½ points out of the possible four in two days and, I hope, fulfilled all our captain's expectations.

'What a pairing they have been!' proclaimed Peter Alliss, on the TV commentary. 'Faldo has been quite magnificent, and Woosnam is a Welsh dragon belching out fire.'

Tony was immediately on hand to offer his congratulations and, to his great credit, Jack also came over and told us we had played exceptionally well. I recently saw Jack quoted as saying he didn't consider himself an effective captain at team events such as the Ryder Cup because he saw them primarily as expressions of international goodwill rather than do-or-die battles. Whether this was the case or not, his conduct at what must have been a difficult time was never less than a credit to the game.

The Americans kept fighting but, when Sandy and Bernhard bravely held off Wadkins and Nelson to win the last match of the day by one hole, we had secured a 10½–5½ lead to take into the 12 singles matches on Sunday. Three and a half points, no more than that, would ensure we retained the Cup. There was still work to be done but, once again, our remarkable team spirit had shone through the foursomes and fourballs and carried us into a commanding position.

'Woosie, I want you to lead us home,' Jacklin told me that evening. 'You've been playing fantastic golf, and I want to put you first in our order of play for tomorrow. Are you happy with that?'

I wasn't going to argue with a man who, over and over again, through three Ryder Cups, had read every situation so carefully and made amazingly few – if any – errors of judgement; and, not long afterwards, I was told Andy Bean would be my opponent in the first match on Sunday.

The difference in height between this gentle giant of American golf and me was no fewer than 12 inches, but I was consistently driving the ball further and, after nine holes, we were still all square. Then, I stood on the 10th tee and looked down the par four . . . there were bunkers down the left of the fairway, and a wonderful palm tree stood at the point where the hole dog-legged left rising to an elevated green.

Right, I said to myself, it's time to take a risk, so I decided to aim my drive over the bunkers, over the corner of the dog-leg and left of the palm tree. It seemed to be within my range. It was ambitious, particularly since Andy had already put his drive in the middle of the fairway, but I uncoiled my swing perfectly and the ball flew off the driver, past the palm tree and settled in the light rough beyond.

It had been a tremendous blow and I walked proudly up the fairway, knowing Andy would hit a four-iron to the green and I would only need a wedge. As I reached my ball, I saw a large, middle-aged, square-jawed, brightly clothed American – yep, another one – standing just beyond the ropes.

'Hey man,' he shouted, 'Is that your second?'

'No, it's my bloody drive!'

He was shocked into silence. I took enormous pleasure from surprising the Americans with my distance off the tee, especially when they seemed unable to get their heads around the fact that such a small man could strike the ball such long distances. The looks on their faces were worth seeing!

There was never much in my match with Andy Bean: we ended up halving the 10th, he went one up with a birdie at the 14th, I missed an eight-foot putt to draw level at the 17th and two solid pars at the 18th left me on the wrong side of a tremendous contest, beaten by one hole.

Just as at The Belfry two years before, I headed back out on the course to support my teammates through what turned out to be a nerve-racking afternoon as the Americans fought back. Each of the first six matches was only decided at the 18th and, in truth, all might have gone either way. Through the next hour at the 18th green, I watched Clark beat Pohl, Torrance halve with Mize, Faldo lose to Calcavecchia; and, when Olazabal lost to Stewart, our once commanding lead had been cut to a precarious 12–9.

Even the calmest characters were struggling to withstand the pressure. Ben Crenshaw snapped his putter after losing the sixth against Eamonn Darcy and had to putt with either his one-iron or the leading edge of his wedge for the rest of the day. Eamonn eventually won by one hole. Who knows if Ben's bad break was the difference between winning and losing for him . . . and, as it turned out, for his team and his country?

The news wasn't getting any better. Rivero lost to Scott Simpson, Lyle lost to Kite and Langer managed a precious half against Mize. We now led 13½–11½, meaning we needed one more half point from three matches left on the course to retain the Cup. With Ken Brown trailing Wadkins and Brand junior involved in a tight struggle with Sutton, our hopes began to rest heavily on the familiar shoulders of Seve Ballesteros.

Holding his game together, Seve sank a three-foot putt on the 17th green to defeat Strange 2 and 1, taking us to the magical 14½ points. With Brand earning a half, we eventually won 15–13.

Defeating the Americans at The Belfry in 1985 was fantastic because it had not been done for 28 years, but the experience of beating them before their own crowd and on their own course felt even better because it had not been done before – ever. We had truly made history. Tony began talking about the greatest week of his life, and everybody in his team understood what he meant.

Our joy was there for all to see. After the formal prize giving was over, Tony and I stood clapping out the rhythm as Jose Maria Olazabal gave an exhibition of Flamenco dancing on the 18th green. Bernhard was waving a German flag and Sam was jubilantly unfurling the lion rampant of Scotland. And we didn't need a second invitation to join a group of our supporters in a hospitality tent, where the drink flowed fast, songs were bellowed into the Ohio night and players were carried around shoulder-high. The Ryder Cup was fast becoming renowned among European golfers not only as an event of intense pressure and world-class golf but also as the time and place of the best parties in the game.

We flew home to a heroes' reception, although not everyone was impressed, notably the policemen who pursued me for 35 miles on the M1, M6 and M54. With Glen asleep in the passenger seat, and Daniel suffering earache at home, I was speeding from Heathrow straight home to Oswestry and it was 1.30am when the police clocked me at 122mph. After an appeal, I was banned from driving for six months.

My celebrations had come to an abrupt conclusion, but the memories of The Belfry and Muirfield Village will live long in my memory. I had been involved in something extremely special.

Against the odds, against America . . . we had won, at home and away; and, in victory, we had demonstrated that European golfers could hold their own on both sides of the Atlantic.

CHAPTER SIX

Number One in the World

The Bowmere Pool might not be renowned as one of the largest water sports centres of Europe but, so far as we were concerned, this large pool, almost a lake, in Shropshire was more than adequate.

Some friends of mine, John and Terry Wilson, kept a boat on the lake and, every Monday during the summer, whenever it was possible for me to get home from the tournament ending the previous afternoon, we would drive out to the Pool and spend the day water-skiing. The sense of speed and power on the water was exhilarating, and I constantly used to urge John to drive the boat faster.

If someone had been sitting on the bank of this little-known lake on one of these long summer Mondays, and if they had happened to be watching the enthusiastic, short guy clambering around in the water . . . well, I don't suppose they would ever have believed that he could become officially ranked as the world's No.1 player in one of the world's most popular and competitive individual sports.

It had been the same at school, and it had been the same during my early years on Tour: to most people, I looked like Joe Bloggs, not any kind of champion. It didn't matter to me.

I have never wanted to be a celebrity and, on the contrary, I have always enjoyed nothing more than to melt into the background, whether it be water-skiing or having a quiet pint in the pub. These days on the lake, as just another fool on the water, when nobody was watching, were perfect.

Some journalists have suggested it is precisely because I am not 6' tall with a perfectly formed six-pack that so many people have felt able to identify with me, and support me through the years. If that is the case, then I am pleased. Playing golf for a living might mean you get more attention than most, but it doesn't make you any different or better than anyone who does anything else for a living.

In any case, it didn't matter what I looked like. By the end of 1987, I was playing well enough to make the idea of becoming number one in the world seem a realistic prospect.

Even now, it feels extraordinary to put those words on paper. You think of so many millions of people playing golf, across Europe and Asia, through America, Africa and Australia, and then you contemplate that an official ranking system singles you out as the best golfer of them all. I was, and still am, awed by the concept of being number one in the world. 'Naughty Ian Woosnam, the farmer's son hurling his clubs into the bushes at the Llanymynech Golf Club, as number one in the world.' The idea made me smile.

Yet there I was, in ninth place. The official world golf ranking lists were produced every Monday and, at the end of 1987, the name 'Ian Woosnam' was there, in ninth position, eight places away from where I wanted to be, eight places from being the number one golfer in the world.

The rankings were calculated by a complicated, and sometimes controversial, method of allocating points to every single performance in most professional tournaments played throughout the world. But I was not so much concerned by the means as the end; and, every Monday, wherever in the world I might be, I would look out for the ranking lists, check my position, and work out what I needed to do.

Yes, of course, I wanted to win a Major tournament, but I reckoned that was bound to happen sooner or later if I continued playing well. Above all, I wanted to be ranked number one.

It seemed a good idea to start 1988 as I had started 1987, by preparing for the year under the warm Australian sun. So, Glen, Daniel and I escaped Oswestry in January and flew to spend some time on the Gold Coast of Queensland. I played quite well in two tournaments on the Australian Tour and missed the cut when trying to defend my title at the Hong Kong Open.

However, by this stage, it had become clear that my best route to the top of the world rankings would take me through the United States. At that time, it was notoriously difficult for European players to get invitations to play on the American tour – far more difficult than for Americans to play in Europe, so it was reckoned that, now my 1987 form had earned the opportunity, I should grasp it with both hands.

In truth, I was perfectly happy on the European Tour, but I understood the need to prove myself on the world's richest golf tour and, following advice, I entered three USPGA tournaments as preparation for my first US Masters. In March 1988, I flew across the Atlantic to acclimatize and get acquainted with American conditions.

At the Bay Hill Classic, I finished tied for 19th; at the Players Championship, I missed the halfway cut; at the Greater Greensboro Open, I missed the halfway cut. This was not love at first sight. My driving wasn't bad, and my iron shots were fine, but I just couldn't get the measure of the course.

'Calm down,' I told myself. 'It's still the same game.'

My confidence was wavering when I arrived for the first time at Augusta National, but nobody fails to be impressed by their first experience at the US Masters. The huge crowds, the sense of tradition, the manicured course and the high quality field combine to make everything very special.

Desperate to find form, I played an encouraging

practice round with Seve, Sandy and Greg Norman, and tapped into their knowledge of the course. Seve had won the Masters in 1980 and 1983, and finished in the top five in six of the previous eight years. Greg had come second in the two previous years, and, although none of us knew it at the time, Sandy was four days away from winning a green jacket of his own. We talked and played our way around the course, discussed the best lines off the tees and the contours of the greens. I was learning quickly, memorising the best positions on the fairways, the way to play the course. Before long, I was raring to go.

It was all in vain: I missed the halfway cut at Augusta. After missing yet another cut the following week, I was greatly relieved to fly home. Three consecutive missed cuts in America sent my name sinking down the world rankings.

There is much I admire about professional golf in the States. Almost without exception, the tournaments are fantastic because they are set up exclusively for the benefit of the players. In Europe, the harsher financial realities meant many tournaments were set up for the benefit of the sponsors.

Things have changed now but, in the late 1980s, it was the small things that made a difference to the players. When you played in America, you were usually given a complimentary car for the week; in Europe, there were times when you were pleased to get a parking place. In America, there was always somebody in the locker room offering to clean your shoes; on occasion in Europe, I changed my shoes in the car park. American clubs always laid on outstanding food for the players in the locker rooms; players wanting something to eat in Europe would often have to queue with the punters in the public bar.

In Europe, many of these issues have now been addressed, for which much credit is due to John Jacobs, founding father of the European Tour, and his successor Ken Schofield, and the gap is much closer. In America, professional golf remains a game run for the players, with the players and by the players. You can't fault the nuts and bolts of the organisation.

And, of course, there are many world-class golf courses in America. Of those that I have played, perhaps three stand out as both an enjoyable experience and an outstanding test of golf.

At Muirfield Village, venue of the 1987 Ryder Cup, Jack Nicklaus has meticulously taken what he sees as the best elements of his favourite courses around the world and put them all together on a piece of rough land a few miles north west of Columbus, the state capital of Ohio. He risked an enormous sum of money to create his 'baby', then christened the place after the course in Scotland where he won his first Open Championship, and the result of his labour is a majestic, tough and fair golf course.

Pebble Beach is rightly included in most lists of the world's finest courses. It is exceptionally difficult and exceptionally beautiful, although I didn't endear myself to local officials when I first played there. The weather was unusually calm that day, and I was being interviewed after my round.

'So, what do you think of our Pebble Beach?' a journalist asked.

'Well, it's all right until you come to that practice hole,' I replied, tongue firmly in cheek.

Well, sarcasm and irony don't always register with Americans and, the following morning, I was asked to apologise to the committee for my remarks about the course. This gave me an opportunity to explain how I had been referring, in humour, to the signature hole at Pebble Beach, the short par-three 7th where the green is spectacularly placed on a small piece of land jutting out into the sea. When the wind blows, you could easily require a seven-iron, or more, to reach the flag, but it just so happened that I had played the hole on a day so tranquil that I could have thrown my ball on to the green. It had felt like target practice, so I made the joke. I had not realised how difficult the hole could play when the wind got up. In any case, my apology was accepted.

The third of my favourite golf courses in America – and probably my favourite course anywhere – is, of course, Augusta National for reasons that would become obvious during April 1991.

There have been times during the past 14 years when I have seriously considered playing more often on the American tour, but the clinching argument for staying in Europe has always been my desire to be close to home and to spend as much time as possible with my young family. Playing in Europe, more often than not, I could get back to have Monday and half of Tuesday with Glen and the kids.

And I must be honest: I didn't enjoy the daily life on the US Tour. I couldn't handle the idea of spending each day between the tournaments sitting around the hotel. There would be times when I strolled down to the foyer, and looked around and wondered where everyone had gone. In the US, you leave the golf course and you don't see anyone till the next day. Maybe they stay in their rooms. I don't know. So, I would wander into the bar, and order myself a drink, and there would be someone there who just wanted to talk about golf and, more often than not, I would end up back in my room with only the television set for company. I was often bored.

It was probably my fault for not looking hard enough, but most American cities appeared to be built on the same vast grid of boulevards linking shopping malls and residential areas. You needed to get in a car to go anywhere, and everywhere looked the same. It just wasn't my life.

In contrast, playing in Europe, you could almost always walk around a decent town centre near the tournament venue, and there would usually be something interesting to see or do. And there was constant variety; one day it would be pasta in Milan, the next week it would be paella in Madrid, then it would be Guinness in Dublin. At the hotel where the pros were based, you would find guys having a drink or two, cracking jokes or going for a meal. The European Tour somehow seemed a more sociable place.

My disappointing form at the start of 1988 obviously became a talking point, and the consensus quickly developed that the cause of all my problems was my new clubs. People said I had stopped playing with Dunlop Maxfli clubs only because I was offered more money by the Japanese manufacturer, Maruman. As ever in these situations, there was an element of truth in the rumour, but only an element. Maruman did put a fantastic offer on the table, but I did not knowingly sacrifice success on the course for money in the bank. After my successes in 1987, I believed I could hit the ball with a stick.

The new clubs did not feel right – in my first competitive round of the year, I had shot a catastrophic 79 at the Hong Kong Open. Yet I did not believe there was anything wrong that could not be put right – after all, I had produced a second round 67 to make the cut at Fanling Golf Club. I had just lost the feel.

Maruman could not have tried harder to put things right. When the grooves started shearing the cover off the ball, they sent technicians over to alter the clubs to my liking. As each problem arose, the team working on making the changes back in Japan seemed to grow larger and larger. The issue rumbled on through 1988 and the next few years, and the clubs did eventually start to feel better. The last word on this particular saga has to be that I used Maruman clubs at the Masters in 1991, so they can't have been too bad!

As I settled back into the familiar routines of the European Tour, I knew deep down that the clubs were only part of my problem. There was something wrong with my swing. I started to practise longer and harder than I had ever practised as a professional. My confidence was draining away, I was slipping down the world rankings, and I desperately needed to get back on track as soon as possible.

One bright morning in Monticello, Italy, just after waking up on the second day of the Italian Open, I was standing in my hotel room, absent-mindedly rehearsing my swing in front of the mirror. I was just swinging my arms, turning my body, trying to 'feel' right.

Hold on! I looked again, double-checked. Yes, that's wrong. My hips were in the wrong position when I addressed the ball and, as a result, I was swinging the club from out to in. An hour or so later, on the driving range, I changed my hip position and started hitting balls more solidly.

People had said some very kind things about my swing. Seve Ballesteros called it 'the sweetest swing in Europe'. Some players noticed the speed I generated in the club through impact, and others admired how my head managed to stay perfectly still while the rest of my body turned. Such remarks boosted my confidence, but the battle to get my swing 'right' was never won. This wasn't something you achieved, and then moved on. On good days and bad days, it was an ongoing struggle to keep every element in its place. There were hot streaks when I got into a groove and played well for several weeks, but sooner or later things would go wrong; and then, all over again, I would stand in front of the mirror, or consult Bob Torrance, or a friend, or anyone, and make a change to this or alter that. My swing was a jigsaw puzzle that, once in a while, fell apart and needed to be put back together.

The improvement in my form this time was immediate. Rounds of 68-68-69-69 at Monticello carried me to sixth place at the Italian Open and suggested I was rediscovering some consistency. The following week, playing in the inaugural Volvo PGA Championship at Wentworth, I started with a 67, sustained my challenge in a quality field with 70 in the second round and another 70 in the third round. I was pleased because the alterations to my swing were holding together under pressure. Everything was feeling good.

One shot behind Seve going into the last day, I produced another 67 and then watched from beside the 18th green as Seve missed a chip that would have forced a play-off. From hopeless despair to the mirror in my hotel room at Monticello to the driving range to another large silver trophy at another prize-giving: this would be the pattern of my journey up the rankings to be number one in the world.

I was competing again, stomping up and down the fairways of Europe, feeling strong and, in the middle of August, I arrived to play the Irish Open at Portmarnock. Perhaps it's the Gaelic solidarity between the Welsh and the Irish, but I have always enjoyed playing in Ireland, and meeting up with friends over there, particularly Tony Higgins, a butcher who I first met at Hill Valley in 1979.

On the evening before the tournament, I arranged to go out for a couple of pints with Tony in Dublin. The following day I shot 67, seizing a lead that I never lost on my way to my second title of the year. As a Welshman, I have always felt something of an honorary Irishman in Ireland and my decisive seven-shot victory over Olazabal, Faldo, Pinero and Des Smyth was greeted like a hometown win.

Rolling again, I tied for second place at the Swiss Open two weeks later and then came back home to win the European Open at Sunningdale. By the time I returned to Sun City and finished fourth in the Million Dollar Challenge, I was pleased to have successfully turned the year around. Three titles, worldwide prize money of £270,674 and fourth place on the European Order of Merit seemed to be a reasonable return.

Into 1989, the pattern remained the same: a quiet start was followed by a burst of mid-summer form, highlighted by the successful defence of my Irish Open title at Portmarnock. I finished in the top five in eight successive tournaments, but repeatedly fell on the wrong side of the famously thin line between triumph and runner-up. Nonetheless, second places at the PGA Championship, the Wang Four Stars Pro-Am, the Scottish Open and the European Open sustained my earnings and my world ranking.

My form in America was tremendously improved. Tied for 14th was a respectable result at the Masters, and I surprised even myself in my first US Open by finishing second to Curtis Strange at Oak Hill. Two months later, I came sixth in the US PGA Championship when Payne Stewart won at Kemper Lakes. Such strong, consistent performances served to enhance my reputation in American minds ahead of what loomed as my big challenge of 1989: to help Europe successfully defend the Ryder Cup at The Belfry.

Ray Floyd had been appointed as the US captain, and this formidable and competitive man threw down the gauntlet during the Opening Ceremony when he introduced his team as 'the 12 greatest players in the world.' Ben Hogan had used precisely the same words on the eve of the 1967 Ryder Cup in Houston, and the Americans had gone on to win 23½–8½.

However, times had changed. Ballesteros raised an eyebrow, Faldo smiled dryly and Tony Jacklin, captaining the European team for a fourth successive time, seemed to take no notice of the remark. However, the general muttering and shuffling among the Europeans suggested Floyd had successfully stoked the fire.

The lesson of our victories in 1985 and 1987 appeared to be that Europe's strength lay in the foursomes and the fourballs. In both matches, we had established such a commanding lead during the first two days that the Americans had been unable to rescue the situation in the Sunday singles.

In our view, this pattern was explained by the phenomenal family spirit within our group and the strong bonds that developed between certain pairs. While the Americans appeared to operate as individuals, spending evenings with their wives rather than their teammates, we were socialising together, cementing the confidence in each other that, we hoped, would reap dividends in the fourballs and foursomes.

'OK, guys, settle down please.'

Another Ryder Cup, another team meeting, Jacklin speaking again.

'The pairs for tomorrow will be . . . well, obviously, Seve and Olly, Nick and Woosie . . .'

Obviously. Two years before, Ballesteros and Olazabal had produced three points out of a possible four, while Nick Faldo and I had scored 3½ from our four matches. It was therefore no surprise to anyone that the captain wanted these same combinations to do the same job at The Belfry.

It wasn't difficult for Nick and me to pick up where we had left off at Muirfield Village. We were both playing well – he was the reigning Masters champion and had won three times on Tour – and the Ryder Cup seemed to bring out the best in both of us, on the course, off the course and as partners.

The Belfry was buzzing again on the morning of 22 September, 1989, and another huge, enthusiastic crowd poured onto the course in anticipation of seeing more European success. Our triumphs in 1985 and 1987 had created a level of expectation that sometimes seemed a burden. It had been easier to take on the US team when we were the underdogs. In 1989, many people were talking about us as favourites to win again.

At least, we were favourites until lunch on the first day. By then, the Americans had grabbed a 3–1 lead, winning two of the morning foursomes and drawing the other two. Nick and I had played steadily to halve a close match against Curtis Strange and Tom Kite, while Seve and Ollie were held by Tom Watson and Chip Beck. We were in a battle. That much was clear. Any complacency evaporated like the morning mist.

Encouraged by Jacklin and chastened by the morning's defeats, we collectively ripped into the afternoon fourballs, with the result that only one of the four matches reached the 18th green.

Sam Torrance and Gordon Brand junior flew the Scottish flag with victory over Strange and Azinger, then Howard Clark and Mark James, both of England, closed out Wadkins and Couples. Nick and I held firm against McCumber and Calcavecchia, winning by two holes; and that left Ballesteros and Olazabal to complete a great afternoon by routing the experienced Watson and O'Meara by 6 and 5.

That was more like it! We led 5–3 on the Friday night and the crowd went home happy. A similar result on the Saturday would have given us the kind of lead that we were looking for to take into Sunday, but Floyd's tough approach had rubbed off on his team and nothing came easy. The morning foursomes were shared 2–2, with Nick and me overcoming Wadkins and Stewart 3 and 2, and Seve and Olly squeezing home by one hole against Kite and Strange; and there was nothing between the two teams in the afternoon, when the fourballs were also shared with two wins each.

Nick and I had been confident of beating Paul Azinger and Chip Beck in the first match of the afternoon, and we hardly hit a bad shot in compiling a betterball score of 11-under-par by the time we reached the 17th green. By then, however, we had lost 2 and 1. The Americans were 13-under. Sometimes, you just have to put your hands up and concede the other guys deserved to win a fantastic match.

So we led 9–7 with the singles to come and Tony decided to place Nick and me in the anchor positions, at 11th and 12th on his order of play; perhaps this was a kind of insurance, executed in the hope that, if the match was tight at the end, we would be able to pull through and deliver. I was flattered, even though I didn't need to be reminded of my Ryder Cup singles record so far – played 3, lost 3. In the event, the insurance policy was not required. We needed just five points to retain the Ryder Cup and, although Seve, Bernhard, and Howard Clark lost the first three matches of the day, a heroic succession of European players came down the 18th hole and held their nerve under pressure. Olazabal beat Stewart by one hole, Ronan Rafferty beat Calcavecchia by one hole, Mark James overcame O'Meara at the 16th, Christy O'Connor junior produced a glorious two-iron second shot at the 18th to upset Fred Couples by one hole; and so it was left to the veteran Jose Maria Canizares to defeat Ken Green by one hole and take us to 14 points.

By all accounts, it had been a nerve-racking hour and a half on the 18th green with the European players holing crucial putt after crucial putt and, amid great relief, safely achieving our goal, to retain the Cup.

Unfortunately, I missed these scenes and celebrations because I was still out on the course, continuing my match against Curtis Strange. We had just teed off at the 16th hole when news arrived that Canizares had beaten Green and that, officially, Europe had retained the Ryder Cup.

'Well done, Woosie,' Curtis said, walking towards me with his hand outstretched. I sensed that he wanted to concede the match, so we could make our way straight back to the clubhouse.

'Thanks,' I replied, 'but do you mind if we play on and finish?'

I was thrilled by the news from the 18th, and eager to join my teammates, but, although we had reached 14 points and safely retained the Ryder Cup, we needed one more win to actually win the match outright. And, on a personal level, I was one-up at the time and I desperately wanted to win a singles match in the Ryder Cup. Would it still have counted as a victory if Curtis conceded? It probably would have, but I wanted to win properly.

'Sure,' he replied amicably. 'No problem.'

So, we played the 16th, and he holed a 25-foot birdie putt to win the hole. Now we were level. Curtis was enjoying himself, and he birdied the 17th to go one-up. I had been playing steady golf, making two pars in a row, but it wasn't good enough.

By the time we reached the 18th tee, it was about an hour since Canizares' win had drained the snap and tension out of the afternoon. Many spectators had already left for home, celebrating the European success, and there was an empty atmosphere on the course. Gordon Brand junior, Sam Torrance and Nick Faldo had all lost their matches, yet I was still out there, still fighting my personal battle.

'Just win the last,' I told myself. 'At least, you'll get half a point.'

I launched myself into a powerful drive straight down the middle of the fairway, way past Curtis' ball, but he then spoiled everything by nailing an unbelievable two-iron four feet from the flag. To say I was cheesed off is a major understatement. Curtis holed his putt for a third birdie in a row, against my three pars, and ended up winning our match by two holes. At a time when I wanted to be entering into the spirit of our team celebrations, I was feeling bitterly disappointed that I had lost my match.

'Don't worry, Woos,' said Sam Torrance, smiling as he wrapped his arm around my shoulders. 'You'll probably never win a singles match in the Ryder Cup. That's your fate!'

I wasn't laughing, but Sam didn't mind; he was. So, Europe and the US finished at 14–14, and we retained the Cup.

When we arrived back at our team room later that night, we were greeted by the soothing sounds of Chris de Burgh playing the piano. The Irish singer had performed at the opening banquet, and then stayed to watch the golf. I enjoyed his music, so I introduced myself and we started chatting.

It turned out we had a great deal in common. Like me, he had also taken a long time to reach the top of his profession. While I was driving around Europe in a caravanette, he was singing in pubs and clubs. Then, his song, 'Lady in Red', became a worldwide hit, and he has never looked back. Chris and I have since become good friends and, our schedules permitting, we meet on a regular basis.

The effect of this sustained Ryder Cup success on the European Tour can be likened to adding three turbo engines to a glider. Three times, the best players in Europe had overcome the best players from the PGA tour in America. Everyone took notice. Above all, the sponsors took notice . . . with the result that the late-1980s and early-1990s soon became recognised as a Golden Age of European golf.

It is easiest to measure the phenomenal growth of the European Tour during this period by the number of events played and the total prize money offered in these tournaments. These statistics, at least, don't lie.

In 1983, when Tony Jacklin first took his optimistic team to contest the Ryder Cup at West Palm Beach, European pros played 27 events for total prize money of £2,819,185. By 1990, three successful Ryder Cups later, there were 37 events on the Tour schedule with total prize money of £16,100,425.

The Ryder Cup effect fuelled progress during the

next decade as well: by 2000, the European Tour comprised 44 events worldwide and offered total prize money of £56,812,679.

And yet, throughout this period and despite the introduction of co-sanctioned events in Australia, Africa, Asia and the Middle East, the European Tour has not matched the levels of prize money available on the American tour . . . partially because the leading companies still perceive the USA as the world's largest golf market, and partially because of the enormous television income generated by the game in the United States.

This relative poverty – and, of course, it was only relative – led European golf towards the necessary evil of appearance money as the only way of preventing a migration of top players to the States. It is common knowledge that big name players have been offered substantial sums simply to compete in a specific tournament, irrespective of where they finished and additional to any prize money they might earn.

The first offers of appearance money emerged in 1988; and, in a sense, they changed the nature of the tournament for me. If I was being paid to play, I felt obliged to offer decent value for money and, at least, get myself into contention on the Sunday afternoon.

So, while it is true that this Golden Age was prompted by the Ryder Cup successes – and then sustained by European players regularly winning

American events such as the US Masters and the Open Championship – it was also underpinned by the payment of appearance money to leading players.

And I was a prime beneficiary. I don't apologise for that. I understand the arguments of people who say these large sums of money should have been added to the total purse. Yet the simple realities of the situation were that, without appearance money, the leading players would have gone to compete in America where the prize money was three or four times larger, and golf in Europe would have suffered. This struggle continues today, and the battle is gradually being lost. As purses soar in the US, not even the appearance money can keep the Europeans at home, and more and more leading players, such as Parnevik, Garcia and Olazabal, are competing more and more regularly on the US PGA Tour.

During the late 1980s, however, the stars stayed at home, and the spirit of the European Tour was built on the inspiring achievements of its great players, on the unfolding legends of Faldo, Lyle, Ballesteros, Langer, and others . . . and, although it's not really my place to make this judgement, me.

As I prepared for the 1990 season, my main ambition burned brighter than ever. I wanted to work hard, to practise more . . . and I desperately wanted to wake up one Monday morning, and see the rankings, and see my name in the top position. I wondered how I would feel. I wanted to know.

The year started with a bit of luck in the pro shop at Oswestry Golf Club. I wasn't looking for anything in particular when I saw this Zebra putter. It was a ladies' club, a little shorter than normal with the grip not quite straight in such a way that, when I putted, I had the feeling of the face staying open. I took it out to the putting green, and was amazed by the results. I was effectively slicing every putt, and this action stopped me from pulling putts left of the hole. I bought the putter there and then, put it in my bag and used it throughout the year. It played amazingly well from the first tournament to the last. In 1990, I seemed to hole almost everything.

In fact, I won the first tournament of the year, the Amex Mediterranean Open in Spain, and secured a couple of second places in May, at the European Open and the Belgian Open, but I had to wait until July, later than I had hoped, before I launched on another excellent run of form. It began in what for me were the unpromising surroundings of the Monte Carlo Open. There was some history involved.

Back in 1984, I had arrived to play in the very first Monte Carlo Open at the Mont Agel course, perched on top of the mountain overlooking the principality. It was just a few months after we were married, and Glen came along to the tournament. On the Tuesday, she went shopping in town and I headed off to the course for a practice round. After nine holes, I had

had enough. To say the least, I thought the course was disappointing and, as soon as I got back to the hotel, I withdrew from the event and then told Glen we were going home. Then, I tried to change our air tickets but the airline said it was going to cost me a couple of grand. Well, that changed everything. I didn't want to pay that much money, so I thought I might as well play in this Monte Carlo Open after all. I phoned the tournament office and asked if I could get back into the tournament.

'Sorry, Monsieur Woosnam?'

'Yes, I would like to play tomorrow.'

'Sorry, Monsieur Woosnam, it's too late.'

My reaction to this perfectly justified decision was to avoid playing in the Monte Carlo Open for the next five years. I just found somewhere else to play during that week, but, now it was 1990, and I was prepared to forget the past; and I discovered the course had been substantially improved.

And I won the tournament. It was only a par-69 layout but I produced rounds of 66, 67 and 65, and then moved decisively clear of the field with a round of 60 on the Sunday afternoon. Adding to the irony, I returned to win the tournament again in 1991, and again in 1992; and then the sponsor withdrew and the Monte Carlo Open disappeared from the schedule. In the end, I was sorry to see it go.

In 1990, however, victory in Monte Carlo launched an exceptional run of form that took me to the top of the European Order of Merit for a second time, and to sixth in the world rankings.

I won the Scottish Open at Gleneagles the following week, and then moved on to the Open at St Andrews, where I played reasonably well without ever threatening to win. Rounds of 68, 69, 70 and 69 left me tied for fourth place behind Nick Faldo.

The prize money was good but, at this particular stage of my career, the world ranking points seemed to be almost as important. I collected 28 at the Scottish Open, and 14 at St Andrews. I had moved up to fourth in the official rankings and still, more than anything, I wanted to be No.1.

After a quick spot of globetrotting to Shoal Creek, in Birmingham, Alabama, where I tied for 31st at the US PGA (scoring only 2 ranking points), and Japan, where I came third in the Maruman Open (4 points), I returned home and finished second in the European Open at Sunningdale (14 points). This wasn't good enough. I needed to start winning tournaments if I was going to threaten the top three in the world.

The World Match Play Championship loomed as an opportunity. After winning the title in 1987, I had lost in the semi-finals but won the third-place play-off in 1988 and was runner-up to Nick Faldo in 1989, losing by one hole in the final. My form was good, and I had always rated the Burma Road course at Wentworth among the best in the world.

There was no lack of surprises in the first few days,

and I found myself drawn against giant-killers fresh from their moment of triumph: Ronan Rafferty had beaten Seve in the first round, but I overcame the Irishman 5 and 4 in a quarter-final; Chip Beck had defeated Faldo, but I won our semi-final contest by 5 and 3. Mark McNulty had beaten Greg Norman in the other semi-final, leaving the talented Zimbabwean and me to contest a 36-hole final for the title. The match swung this way and that: I went two up, he drew level, I then birdied the last four holes of the morning round and ate lunch at three-up.

That should have been a decisive lead, but Mark won three straight holes from the 7th to pull level again. I urged myself on, refusing to let the title or the ranking points slip, won the 10th and the 12th, and eventually secured the title (and 24 points) on the 16th green, winning by 4 and 2.

At the request of the media photographers, Rebecca, our two-year-old daughter, joined Glen, five-year-old Daniel, me and the World Match Play trophy on the 18th green after the prize-giving.

The next week, I played in the Epson Grand Prix of Europe at St Pierre, near Chepstow in Wales, and won again. I had managed to shoot below 70 in no fewer than 14 of my last 16 rounds on the European Tour. I was driving long and accurate, my Zebra putter still felt great and my iron shots were steady.

Into October, I was still seeking tournaments and points. Second place at the German Masters gave me another 12 points and, two weeks before Christmas, second place at the Johnnie Walker Classic in hot, humid Singapore provided a further 10 points. Just before I boarded the plane back home for Christmas, I got news of the latest rankings: I was up to second in the world; not far to go now.

Following the Tour protocol that champions should return to defend their title, I started 1991 by returning to the Mediterranean Open and successfully defended my title at Estoril. Monday came . . . still second. I flew to America to play two tournaments as preparation for the Masters. Tied for seventh at the Nestle International gave me only four points. Monday came . . . still second, but not by much.

I was not named among the favourites before the USF&G Classic in New Orleans, but my form held good and I emerged through a congested field to win in a play-off. Two wins in four events represented a superb start to the year, and soon it was Monday morning, the Monday before the Masters . . .

Official World Golf Ranking

No.1   Ian Woosnam (Wales)
No.2   Jose Maria Olazabal (Spain)
No.3   Nick Faldo (England)

No more dreams. Winston Churchill said facts are better than dreams. On Monday 8 April 1991, I knew he was right.

CHAPTER SEVEN

Green Jacket

The greens were slow and bumpy, not like velvet. The fairways were heavy from the rain, not flawless and lush. Plant life was non-existent in winter, not magnificently colourful. There was hardly anyone around, not 20,000 fans straining for a view.

This was the Oswestry Golf Club in mid-winter, a million miles from Augusta National in bloom.

Geoff Roberts had called and asked if I wanted a round. It was Friday 4 January 1991, and it looked like a dry day. It was also freezing cold but, during winter in Shropshire, if it's dry, it's playable. We met in the clubhouse: Geoff, John Wilson and me. The three of us teed off at noon.

I completed the outward nine in 27 strokes, making seven birdies and one eagle. My longest putt was 15 feet. I hit it close at the 10th, but missed a two-foot putt for birdie. Further birdies followed at the 11th, 13th, 14th and 15th. Then I missed a 10-foot putt for birdie at the 16th, missed a 12-foot putt for birdie at the 17th, and missed an eight-foot putt for birdie at the 18th.

'Not much of a finish,' I said as we shook hands, thinking about my straight pars at the last three holes.

'Woosie, you've just shot a 57!' Geoff replied.

We signed the cards, but my round did not count as the new course record because it was informal. Even so, it could hardly have been more significant in my career. As I drove home that afternoon, I started to reflect on what I'd done. I'd had that ball on a string. My game was exactly where I wanted it to be.

I had won more than 20 professional tournaments around the world, but I was resolutely blocking my mind to one awkward reality. If any journalist dared to raise the subject, I would instantly respond that I was not bothered at all and I would then ask him why he had the right to decide what makes a successful golfer.

The reality? The subject? It was simple enough. I still hadn't won a Major. I had challenged: at the Open in 1986, at the US Open in 1989, at the Open again in 1990, but I hadn't won a Major. As I arrived home after shooting 57, I muttered to myself: 'Come on, you've got to do it this year.'

Three months later, it was Monday 8 April 1991, and the greens were like velvet, the fairways were flawless, the magnolias were magnificent, there were 20,000 fans on the course, and it was only the first day of practice. This was the US Masters.

That same morning, the Official World Golf Rankings had been released and I had achieved my goal of becoming the number one golfer in the world. So, there had been an extra spring in my step as I walked down to the driving range, at least until I was approached by an American golf writer.

'Hey, Mr Woosnam?'

'Yes?'

'Did you know that nobody has ever won the Masters while being ranked number one?'

'No.'

'Well, that's a fact!'

I carried on walking. So what, I thought to myself. What's being number one got to do with winning the US Masters? Nothing at all. In any case, there was always a first time for everything.

As I practised around Augusta National, a course I had grown to know reasonably well during my three previous visits to the Masters, I ran a mental check on my preparations . . .

My clubs were now fine. Something had felt not quite right at the start of the year, but I had arranged to put the irons in a 'loft and lie' machine that delofted the heads to make them one club stronger. The effect of this was to make the two-iron play like a one-iron, the three-iron play like a two-iron, right through the set; it was not the most conventional way of correcting the 'feel', but it worked for me and the problem was solved.

In fact, these newly 'bent' clubs felt perfect for me in a way I had not imagined possible. My form had been excellent since the start of the year and, just two weeks before the Masters, I played great golf at the USF&G Classic in New Orleans, ending up in a play-off with Jim Hallet, an American touring pro. The first additional hole was halved.

The second extra hole was the par-three 17th, so I decided to take a seven-iron, which I knocked to 25 feet from the flag, pin high. I could see that Hallet was angling to see which club I had used, and I made no attempt to conceal the number on my club as I slotted it into my bag. I assume copying me, Jim also took a seven-iron, but his ball finished in a bunker 10 yards short of the green. He had under-clubbed because what he did not know, of course, was that my seven-iron had been bent stronger and was playing like a six-iron. While Jim took a bogey four, I two-putted, and won the tournament.

My performances in America had gradually improved since those three consecutive missed cuts on my first expedition to the US PGA Tour in 1988, but this maiden victory in the States had been a massive boost. Now I felt comfortable in the conditions and confident in the environment. I had won once, so I could win again.

And my state of mind was refreshed and relaxed because, between winning in New Orleans and arriving at Augusta, I managed to spend a week away from any golf. Greg Norman had invited me down to his place in south Florida, and we had been fishing and scuba diving off the Florida Keys.

Greg had a fantastic lifestyle: at one point, I was motored out on his fishing boat to some isolated islands, where Greg joined me the next day, arriving in his helicopter after fulfilling some business commitments. We fished for another day, then the helicopter whisked me across to join Glen and the children in Orlando, where they had checked in to the Buena Vista Hotel at Disneyland. Two days later, we all caught a flight to Augusta and settled into a rented house only five miles from the Augusta National course.

I was pleased the whole family could be with me in America. This kind of 'home from home' had always been my favourite environment during a Major tournament because it meant I could arrive back from a tough day's work on the golf course, enjoy Glen's cooking and quickly switch off. Just having Daniel and Rebecca around helped me to relax because, so far as they were concerned, I was just another Dad getting back from work. They had no interest in hearing how I had missed a putt or hooked a drive, and remained wonderfully oblivious to the ups and downs of my career.

Strong families are a stabilising factor in anyone's life and, whenever possible, I have wanted to have my troops around me. So I was happy they were all with me at the Masters in 1991.

As I continued my practice round on this warm, sunny Monday afternoon at Augusta, the preparations were going undeniably well: my golf clubs felt great, I had got used to the pace and slope of the greens, I was hitting the ball well, my confidence was high and my general state of mind was refreshed and relaxed.

People had suggested I would find the number one world ranking a burden, because it would increase public expectation and the pressure to succeed, but the reverse had been the case. I had focused my whole mind for so long on being No.1 that attaining this goal actually felt like a relief and liberation. The way I saw it, that was one goal out of the way; now I could concentrate my efforts on winning a Major tournament.

Perhaps it would happen this week at the Masters. I didn't know. Nobody ever knows when they're going to win a Major, but – and this is neither hindsight nor cockiness – I did have a gut feeling from the beginning of that week in Georgia that I was going to play well and that, with a little luck, I could even win. Sometimes you just turn up and feel right. You don't tell anyone, of course, but it happens like that.

My white Cadillac drew up outside the Augusta National clubhouse shortly before seven o'clock on the Monday evening. Each player had been given one of these luxury cars for the week, and I was arriving in time to attend one of the traditional functions that makes Masters week so special.

The International Players Dinner was conceived by Bobby Jones, the founder of the Masters, as a private gathering for the non-Americans in the field, and it was easy to be impressed by the seamless organisation and the classy atmosphere. Golfers, like anyone else, enjoy being made to feel special.

I chatted briefly to Nick Faldo over dinner, and he appeared relaxed about his prospects of becoming the first man to win three Masters in row. His back-to-back wins in 1989 and 1990 matched Jack Nicklaus' victories in 1965 and 1966, and now he was bidding for an unprecedented hat-trick. History is everywhere at Augusta, on every wall, in every custom, in almost every conversation; and it can seem daunting at first until you realise it's history that's still in the making, and that it embraces new names every year. It's my favourite event of the season.

Seven years later, the club would decide to abandon the International dinner because the number of international competitors had grown so large and Jones' original intention – 'to allow golfers from different nations to meet each other' – seemed less appropriate in an era when we virtually lived together for 35 weeks of the year. Nonetheless, it was a pity because the Monday night dinners were always relaxed and enjoyable.

As the 1991 dinner ended, in fact, I was feeling envious of Nick, Bernhard Langer, Seve Ballesteros and Sandy Lyle, who had been invited to return on the Tuesday evening to attend the second function of the week, the Masters Champions dinner. This was an occasion reserved for that elite group of golfers who had won the Masters, men who could comply with the strict dress code, 'Green Jacket'.

These four European players had won no fewer than five of the previous eight Masters between them, a fact that prompted two thoughts in my mind. First, this was a tournament that 'we' could win, as opposed to the US Open, which had produced eight American winners during the same period; second, if I wanted to be respected like these guys, it was a title I ought to win.

I practised again on the Wednesday, playing nine holes just to make sure my game was in shape. There was no doubt in my mind that Augusta suited me because the course seemed to favour players who naturally drew the ball from right to left, although Jack Nicklaus' five titles suggested he hadn't done too badly as a natural fader of the ball. And, as I played round these holes, each adorned with the plant after which it was named, I began to feel more and more comfortable.

On Wednesday afternoon, on the eve of the tournament when your nerves are starting to tighten, another Masters tradition is that players put their name down for a tournament on Augusta's par-three course. Nobody takes it too seriously, and it's only nine holes, but there is always a fantastic atmosphere because as many as 10,000 fans turn out and they're quick to roar when anybody hits the ball close to the flag.

The superstition, supported in the record books, is that no winner of the Par-Three Contest goes on to win the Masters later in the week, so I have always taken care to enjoy myself and not play too well! In fact, I have regarded the event as a chance to invite friends along as my caddie: one year, it was Dennis Taylor, the snooker world champion; another time, Max Boyce; in 1999, it was my son Daniel.

In 1991, we thought for most of the afternoon that Sam Snead would win the contest but, in the end, the 78-year-old, three-times Masters champion was narrowly beaten by Rocco Mediate. It goes without saying that Rocco didn't go on to win the Masters. Come Sunday evening, he tied for 22nd place.

At last, it was Thursday morning.

'Calm down, Woosie, hang in there.'

I was talking to myself again, desperately trying not to get upset because my opening round was battling to get off the blocks. I was hitting the ball well from the tees and fairways, but I had lost count of the six or seven foot putts that rolled tantalisingly past the cup and stayed above ground.

Glancing frequently at the scoreboards around the course, I could see many of the field were dipping under par, but I couldn't find any momentum. I wasn't playing badly, but I wasn't holing anything and I was disappointed to finish with a level-par round of 72, which left me tied in 31st position.

By the time Lanny Wadkins, Jim Gallagher junior and Mark McCumber were confirmed as joint leaders at five under par, I was searching for a solution on the practice putting green. I had used exactly the same putter that had felt so good when I won in New Orleans, but this was another place and another time, and the title-winning putter that had felt so right was now starting to feel not so good.

One hour, two hours, three hours . . . finally, I decided to discard that putter, which was not feeling right in my hands, and return to a very short putter that had been specially designed for me by Tad Moore and delivered to me at the start of the week. Tad had been working with Maxfli since late 1989, and, with his putter, I began to feel more comfortable knocking in the three-footers. That, in turn, gave me the confidence to go boldly for the longer putts because I wouldn't be so afraid of missing a three-footer coming back.

I returned to the golf course on an overcast Friday morning aware that I needed a strong second round to carry me into contention and, early in the day, almost unnoticed, I produced seven birdies and one bogey in a round of 66. My putting was massively improved and, although it had started to rain, I felt much happier as I drove back to our rented house to watch the rest of the day's play on television.

With my feet up, literally, and Rebecca on my knee, I watched an amazing sequence of events unfold on what the Augusta Chronicle later described as the most dramatic Friday in Masters history.

Wadkins missed a four-foot putt for par at the ninth, then tried to backhand the tap-in and missed again. Olazabal needed three pitches to escape from a damp lie beside the sixth, made a quadruple-bogey seven and walked to the seventh tee with what looked like tears in his eyes. Then Jack Nicklaus arrived at the 12th at four-under-par, two off the lead, his best Masters start in some years, and hit two shots into the water. Jack's response to this disaster was typical: birdie at the 13th, birdie at the 14th when he hit his second to three inches from the flag, birdie at the 15th and a birdie at the 16th when he holed a 30-foot 'indicator' putt (so called because they make sharp right turns). Even Rebecca, aged two, kept looking up at the screen as the crowd went crazy. I have played with the great man at the Masters and reckon that, when Jack gets on a birdie roll at Augusta, the sheer noise and overwhelming sense of affection is as exhilarating as anything in sport.

When the dust settled on the second round, Tom Watson emerged at the top of the leaderboard, eight under par, leading by two strokes from a group of four: Wadkins, McCumber, Calcavecchia and me. Quietly and unobtrusively, I had moved from nowhere into what seemed an ideal position.

On Saturday morning, the talk in the locker room was that Augusta had never played easier. Three of the four-par fives were reachable in two, and the whole course had been softened by thunderstorms earlier in the week. As the third round unfolded, an unprecedented 30 players shot below par.

I knew I needed to be among them, but I started cautiously, taking few risks, churning out the pars and making two birdies on the front nine. Faldo had surged up the leaderboard with a 67, Floyd and Olazabal were also making a move, but I needed to be patient, to await my chance and then seize it. The course may have been in a docile mood, but the old lady was still capable of cutting anyone down to size.

My tee-shot at the par-three 12th finished on the apron of the green, but I was able to use the putter and I managed to roll in the 20-foot putt for my third birdie of the day. That felt much better. I felt as if I had been let off the leash. Having remained calm and patient, and having curbed my natural instincts, I walked to the next tee, pumped up to attack the course and take hold of the tournament.

The 13th hole at Augusta, named Azalea after the 1,600 flowers on its borders, is a par-five dogleg left, and my drive ran through the corner of the dogleg, finishing in the pine needles gathered beneath a stand of trees. As I walked to the ball, I knew I would face a difficult choice: play safe, lay up short, chip and two-putt for par or wind myself up and go for the

215-yard carry to the green. If I cleared the creek and found the green, I would certainly make birdie, and maybe even an eagle; if I finished in the creek, I could end up with a six or seven.

I had just about convinced myself that I should play safe when I reached the ball, but then I saw it was lying well, above my feet – that was perfect for my draw. I was being tempted and, as I looked towards the green, I somehow started to visualise the shape of the shot, starting right, around a tree and drawing in to the green.

'Come on, Wobbly,' I said to my caddie. 'We only live once. Give me the two-iron.'

This was the Masters. I needed to make my move. I was going for it. What followed ranks as one of the most satisfying shots of my life. The ball did start right, and it did draw in, clearing the creek and finishing 30 feet from the flag. A steady two-putt gave me a second successive birdie.

At the par-four 14th, the only hole on the course without a bunker, I reached the green in regulation and sank a 25-foot birdie putt that paused before falling into the hole. I was charging.

At the par-five 15th, playing downwind, I reached the green in two and left myself a 30-foot putt for eagle. The putt felt perfect as I made impact but, almost incredibly, the ball rolled right to the lip of the hole and came to a halt. It seemed inevitable that a stiff breeze would blow it into the cup, so I walked slowly forward, giving it time. The ball didn't move and I tapped it in.

'Careful, Woosie!' It was Tom Watson, my playing partner for the day. 'I think you should have marked the ball,' he continued. 'That thing could have moved at any moment.'

The television commentators suggested we were arguing when, in fact, I appreciated Tom's remarks: if the ball had moved while I was removing the flag to tap it in, I would have suffered a two-shot penalty. The correct option would have been to mark the ball, but I had been so eager to secure the birdie that I had taken the risk, vigilantly lifted the flag out of the hole and nudged the ball in for my fourth birdie in succession.

I was on course for another round of 66, but my drive went right at the 18th and landed in the trees; my second went in a bunker and the bogey left me at 204, twelve under par, the leader by two from Watson at ten under par, with Olazabal and Wadkins one shot further back. It had been a long, demanding day, and I was leading the race.

'Daddy, why are you so late?'

As I arrived back at the house, my six-year-old son was more interested in kicking a football around than my battle for the Masters, and that suited me perfectly. Back at the course, troubled Americans were gazing at my name on top of the leaderboard and struggling to accept the prospect of a fourth consecutive

European winner of what they saw as 'their' Masters. Meanwhile, I relaxed and let Daniel take a 3–1 lead in our game of football.

IMG had invited Glen and me to dinner on the Saturday night, but we stayed at home with the children and were soon involved in a serious debate about what shirt I would wear in the final round.

'I think the white shirt would look good with a green jacket,' I said, grinning.

'You can't wear that,' Glen replied. 'It's dirty down the front.'

'Can't you wash it?'

'I'll try.'

She did try, but the marks remained and we finally decided I would wear a dark blue Tacchini shirt with red, lightly checked trousers. People would eventually say these trousers were tartan, but those were probably the same people who thought Wales was part of Scotland. In reality, they were a pair of Tacchini's best checks; they might have clashed with the Masters green, but they would have to do.

It was a strange feeling to wake up on a Sunday morning, and realise that I would lead the field into the final round of a Major tournament for the first time. I had finished the first round tied in 31st position. In 57 years of Masters history, no one had ever come from so far down the field after the first day to win the tournament. I felt incredibly nervous, but various messages of support sustained me through until lunchtime. Greg Norman phoned, wishing me luck; 'Go out and win it,' read another message.

On the driving range, and around the practice green, I started to sense the overwhelming support of the international players. The history of European success at the Masters, combined with recent Ryder Cup history, seemed to have polarised everyone at Augusta and I was caught in the middle. While the handful of Europeans regarded me as the gutsy, wee Welshman out to upset the odds, the massed ranks of Americans saw me as an upstart foreigner trying to deny their much-loved Tom Watson a third Masters title.

I'm sure there were some people among the masses across the course who simply wanted the best man to win – maybe, there were many thousands – but they tended to be shouted down, leaving me with the clear impression of an overwhelmingly partisan crowd. 'Let's show 'em,' I thought.

There is a saying at the Masters that the tournament only really starts when the leaders approach Amen Corner – the infamous 11th, 12th and 13th holes – on the Sunday afternoon and, through the early stages of the fourth round, Tom and I were like boxers circling each other in the ring, trying to avoid mistakes.

Steve Pate had already shot 65 and established himself as leader in the clubhouse at nine under par, but the air was now heavy with expectation.

Something had to happen, something had to give. 'Stay calm,' I told myself repeatedly. 'Stay calm. Hang on in there. Don't give it away.'

Watson was the first to blink, hitting his tee-shot at the par-three 12th into the water. The crowd sighed, I made another solid par and suddenly there was daylight between me and the chasing pack. As I reached the 13th tee, I swallowed hard and looked across at the leaderboard: still 11 under par, I was now two shots clear of Pate, who had finished, three clear of Olazabal and four clear of Watson.

Recalling how I had reached this par-five in two the previous day, I decided this was no time to stop and smell the azaleas. Many would have played safe, laid up and settled for par but, ever since my earliest days in Shropshire, my instinct had been to attack the course. That was my game, even at Augusta, even when I was within touching distance of my first victory in a Major tournament. So I would be strong, and I decided to crack my drive far down the fairway, giving myself a reasonable chance with my second.

I was ready and bristling to drive . . . but the course was congested. Tom and I waited for 20 minutes on the 13th tee, while a four-group pile-up ahead of us on the hole unravelled and moved on. The minutes passed like hours. I have always been a fast player, and standing around drove me to distraction. I hated losing my rhythm, and I started to wonder whether

I should attack or not. Doubt crept into the vacuum of time.

At last, the fairway was clear. No, I would go for it. Flat out.

Hook. Splash.

The spectators standing along the fairway started to cheer. When I heard that, my immediate reaction was that I must have got across the water and be safe. Then, I remembered the people cheering were supporting Watson, not me.

Moments later, as news of my mistake reached the green, I bristled with anger as I sensed the buzz of excitement ripple through the ten-deep gallery. My tension bubbled to the surface, and I was fuming. The spectators had applauded when my ball rolled off the green at the 10th, and now it felt as though they were all laughing again.

'I suppose people enjoyed that, me going in the water,' I said, as I found my ball submerged in the dim, murky water of the famous Rae's Creek down the left of the fairway. My words were picked up by the television microphones, and broadcast around the world.

There was no option but to take the penalty drop and play up short of the creek. Meanwhile, Tom drilled his second onto the green, leaving himself a 15-foot putt for eagle. Back on the tee, the Masters had seemed mine for the taking; within eight hectic minutes, I was right back in the battle.

As I walked down the fairway, I became aware of Tom walking beside me. This was unusual. The friendly chat between players generally stops at the business end of the week.

'Hard luck,' he said, smiling generously.

'Oh, thanks.'

Tom continued: 'You know, when I first came on Tour, there were players who used to say some negative things to me, and I decided the best way of dealing with them was just to turn around and say "thank you very much, thank you very much". They didn't like that at all.'

'Oh really?'

'Yep, that became my way of dealing with hecklers.'

He grinned again, and walked on towards his ball. I proceeded to pitch to the green and two-putted for a bogey but, amid more thunderous roars from the now ecstatic crowd, Tom holed his eagle putt. The three-shot swing at the 13th meant there was now just one stroke between us.

I glanced across at the leaderboard and noticed that, while I had been suffering at the 13th, Olazabal had made a couple of birdies and now shared the lead with me at ten under par. The contest was tightening, and I prepared myself to put things right with a solid drive down the 14th fairway.

'Hey, Woos-man,' bellowed another American voice from the back of the tee. 'This is Amen Corner at Augusta National, not a links course.'

I had heard every word, but I didn't move an inch from my position of address, and I swung, turned and followed through, and the ball soared away, straight and true. As I bent to collect my tee, I turned towards the back of the tee, and resolutely pointed my finger towards the man who had shouted.

'Thank you, very much,' I said. 'Thank you very much.'

Tom heard me, and smiled in my direction. As my father pointed out in 1982, Tom Watson does not have three arms and four legs, but his sportsmanship during this fourth round at the Masters confirmed his status in my mind as one of the great gentlemen of our sport. Under intense pressure, he had shown great compassion and understanding towards his closest rival, and further enriched the game of golf.

Emboldened and encouraged, I felt upbeat and positive again. As I would repeat endlessly in interviews at the end of the day, the angrier I became, the better I played. It was true.

As we both made par at the 14th, news arrived from ahead that Olazabal had posted a third consecutive birdie and moved clear at eleven under par. I had lost the lead for the first time since Saturday afternoon, but there was no need to panic: the par-five 15th was reachable in two.

Every shot now felt crucial. I pushed my drive right and, with 218 yards to the pin and water in front of the green, I struck a solid four-iron towards the back of the putting surface. Tom put his second closer. My putt for eagle slipped by on the right, but I tapped in for a birdie. Tom holed for his second eagle in three holes. The gallery erupted once again and, this time, I was happy to join in the applause.

Three holes to play, and three of us shared the lead at 11 under par. While Olly and I were both seeking our first Major victory, Tom was bidding for his ninth but the American's advantage in experience was balanced by the fact that he hadn't won any title since 1987. We all had demons to slay.

Whatever we were doing, we did it incredibly slowly. I wanted to race through the closing holes, to get rid of the tension, and finish the thing, and see what happened, but the congestion on the course was heavy and we were being made to wait before every stroke. The day crawled towards its conclusion.

Tom and I both hit reasonable shots to the back edge of the green at the par-three 16th, but our downhill birdie putts accelerated past the hole on the fast surface. Either of us might have buckled at that moment and missed the putts coming back but, amid incredible tension, I holed an eight-footer for par, and Tom holed a six-footer for par. There was nothing between us at the 17th hole either, where we both hit a big drive, wedge and two putts for par.

So, the 1991 Masters arrived at this simple conclusion: three men came to the 72nd tee tied at 11 under par, and the outcome of the tournament hung precariously on three pressure-laden drives.

Olazabal, playing ahead of us, wanted to fade his tee-shot to the right of the steep-faced bunkers on the left of the fairway, but he didn't get enough fade and his ball finished in the bunker. While Tom and I watched from the tee, the young Spaniard's second shot found a bunker to the front left of the green; his sand shot came out 40 feet short of the flag, and two putts gave him a bogey at the last.

Tom then blocked his drive into the trees on the right. I swallowed hard. Olly had finished at ten-under, and Tom was in trouble. I didn't dare believe par at the last hole would be enough to win, but this now seemed possible.

I had taken a long, hard look at the 18th during the week, and finally decided to play the hole the same way as Greg Norman had done. I would power the ball over the bunkers on the left, taking them out of play, and into the wide-open spaces beyond. This line was not conventional, but it gave me a clear second to the green.

Pumped-up beyond words, I launched myself into a full-blooded drive and ripped the ball way left. The carry was later measured as being 286 yards, and my ball had finished exactly where I intended, away on the members' practice area between the 9th and 18th holes. Our problem now was persuading the crowd to move from their places along the fairway, and give me a shot to the green.

'Excuse me, would you move back please?'

Spectators who had arrived early in the morning and put their collapsible Augusta seats in this prime position were not enthusiastic about losing their places for the climax of the tournament, but there was not much I could do about it. 'Come on, please . . . thank you . . . yes, you Sir . . . to the left, please . . . thank you.'

It took Wobbly, a couple of marshals and me more than 20 minutes to clear a gap through the hordes of fans but, when they had finally moved back, I sent my approach soaring over the rise. It felt a bit heavy, but I walked forward to find it had finished on the left apron on the lower tier of the two-tier green. By this time, Tom had found a line out of the trees and landed in the same greenside bunker visited by Olazabal moments earlier.

Everything had come down to this. As excited spectators pressed in from all directions, I stood quietly to one side while Tom steadied himself in the bunker. My mind darted back to his famous chip to win the 1982 US Open at Pebble Beach, and to the Ryder Cup in 1983 when he holed a chip to beat Sam Torrance and me. Surely, he was not going to perform some kind of last gasp miracle all over again.

The ball emerged from a spray of sand, and flew straight at the hole. My heart seemed to leap in my mouth when Tom's sand shot nearly pitched in the cup, but the ball raced 25-feet past the flag.

As the crowd quietened in their disappointment, I didn't waste any time in stepping up to strike a steady 35-foot putt from just off the green to the upper tier. It looked excellent at first, but the ball swung away to the right and it agonisingly kept rolling until coming to rest a little more than six feet from the hole.

Once again, I stepped back as Tom moved forward to prepare his long putt for par. He produced a steady stroke, and the ball seemed to be rolling well, but it slipped left and went five feet past. The spectators had tried to roar the putt home, but their cheers evaporated into groans of disappointment.

I had been up, I had been down. I had been furious, I had been happy . . . and all that was in only the past hour and a half. It was simple now: I had a six-foot putt to win the Masters.

'It's this putt to win the Masters!'

How many times had I said those words before? Probably a thousand and one times, as a scraggly lad stooping over my ball on the deserted, windswept 18th green at Llanymynech Golf Club, challenging myself to hole a putt to beat my mates. 'This to win the Masters,' I would say, and we would all laugh.

Now, on 14 April 1991, this *was* the putt of my wildest dreams. Everything had come true. Here I was on the 18th green at Augusta, with the crowd hushed, with millions around the world watching live on television and with my parents following the action from their living room in Oswestry.

It really *was* this putt to win the Masters.

The line looked clear . . . outside the right lip. I had two practice strokes, then hit the ball . . . smooth, no problem, it was breaking perfectly, dead centre. Eighteen inches from the cup I knew it was in. Yes, yes, yes! I went down on my right knee, let out a roar of delight and punched the air so hard that I actually managed to pull a muscle in my arm.

I looked across to see Wobbly virtually in tears, and we were soon hugging each other. He lifted me clean off the ground. 'Put me down, you fool,' I said. 'You're hurting me!'

I had won the Masters, but the Masters was not over because Tom needed to hole his four-foot putt to tie for second with Olazabal at ten-under. Wobbly and I quickly regained our composure, and I felt a sincere pang of regret when Tom missed his putt and finished joint third with Wadkins, Pate and Crenshaw.

'Where's Glen?' I asked.

Wobbly didn't know.

I looked around the green because I wanted to share this moment with my wife, but she was nowhere to be seen. I was led away to check and sign my card. Still no sign of Glen. Everything was happening so quickly. I was being pushed this way and that, told to do this and do that. Where's Glen?

After officials had found a jacket to fit me, the traditional ceremony took place in the Butler Cabin, where Nick Faldo, the 1990 champion, held out the green jacket as I slipped my arms into the sleeves. It was not exactly a perfect fit, but I was not complaining.

The usual series of media interviews followed, where I was asked how I thought winning the Masters was going to change my life. 'I'm not going to change my life for anybody,' I replied firmly. 'I just want to be the best and to do it in my own little way . . . drinking a few beers and having fun.'

More than an hour had passed since the winning putt but there was still no sign of Glen. I was getting worried, until I eventually found her with my manager, David Barlow.

'Well done,' she said and, as we held each other, my world seemed to come back into focus for the first time since I had holed the putt at the 18th.

'What do you want to do now?' she asked.

'I could do with a drink,' I replied.

Settled in a bar, Glen proceeded to relate what had happened to her . . . she had been stuck at the clubhouse because an official had refused to let her down to the 18th green to witness the end of the tournament. Then, she hadn't been able to find a television to watch the winning putt and had only guessed what happened by the reaction of the crowd. She eventually managed to find a television in another room at the Butler Cabin, where she and Daniel had been able to watch the green jacket ceremony, and there, amid the exasperation, Daniel had raised a smile when he asked: 'Will Daddy have to wear that jacket all the time?'

In any event, I had won the Masters! So, we celebrated long into the night and, when we got back to Oswestry two days later, we held another party at our house for family and friends.

Officially ranked as the number one golfer in the world.

Now the Masters champion.

Thank you very much, thank you very much.

CHAPTER EIGHT

Walking with Wobbly

Most professional golfers treat their caddies like friends. Some treat them like employees. A few treat them like children. Through 14 years together, Wobbly was more like a brother to me.

This lanky, permed, curly-haired Yorkshireman was christened Philip Morbey, but most people in the golfing world know him as 'Wobbly'. In fact, that's his full name. Usually, he's just 'Wobs'.

He apparently earned this nickname because of the way he walks, but there was nothing wobbly about his performance at my side, carrying the bag. From 1987 until 2001, he was a rock of knowledge, commitment and support. In so many ways, Wobbly was a massive part of my success in golf.

It was true that we came from similar backgrounds, and that we laughed at the same things and we both enjoyed a pint or two but our partnership worked, above all, because we got along.

Through thousands of hours on driving ranges and

putting greens, through hundreds of golf courses, through great days and awful days, we worked side by side. We stooped to judge putts, we measured yardage and wind, we moaned and groaned, and we partied . . . and we got along.

Moving through many hundreds of hotels and airports, passing dull days off in far-flung places, playing golf tournaments in every corner of Britain and Ireland, throughout western Europe, across the United States, in the Gulf and in South Africa, in the Far East and Australia . . . we got along.

There was a chemistry, a degree of mutual understanding that enabled us to bring out the best in each other under enormous pressure, and this ability simply to get along endured for round after round, week after week, year after year; in fact, it lasted for longer than many modern marriages.

The relationship between a player and his caddie, and a caddie and his player, is complicated. There has to be an element of employer-employee because the player pays the caddie (rates vary but the norm is a retainer plus 5% of prize money or 10% of prize money for a win). The player will always take the final decision, play where he wants and how he wants, and be the boss.

And it can never be a true partnership because the perceived division of responsibility is not equal. It is the player's name on the leaderboard, the player's score on the card, the player's name in the newspaper and the player's hands on the trophy . . . while the caddie remains largely unnoticed and unheard.

In days gone by, the traditional approach was for players to be courteous but remote. At the end of the round, they would thank the caddie for his efforts and part with a cheerful 'see you tomorrow morning.' The player would then go for a whisky in the clubhouse, while the caddie went drinking in the pub.

It was never like that between Wobbly and me. We enjoyed each other's company so, if we were on Tour, we would generally go out together. Of course, there were times when we needed our own space, but that didn't matter . . . we just got along.

In recent years, most leading golfers have recognised the benefits of developing a strong relationship with one caddie, and partnerships like Nick Faldo and Fanny Sunesson, or Bernhard Langer and Pete Coleman, even Woosie and Wobbly have become part of modern golfing folklore.

Everybody knows a top-class player needs a top-class caddie. Quite apart from the benefits of constantly being around someone who you know and trust, if he or she can save you only one shot each day, that's going to be four shots in a tournament, and that equates to a lot of prize money. So, if a player finds a good caddie, he will usually want to look after him (or her), and they will travel the world together.

In my early years as a professional, when I could

scarcely afford to feed myself, let alone take a full-time caddie on Tour with me, I would rely on caddies arranged by the club hosting the tournament. However, when I started earning properly in 1982, I hired a guy called Mark Gardner, an amiable Australian, as my first caddie, and he did an excellent job for a couple of years on Tour.

I then employed John Davidson, a remarkable man from Manchester who was widely known as 'The Prof'. Well-educated, he used to write articles for various newspapers and, for three successful years between 1984 and 1987, he emerged as a fantastic caddie for me.

'Woosie, take a four-iron and hit it three-quarters,' the Prof would say.

Round by round, he helped me learn the benefits of working your ball around the golf course, keeping it under control and managing my game. These were valuable lessons.

It took me far too long to realise golf is not a game where you hit every shot flat out. Today, when I see youngsters trying to smack everything, I find myself thinking they have a lot to learn. We might be playing into a strong wind with, say, 100 yards to the flag and it would be typical for a young pro to take his wedge and hit the ball hard, and the ball would fly high with too much spin into the wind and fall short of the target. What that lad really needed at that moment was an older caddie, just like the Prof, calmly handing him a seven-iron for more control and saying: 'Just punch it into the wind, three-quarters, no more than that.'

I was fortunate to have had such a wise man at my side but, by the middle of 1987, as the demands of my schedule increased, I decided it would be better for me to have someone closer to my age as my constant companion, someone young and fit enough to withstand the physical pressures.

It was my friend D.J. Russell who suggested: 'What about Wobbly?'

The young caddie from Selby had certainly got himself noticed on Tour, invariably smiling, always having something to say, often playing practical jokes or having practical jokes played on him, and he had earned a reputation for being lucky. He had carried David Jagger's bag at the start, then worked with D.J, then moved on to Ian Baker-Finch and he had also caddied for Howard Clark; and, wherever he had been, there seemed to be a spark of inspiration. Things had gone well when he was around.

Eager to make the right decision, I asked some of these guys about Wobbly, whether he was as good as people said and whether they thought we might be suited to each other, and David Jagger was kind enough to tell me exactly how this lively, young character had got started as a caddie on the Tour.

Wobbly was just 17 at the time, earning a living by stocking shelves at his local supermarket, but he had set his heart on being a caddie. One afternoon, he plucked up the courage to approach 'Jags', who happened to be the touring professional attached to his local golf club in Selby, East Yorkshire.

'So you want to be a caddie on the professional Tour?'

'Yes, Mr Jagger,' Wobbly replied.

'All right,' Jags replied. 'Well, there is a strict procedure for caddies. First, you have to take a test; and if you do well, you get a pass; and you need that pass before you can caddie on Tour.'

'I see.'

'So, if you want, you can take your test at eight o'clock tomorrow. Can you be here?'

'Of course, I can.'

Wobbly was excited and nervous when he arrived at the club the following morning. Jags appeared and asked him to fetch his bag of clubs from the boot of his car. As soon as he lifted the bag on his shoulder, Wobbly thought it seemed strangely heavy. In fact, it was unbelievably heavy, but he didn't say anything because he wanted to pass his test and he was desperate to make a good impression.

By the time he reached the fifth green, Wobbly was clearly breathing hard. He was sweating at the ninth tee and, approaching the 18th, he was scarcely able to walk. Jags had led him all over the course, up and down hills, through trees and bunkers, but Wobbly shouldered his burden and followed.

'Well done, Wobbly,' said Jags at the end of the round, as the young caddie stood exhausted in the car park. 'You have done very well. I will send a full report to the PGA and, hopefully, they will agree to issue you with a pass. You will then have to wait until it arrives in the post.'

'OK, Mr Jagger. Thank you very much, Mr Jagger.'

As soon as Wobbly was out of sight, Jags took the clubs out of his bag and carefully removed the three bricks he had placed at the bottom of the bag earlier that morning!

Jags took Wobbly as his caddie on Tour soon afterwards, but almost a year passed and Wobbly was still anxiously checking his post, waiting for his caddie pass to arrive from the PGA. Only then, one night in the pub, with people laughing so hard they were falling off chairs, did Jags have the heart to tell Wobbly that, in fact, the whole test had been a joke and there was no such thing as a caddie's pass.

Even then, Wobbly looked more disappointed than angry.

That story made the difference. I arranged to meet Wobbly soon afterwards, quickly agreed terms and our partnership thrived during the closing months of 1987: the Ryder Cup at Muirfield Village, the World Match Play at Wentworth, the World Cup in Hawaii, the Million Dollar Challenge at Sun City. Winning so regularly together brought us closer together in a short space of time, and we simply clicked.

When I won, he won. When I earned a lot of money, he earned a lot of money. As the years passed, we began to understand each other so well, that words often seemed unnecessary.

He was extremely well organised on and off the course, to the point where I didn't have to worry about anything like how many clubs were in my bag or whether I had enough tee pegs and balls. This was ideal, just the way I wanted it. I needed him to eliminate hassle, and he did that.

In 14 years together, I don't remember one occasion when he was late on the tee, and there were only a couple of days when he didn't appear on the practice ground at the appointed time. Wobbly enjoyed a joke, but he also demonstrated a serious, professional pride in doing his job properly.

It didn't take him long to realise I'm not always the easiest person to deal with on the course, and he quickly learned how to handle both my bad swings and my mood swings. He was clever, knowing just when to talk and when to say nothing, always aware how to keep my mind right.

For example, we might be standing on the tee of a par-three and, as usual, Wobbly would wait for me to make the first move. If I immediately took a club, he would back away and say nothing. Even if he reckoned it was the wrong club to play, he would say nothing because a contrary opinion would sow doubt in my mind and that was the last thing I needed. If

I had decided, there was no discussion.

On the other hand, if I asked him what he thought, he would give his opinion, and sometimes I would do what he suggested, but there would never be any kind of argument.

We established a similar routine on the greens. He would only look at the line of a putt if I asked and, in these tense situations, he understood that I wanted him to read the putt like me because that would boost my confidence. If I thought it was two inches left, I needed to hear him say it was two inches left. However, if we did disagree, he would quietly back away and leave me to get on with it.

Set down on paper, my behaviour may seem quite unreasonable but this was the way we operated. There are few things as fragile as a sportsman's confidence, and Wobbly became expert in saying and doing the right things to keep me feeling as positive as possible during every round.

On those mercifully rare occasions when I did lose my temper and control, Wobbly knew how to defuse the situation with a wry remark. There was one time in Ireland when I was playing badly, and I hooked a drive into a river. Enraged, I stormed down and hurled my driver into the water as well.

'That's a pity,' Wobbly said blankly. 'That was the best driver we had.'

And I would stare at him, and laugh, and move on.

Wobbly was a great caddie, but not much of a golfer. He often used to tell me how he had shot one over par when playing at home in Selby, but every time we played together he seemed to lose ten balls in the first nine holes. He had this strange kind of short, fast swing and he kept shanking or hooking the ball. In any case, he never tried to coach me, which was lucky because there might have been trouble between us if he had.

In fact, looking back over those 14 years together, it is remarkable that we argued so rarely, and that we irritated each other so seldom, and that we just seemed to get along.

Victory at the Masters in 1991 was undoubtedly the highlight of my time with Wobbly, and probably the highlight of his years with me as well, but the reality was that we both needed a rest after such a demanding, draining week in Augusta.

Unfortunately, you don't know when you're going to win your first Major, and the reality was that I had previously committed myself to playing the following week in the Benson and Hedges International at St Mellion. I could have simply withdrawn from the tournament, but I didn't want to let anyone down. It was cold, wet and miserable when we arrived in Cornwall, and I asked the organisers if I could be excused from playing in the pro-am on the Wednesday. I was slightly taken aback when they said no.

Clearly, however much I had declared that winning

the Masters was not going to change me, it was going to increase what certain people expected of me. The organisers had understandably hyped the theme of the Masters champion coming home, so I had to satisfy their sponsors. I was cheesed off, but I did play in the pro-am.

Next, even though I was suffering with a cold, I was given one of the earliest tee-off times on the Thursday morning. Again, I asked why. The organisers wanted me out before breakfast on the first day, so I would be playing during the late afternoon on Friday and perhaps draw more people to leave work early and come to the golf.

After all this, I was not in the right frame of mind to play golf. I shot 82 on the Thursday, another 82 on the Friday and, at 20 over par, missed the cut. The organisers were upset with me, and they said so. I felt they had treated me harshly. Either way, barely six days after feeling on top of the world at the Masters, I had found myself embroiled in an unpleasant, unnecessary row . . . and the worst part of the whole thing was that I had insisted on playing because I didn't want to let anyone down.

'Take some time off,' Wobbly suggested.

It was a good idea and, revived by a two-week break, we rediscovered some form in the Italian Open at Castelconturbia, and finished second by one to Craig Parry, the Australian.

However, the rest of 1991 did unfold as an

anti-climax after the excitement of Augusta. Maybe that was inevitable. Maybe it was my fault because, subconsciously, I took my foot off the accelerator. Number one in the world, winner of a Major tournament, millionaire: I seemed to have achieved all the ambitions that had driven me through my youth, the caravanette, playing around the world, right to the top of the game.

Whatever the reason, we failed to generate that kind of sustained run of form that had been a feature of previous years. Instead, we produced only tantalising flashes of my best.

A third round 61 took us clear of the field at Mont Agel, and enabled us to retain the title at the Monte Carlo Open. A month later, a third round 63 in Stockholm gave us a four stroke lead going into the final round of the Scandinavian Open, but we could only score 73 on the Sunday and tied for third.

It was frustrating, but not that frustrating because the official World Golf Ranking came out every Monday morning and repeatedly confirmed I was still number one in the world. In fact, I retained that elevated position for 51 successive weeks, through until a fortnight before the 1992 Masters.

Life was undeniably good.

Midway through 1991, I had decided to spend more than £400,000 on an airplane, a Cessna 421 Golden Eagle. That was a lot of money, but it essentially bought us an extra day at home each week.

Now, wherever we were playing in Western Europe, it would be possible for Wobbly and me to avoid waiting at airports and get back to our families straight after the final round on the Sunday night.

In an average week, I would not have to leave home until lunchtime on Tuesday, so the plane effectively gave me an extra 20 days every year with Glen and the kids. Most professional golfers don't hesitate to look for a private plane as soon as they can afford one, and neither did I.

Robin Richards took responsibility for the plane, and he remained my full-time pilot for many years. When I wanted to travel anywhere in Europe, I only had to call Robin and he would drive through to collect the plane from its hangar, make the arrangements and pick me up at Oswestry. It sounds glamorous, but it was simply a sensible solution to make an extreme lifestyle more tolerable.

In due course, I would replace the Cessna with a BeachKing Air 200, and then a Citation Jet and, as the years have passed, I have become more fascinated by planes and less interested in cars. Of course, every form of travel carries a risk but it's important to keep things in perspective. Official statistics consistently suggest it's much safer to travel long distances in a light aircraft than by car on the road.

Even so, this doesn't reduce the impact when things go wrong. The entire golfing world was stunned by the death of Payne Stewart on 25 October

1999, four months after he won the US Open at Pinehurst. Payne was a fantastic person, a true gentleman in every respect, and he died when his Lear 35 Jet came down in an isolated field somewhere in South Dakota. Initial reports mentioned his jet had lost cabin pressure soon after taking off in Florida, causing everyone to lose consciousness long before impact.

Two days later, Robin, Wobbly and I were flying in my BeachKing to compete at the Volvo Masters in Jerez, south-western Spain, and we happened to be discussing what had happened to Payne when we seemed to lose cabin pressure. The oxygen masks dropped down and we all pulled them over our mouths. Robin took control of what had become an alarming situation, diving down to equalise the outer and inner pressures.

We landed soon afterwards, put the plane through a detailed check and only then resumed our flight to Spain, where a tiny fault in one of the compression seals was corrected.

News of our experience spread around the clubhouse in Spain but, with everyone mourning Payne's loss, we wanted to minimise any publicity. In fact, a journalist approached Wobbly, and he replied in typical fashion, saying: 'We don't want any rubbish in the newspapers. It was nothing.'

I still think of Payne, and the exemplary way he conducted himself in pressure situations at Ryder

Cups, but I still travel regularly in light aircraft. It's part and parcel of my profession.

By the end of 1991, Glen and I had also started to enjoy increasingly regular visits to Barbados. I first visited the Caribbean island in 1983, to play in the Robert Sangster pro-am tournament, and I was impressed by the perfect climate and the relaxed atmosphere. The T-shirt and shorts lifestyle appeals to both of us and, ever since 1987, we have arranged to spend part of the British winter in Barbados.

The children tend to enjoy spending most of their time on the beaches and, one day in January, 1996, bored with lying on the sand, I decided to go for a walk and have a look around the new Royal Westmoreland golf course, with its lush green fairways overlooking the deep blue sea.

It was a beautiful spot, and I noticed they were selling properties around the course. One thing led to another and, later that evening, Glen and I ended up at a cocktail party held by the agents. The show-houses looked incredible and we were soon making the biggest purchase of our lives.

Our house in Barbados stands at the top of the 18th fairway at Westmoreland. Built in what they call the 'Begonia' style, it's designed so that most of the rooms open on to balconies or the large veranda which enjoys views overlooking the course rolling down to the sea a mile away. We're very fortunate and, as I grow older and play fewer and fewer tournaments, I imagine we'll spend more and more time in Barbados.

Buying my own plane and flying away to a paradise home in the sun . . . I can see why many people began to accept the popular view around the Tour that I had won the Masters, relaxed, put my feet up and decided to enjoy the rest of my life. People started saying how a first Major victory seemed to inspire many golfers to seek a second and third, but the little Welshman seemed satisfied with just one.

I suppose I should sound indignant at this stage, and insist this was not the case. However, the truth was that my approach had remained constant since my earliest days in the game.

Other guys might have been prepared to sacrifice their home lives and everything else by embarking on a single-minded, one-tracked pursuit of Major titles and the number one ranking, but that was just not me.

My wife, my children, my family, my mates, having fun . . . these were always more important than winning golf tournaments. If that approach makes me any less of a player, then so be it.

Having said this, I certainly did not make any conscious decision to sit back after the Masters and relax. I kept practising, I kept working at my game and I desperately wanted to win every tournament I entered. I am competitive by nature. It's inconceivable to me that I would ever not try to win. Of course,

I wanted to win yet more titles around the world, and hopefully more Majors . . . but not at any cost.

In any case, by the last week of September, this nonsense about my supposed lack of commitment and motivation completely evaporated in the hype leading up to the 1991 Ryder Cup. I duly took my place in the European team that travelled to Kiawah Island, South Carolina, as grimly determined as anyone to defeat the Americans and retain the trophy for a third successive time.

It would be my fifth Ryder Cup and Wobbly's third, and he seemed to relish the unique atmosphere, and the pressure, and the camaraderie just as much as me. Whenever I played in a professional event, he carried my bag. Whenever I walked on a golf course, I was walking with Wobbly.

At Kiawah Island, I was also walking with Nick Faldo. Bernard Gallacher had been appointed to replace Tony Jacklin as captain of the European team, and he appeared to share his predecessor's confidence in the tried and trusted Faldo-Woosnam and Seve-Olazabal combinations. It soon became clear that, once again, we would lead the fight in the foursomes and fourballs on the first and second days.

As we practised on this newly established seaside links course on a windblown stretch of coast, some of us started to wonder why the United States PGA had chosen Kiawah Island to host the event, since it didn't seem to give the home side any particular advantage. Where we had feared unforgiving rough and slick greens, we were pleased to discover exactly the sort of rough and ready coastal conditions that many people said we should arrange, to our advantage, whenever the matches were played in Europe.

However, by lunchtime on the first day, I don't think Nick Faldo and I would have agreed. We had played foursomes against Payne Stewart and Mark Calcavecchia, and struggled on the greens. We would be studying a putt together: Nick would see it inside left, and I would see inside right.

Just as everything had seemed to click between us in the 1987 and 1989 Ryder Cups, we appeared to be broadcasting on different wavelengths now. We battled on, tried our best and were perhaps a little unfortunate to lose by one hole, but the team had needed our point. Seve and Olly had beaten Paul Azinger and Chip Beck, but defeats suffered by Langer and James, and David Gilford and Colin Montgomerie left us trailing 3–1.

I remember feeling somehow uneasy on this opening day. It was hard to explain the precise reason, but some of our guys agreed the atmosphere on the course was different from previous Ryder Cups. This was more than merely competitive; it was bordering on hostile and unpleasant.

Only six months had passed since Iraq accepted a ceasefire at the end of the Gulf War, and some people in the American media and crowd appeared keen to carry the patriotic spirit into the Ryder Cup. The press were calling the event the 'War on the Shore'. So far as we were concerned, this kind of jingoism was inappropriate at a sporting event and would spoil the special atmosphere of the week.

Of course, we relished the prospect of a tough, fair struggle, but this was golf, not a war to be won at all costs where any means were going to be justified by one end – an American win.

Nick and I played a fourball against Raymond Floyd and Fred Couples on that first afternoon, and quickly fell behind as we continued to struggle on the greens. It was frustrating. We tried to get each other going, but somebody seemed to be calling time on our successful Ryder Cup partnership.

Our cause wasn't helped when, on one or two occasions, the Americans seemed to hit shots into the crowd that amazingly 'bounced' off spectators and landed back onto the fairway. This would become a feature of the Ryder Cup in 1991.

We eventually lost 5 and 3 and, that evening, I told Bernard my putting had got so bad that I should be rested for the following morning. The rest of the team had seized 2½ points of the other three on the first afternoon, leaving us trailing 3½–4½ overnight, but our pairing was not firing. We were both sorry but, in the Ryder Cup as in everything else, all good things must come to an end.

I was rested during the foursomes on the Saturday

morning, and was disappointed when the Americans took three of the four points. Bernard had put Nick with David Gilford, but the pair lost 7 and 6 to Paul Azinger and Mark O'Meara. We were all struggling. Only Seve and Olazabal kept us in contention, decisively beating Couples and Floyd to secure their third point out of three.

It was obvious we needed a huge afternoon in the foursomes, and Bernard asked me if I would play with Paul Broadhurst in the lead match. I immediately agreed. 'Broadie' was a friend of mine, playing his first Ryder Cup and the fact that he was recognised as one of the most consistent putters on the Tour made me feel more confident that we could combine and conquer the greens at Kiawah Island.

That's exactly what happened. I stayed solid from tee to green, Broadie holed the putts, and we led the European revival by defeating Azinger and Hale Irwin 2 and 1. Bernhard and Monty beat Pate and Corey Pavin, Mark James and Steven Richardson beat Azinger and O'Meara, and, even though Seve and Olazabal were held to a half by Couples and Stewart, we were back in the match at 8–8 with the singles to come.

Our spirits were soaring in the team room that evening. If the Americans wanted a battle, then they were going to have a battle. For the first time in my experience, relations between the two teams were not as cordial as usual, but the real fun and games was only just beginning.

As usual, the two captains submitted their team sheets for the singles and the draw was distributed soon afterwards. It was generally accepted that if any player was injured, he would withdraw before the team sheets were submitted. However, in 1991, Steve Pate withdrew afterwards.

We had heard during the week that Pate had been involved in some kind of car accident, but he played in the fourballs on Saturday afternoon. His withdrawal was announced after he had been drawn to play Seve, our top player.

In such circumstances, the opposing player to step down is determined by a name previously placed in an envelope by the captain. This turned out to be Gilford. So, he was forced to withdraw, and his matchup with Pate was marked down as a half.

And the American names all moved down one slot against our list, creating a revised draw for the singles. Seve would now play his singles match against Wayne Levi, a Ryder Cup rookie.

A siege mentality was developing at our hotel, and our frame of mind was not helped when several guys were regularly woken during Saturday night by telephone calls from local radio stations asking for interviews.

In each of the previous three Ryder Cups, we had carried an advantage into the singles; now, we were level. Under the circumstances, everybody understood it would require a huge effort to retain the Cup, but our resolve was strong. You only had to look at the expressions on the faces of senior players like Seve, Bernhard, Nick and Sam to realise how important the Ryder Cup had become.

The final day started well. Nick defeated Floyd; David Feherty surprised Stewart. And, when Montgomerie fought back from four down with four holes to play and secured a half against a distraught Mark Calcavecchia, whose game collapsed when he hit his ball into water at the 17th three times, it was starting to seem as though, despite all the setbacks, we would win through.

However, the Americans fought back: Azinger beat Olazabal and Corey Pavin, who had decided to wear what looked like a US military cap for the occasion, beat Richardson. When Seve had overcome Levi, we were leading by 12–11 as my singles match against Chip Beck swiftly moved towards a conclusion.

Not for the first time, nor the last, in a Ryder Cup singles, I found myself drawn against an opponent who happened to be playing particularly well. Beck and I were both around level par by the time we reached the awkward par-three 14th hole, and I was hanging in there, only one down.

The green was raised, falling away all around, so if you missed the middle section at the front, back or side, your ball would roll down a bank. Once Beck had missed the green to the right, I planted my ball 20 feet from the pin and seemed in good shape because chipping to this green was notoriously tough.

Beck's chip flew right across the green, and his third shot flew back to near where his tee-shot had finished. I appeared certain to win the hole and draw level.

Then, from down the bank, and out of the blue, Beck chipped in; and I somehow managed to three-putt, and the hole was halved with bogey fours and I was still one down. Somewhat stunned, I hit my ball into the water at the 13th hole and quickly found myself in a crisis, two down with five to play.

A couple of chances slipped past at the 14th and 16th, and Beck finally closed out the match when he won the 17th, and took the point with a 3 and 1 victory. Defeat left me disconsolate.

'Do you think we'll ever win a Ryder Cup singles?' Wobbly asked bluntly.

There was no need to answer.

Still, there was a Ryder Cup to be won. Paul Broadhurst won through against O'Meara, but Torrance and James were beaten by Couples and Wadkins respectively and we trailed by 13–14 with one more match out on the Ocean Course at Kiawah Island. Amid unbelievable tension, we needed Bernhard Langer to win his match against Hale Irwin, and take the point required to draw 14–14, and retain the Cup.

I joined the rest of the European team, following the closing stages of this crucial match as we picked our way through the fiercely partisan American galleries. There had been several unpleasant incidents during the week when wives of European players had reacted to some of the taunts from local spectators, and, once again, the mood on the course seemed more menacing than at any previous Ryder Cup.

'U-S-A! U-S-A! U-S-A!'

'Come on, Bernie!'

Much has been said and written about what took place during the dramatic 45 minutes or so that it took for Langer and Irwin to play their way down the 16th, 17th and 18th holes, and decide the outcome of this incredibly close contest. I only know what I saw with my own eyes.

Standing just short of the 16th green, I watched Hale slice his third shot away to the right and saw the ball land at the top of a sand dune. I looked away for a few seconds, and then turned back to see the ball sitting in the middle of a hollow, pin high, right of the green, in a decent lie.

One or two individuals in the crowd were clearly interfering with the game, but there was nothing anyone could do. If the match referee had seen the ball come to rest before it was picked up and thrown to the fairway, he could order it to be replaced, but he had been too far away.

Even in this environment, Bernhard held firm and the contest seemed to have swung his way when

Irwin hooked his drive into the crowd at the 18th but once again the ball ended up in the semi-rough in a decent lie. With the match all-square, the American hit his approach short, chipped on and ultimately missed a putt for par. His tap-in was conceded, leaving this simple equation: Bernhard needed to get down in two from just off the edge of the green and we would retain the Ryder Cup.

I was kneeling no more than a few metres away and I could see Bernhard wanted to use his putter, but there was a sprinkler head on his line and it was too far away for him to get relief. So, he had to play a delicate chip and he pushed the ball agonisingly six feet past the hole. I still felt everything would be OK. Bernie's temperament was second to none. If anyone could withstand this pressure, it was him.

There was a further twist. As he studied his putt, he found a severe spike mark directly on his line. Now, he faced a decision: did he putt over it, or did he putt softly around the mark and allow the ball to take the break? We sensed the problem from the edge of the green, and we all agreed he was right to try and putt around the mark.

The image of what happened next will never be erased . . . the smooth stroke, the ball rolled but stayed above ground; Bernhard's knees bending and his hands clutching his head; Americans starting to cheer, louder and louder, falling into each other's arms, celebrating a 14½–13½ win.

Many tears were shed in the privacy of our team room that night. Golfers sobbed, household names sat with red eyes, devastated in defeat. After our successes in 1985, 1987 and 1989, we hated to lose. It was like the end of something special. I had never known, or indeed felt, such despair.

'Come on, guys,' I said, getting to my feet. 'We all know what has happened this week, but that is gone now. This is only a temporary setback. We can put everything right in two years' time.'

My form remained respectable, if not spectacular, for the rest of the year, but 1991 ended on a high note when I was awarded an MBE in the New Year's Honours list. I was thrilled. As usual, I had been told a couple of months earlier and been asked to tell nobody beyond my close friends and family.

Then, I was running late on the day when I was due to receive the medal at Buckingham Palace. Daniel was with me, and we made this mad dash from the airport through the London traffic and arrived just as they were closing the main gate. 'I recognise you,' said the guard, as he let us through.

So, we duly joined the queue and, once I had been given a quick lesson in how to bow to Her Majesty, I stepped forward to meet The Queen. She said she had seen me on television, somehow managing to play well in a strong wind. I replied that playing in a wind was easier when you're small.

She was very knowledgeable and relaxed. In fact,

I have been privileged to meet The Queen on a number of occasions: once I was invited to attend a lunch for 12 people, and once with the Ryder Cup team, and I have always been overawed. Queen Elizabeth II is a truly remarkable person.

I was still officially ranked number one in the world at the start of 1992 and, although I lost the top spot in April, I remained competitive on the European Tour, producing nine top-10 finishes from 16 starts, including victory at the Monte Carlo Open for the third year in succession. However, 1992 stands out in my memory as a year when I produced strong challenges in three of the four Major tournaments.

Returning to the Masters was always going to be an important week for me because I was determined to show the Americans my win in 1991 had not been a flash in the pan. My prospects were not looking good when I arrived in the States and missed the cut in two warm-up tournaments, but I settled down as soon as I arrived at Augusta and thoroughly enjoyed the dinners at the start of the week.

As the defending champion, I was invited to choose the menu at the dinner for former champions on the Tuesday evening, and Welsh lamb was duly served to the assembled legends of golf: Snead, Palmer, Nicklaus, Player, Watson, Ballesteros and the rest. It was a wonderful experience to sit in this elite company, and discuss the game, and chat. This was an occasion I would enjoy for many years to come.

Out on the course, I took few risks in an opening round of 69 and then started to produce my best form on the Friday. Pounding up and down what seemed increasingly friendly fairways, I collected seven birdies in a second round 66 that carried me into the halfway lead with Craig Parry at nine under. Some of the previous year's hecklers in the crowd must have looked up at the leaderboard and sighed: 'No, not again!'

They need not have worried. After a rain delay on the Saturday, I returned to the course and went double bogey, double bogey at the fourth and fifth, which effectively took the wind out of my sails. My closing round 73 left me tied for 19th, but I was glad to have made an honourable defence; and I was also pleased that, on the Sunday evening, I was able to help the likeable Freddie Couples into his green jacket after his first Major win.

A couple of months later, I returned to America and tied for sixth place in a bizarre US Open at Pebble Beach. Gil Morgan made the early running and reached 12 under par at one stage – the first time anyone had been below ten-under in a US Open – but conditions deteriorated alarmingly and everyone's scores started to soar. Relatively early on the last day, Colin Montgomerie finished at level par, and watched from the clubhouse as the leaders struggled.

At one point, Monty seemed certain to win – Jack

Nicklaus even congratulated him – but Tom Kite dug deep, and held on to win the tournament by three strokes. I had kept my head down, played solid golf in the wind and was reasonably content to finish two-over par, tied for sixth.

I was playing well, working hard on the driving range, consistently challenging for the major honours in the game and regularly getting my name on the leaderboards that mattered.

The Open Championship was played at Muirfield in 1992 and, once again starting among the favourites, I produced an opening round of 65 to leave me one shot off the lead. However, Nick Faldo shot 64 on the Friday while I managed only a 73. He advanced to win the claret jug, while I tied for fifth.

Or should I say 'we' tied for fifth. Wobbly and me.

Earlier in this chapter, in recalling tournaments in 1991, I used 'we' rather than 'I' when referring to the scores, and missed cuts, and places; and I suppose the 'we' is a more accurate description of what took place because Wobbly and I did work as a team. It's only one of the accepted conventions of the game that players are, almost without exception, recognised, rewarded and blamed in the first person.

Nonetheless, I walked with Wobbly from June 1987 right through until May 2001, when my schedule was reduced to such a level that I suggested he should find a younger player. Wobbly wanted to stay with me, but the time was right for him to move on and he now works successfully with Jose Maria Olazabal.

Fourteen years, we walked together. We worked, we played, we joked, we drank, we shared it all. Fourteen great years.

CHAPTER NINE

Fun Seeker

Perhaps my mind wasn't right. Once I had been desperate to win golf tournaments, maybe now I didn't need to win enough. I had achieved the goals that I set when I turned professional, maybe now I needed to establish some new targets.

Somebody said I should make an appointment to see a sports psychologist. I laughed. It was midway through 1993, barely two years after my victory at the Masters, and I was in contention on Sunday afternoons more often than not. I didn't think I needed to see a sports psychologist, but the suggestion persisted. John Allsop had started to work on the Tour, and was available to the players.

'Good afternoon, John.'

'Good afternoon, Woosie,' he replied. 'How are you?'

Well, there didn't seem any harm in giving it a go. I had just shot 75 in the third round of the Scottish Open at Gleneagles, tumbling down the field. In my disappointment, I thought I might as well try some sports psychology as smash a few hundred more balls on the driving range.

So I had made an appointment and we talked for more than four hours, about the game, and the way I felt about my game; and, at the end of the session, John made some suggestions, including the idea that I should just concentrate on being myself.

'From what you have said,' he concluded, 'you seem to play better when you're enjoying yourself on Tour. That's what makes you tick. Don't try and be someone who practises endlessly, and thinks about golf 24 hours every day, when that's not you. You should just be you. Enjoy yourself.'

With these words ringing in my ears, I walked downstairs to the hotel foyer and, as a creature of habit, I popped my head into the bar to see if anyone was about. D.J. Russell and Barry Willett happened to be sitting there and, since I had been instructed to enjoy myself, I joined them for a couple of drinks.

I didn't stay long and, at about ten o'clock that evening, I went up to my room because I wanted to make a business call. I dialled the number. Engaged. I waited a few minutes. Engaged. Another five minutes passed. Engaged. I waited ten more minutes. Still engaged. I was starting to get frustrated.

All right, I told myself, try one more time. Engaged! In a flash of irritation, and frustrated by not playing well, I banged the side of the door with my right hand, but this wasn't a normal door; it was a large, heavy, panelled slab of oak and I succeeded only in breaking the knuckle on my right hand.

It was extremely sore, but there was the final round of the Scottish Open to be played the next day, and the Open Championship at Sandwich the following week. I decided there was no way I could tell everyone I had broken my knuckle and withdraw, so I had no option but to play through the pain.

And it was agony, every time I took a divot. My hand was swollen and I could hardly hold the club on the Sunday, but I managed to get around Gleneagles in what, under the circumstances, was an unbelievable 69.

I then travelled down to Kent and, still not wanting to tell anyone about the injury, I competed in the 122nd Open Championship. Using ice packs discreetly on my damaged hand, I eventually tied for 51st place at a five over par, although rounds of 72, 71, 72 and 70 represented a victory of sorts.

Several weeks later, I was telling this tale to a group of friends over lunch at home in Oswestry, and one of England's greatest cricketers replied by saying he understood how I must have felt. He, too, had approached his career determined to enjoy himself; and, like me, he had played through the often painful consequences of his actions. 'In fact,' he said, 'I generally played better after a relaxing night out!'

Ian Botham and I, we were kindred spirits.

We first met during a pro-am tournament hosted by the Welsh Rugby Union at Chepstow, Wales in mid-1983, and our similar approach to sport, and life in general, has cemented our friendship ever since.

Above all, Beefy is a fantastic competitor, a truly great competitor. He wants to win every game he plays, and he wants to win properly. We have played a lot of golf over the years, and I have always enjoyed watching him try to whack every ball. It's invariably a good 'un or a bad 'un – there are no half measures – but he's not all power because he has a deft short game as well. Playing off five, he can be dangerous.

He's so whole-hearted and direct; I would love to have seen him playing in his prime, although the fact is that I have never attended a single cricket match in my life. During the years when we were both living in the Channel Islands, he regularly used to bring Kathy and the kids from Alderney over to our home in Jersey, and we would all have Sunday lunch. We spent some wonderful days together.

The nights out with Beefy have not been bad either, even though he's way out of my league in terms of capacity. There was a time when I would try and keep up, but now it takes me a few days to recover, so I sit back and watch; at least, I try extremely hard to sit back and watch.

In any event, my broken hand healed as 1993 wore on and, by August, I was back at my best, taking care to enjoy myself, just as the psychologist had said, and playing well.

At the BMW International in Munich, I only finished second when Peter Fowler went mad on the last day and shot a 63 and, after nipping over to Inverness, Ohio, for the US PGA Championship, I returned home to win the English Open at the Forest of Arden. A couple of weeks later, I tied for fifth at the European Open and then chipped and putted my way to victory at the Lancome Trophy, near Paris.

Peter Baker, a close friend from Wolverhampton, was enjoying his best year on Tour, and he was pleased to point out the significance of the Lancome win because I was not exactly known for my short game or my putting, but I was pleased with my second title of the year. Third place on the Order of Merit set the seal on another successful, enjoyable and rewarding year on Tour.

By the end of September, all someone had to say was 'Kiawah Island' and I was fired up to join the European team for the 1993 Ryder Cup at the Belfry.

Each Ryder Cup picks up the memories and emotions left by the previous contest; and, in 1993, nobody felt this quiet sense of unfinished business more keenly than my partner in the foursomes on the opening day, Bernhard Langer. Together, we set about our challenge with quiet purpose.

Bernhard is only six months older than me, but he turned professional at the age of 18 and made his first appearance on Tour in 1972. Incredibly, he finished in the top five on the European Order of Merit in 12 of the 15 years between 1981 and 1995, emerging as a remarkably consistent, dedicated player. There are no sides to Bernhard at all: he works hard, and he remains constant, unchanged and unfailingly friendly.

Famous for using a compass to check the direction of the wind during practice rounds, his preparation is meticulous to the point of being scientific. He notes every yardage. There is a story that Bernhard once asked his caddie for the distance from a sprinkler head in the fairway to the front of the green.

'It's 114 yards,' Pete Coleman, his long-time caddie, replied.

'Is that from the front or the back of the sprinkler head?'

Personally, I found this story hard to believe, at least until I teamed up with Bernhard to play four-somes against Paul Azinger and Payne Stewart on the opening morning of the 1993 Ryder Cup. We both started strongly, and were two up on the Americans by the time we reached the fourth tee.

He drove well but, at the par-five fourth, as we walked down the fairway, I sensed Bernhard was anxious about something. 'Ian,' he finally said, in his gentle German accent, 'I would like to have either 75 yards or 104 yards left to the pin.'

'Sorry?'

'Yes, I would like you to lay up and leave me either 75 yards or 104 yards to the pin for the third shot, OK?'

'Sure.'

Typically, Bernhard had worked out his distances and he knew precisely how far he would hit each club. He was carrying two sand wedges in his bag and he knew one would hit the ball 104 yards, and the other would hit it 75 yards, so he wanted me to leave our second shot either of these distances from the pin.

That's what he wanted, so I did my best to oblige. This was a new discipline for me. We halved that hole and, as we approached the sixth tee, my partner approached me and asked how many yards I wanted to be left in case we had to lay up on a particular hole.

'Don't worry,' I replied. 'Just knock it down the fairway.'

He smiled at my lack of precision, but we combined well that morning, winning by the clear margin of 7 and 5, and helping our team end the first session of the match level at 2–2.

Once again, huge crowds had been drawn to this increasingly famous part of Sutton Coldfield, attracted by the prospect of yet another high quality and highly competitive match between two intense rivals.

Bernard Gallacher had been retained as the European captain, and I was delighted when he asked me if I would partner Peter Baker in the fourballs. Aside from knowing we would have a good time together, I was also aware that 'Bakes' was in a fantastic run of form. He was the one competing in his first Ryder Cup but it turned out to be me who spent an enjoyable week being carried on his shoulders.

I need hardly have turned up for our match against Jim Gallagher junior and Lee Janzen, because Bakes was hitting everything so solid and holing every putt. We only won by one hole, but it is no exaggeration to say that, as a team, we only required my score on one of the 18 holes we played.

With Ballesteros and Olazabal, paired together in a fourth successive Ryder Cup, defeating Davis Love III and Tom Kite late in the afternoon, Europe led 4½–3½ after the first day. We knew the score by now: the Americans would be strong in the singles, so we needed to increase our lead on the Saturday.

The day started well. Bernhard Langer and I again clicked neatly in the foursomes, defeating Couples and Azinger 2 and 1, while Ballesteros and Olazabal, and Faldo and Montgomerie also won their points. A similarly strong showing in the afternoon fourballs would have put us where we wanted to be, but Tom Watson, the US captain, had shuffled his combinations, and triggered an American fightback.

Only Peter Baker, still in magnificent form, saved Europe from disaster. He dominated our fourball match against Couples and Azinger in a way that meant all I had to do – and this is no exaggeration – was talk to him now and then, pick his ball out of the hole and pat him on the back. By the time Bakes had birdied the 13th, his individual score was eight under par and we had won the match 6 and 5.

Otherwise, the scoreboard turned red . . . and our lead that had seemed so commanding at lunchtime was relentlessly reduced to a precarious 8½–7½ with the Sunday singles matches to come.

It had been an extraordinary couple of days for me. People were congratulating me, and shaking me by the hand because the results indicated I had won four points out of four on the opening two days, but I knew I had not played especially well. Bernhard had been terrific in the foursomes and Bakes would have won his two fourball matches if he had been playing with Mickey Mouse as his partner.

In any case, the 100% record did wonders for my confidence and I eagerly looked forward to Sunday as the day when the European team would regain the Ryder Cup and also, on a personal level, when I would get a break and end my frustrating run of five straight defeats in singles matches.

Bernard Gallacher placed my name at the top of our team sheet, and this brought me up against Freddie Couples in the opening singles match of the day. That suited me. We both played fast, so we both appreciated the opportunity to get round the course without anyone ahead of us.

Everything seemed to be going well for me by the time we reached the par-four 13th. I had played steady golf, holed a couple of putts and was two-up on Freddie, seemingly in control. Then, some fool in the crowd around the tee shouted abuse at my American opponent. I turned to try and identify the guilty man.

'Fred, I'm sorry about that,' I said, as we walked towards the green. 'That's not what the Ryder Cup is all about. Don't bother about the idiots. Just ignore them.'

'Thanks,' he replied, and he proceeded to win the next two holes.

We were still all square when we reached the 18th hole. Fred then hit a good drive down the middle of the fairway, but I managed to drive my ball 15 yards further. I was pumped up, and I thought I had delivered a decisive blow when I hit my second close to the flag, inside his ball. The spectators behind the green were cheering, and I sensed my luck on Ryder Cup Sundays could finally change.

With the balls sitting side by side on the green, Fred glanced towards me in such a way that I thought he was suggesting we should concede each other's putts and take the half. However, nothing was said, and he promptly rolled his ball to the side of the hole, and I conceded his par four.

Right, now, at last, I had a putt to win a singles match. I took my time. I wanted this putt. I needed this so badly. There was a left to right break, and I felt pretty confident as I stood over the ball . . . I hit it firmly, too hard, much too hard. Stop! The ball went through the break and ended up six feet past the hole.

I couldn't believe what had happened. Even Fred looked aghast, with an expression that asked: 'What on earth is this guy doing?' He looked at me as though he wanted to concede the putt, and walk away from what had been a great match with the half that we both deserved, but he knew the six-footer was too much to give.

This was no fun at all. I was very nervous as I aimed the putt one ball outside the right edge. Was it going to turn? I glanced up at Fred, and saw he was living through this nightmare with me. Finally, I stroked the ball and it appeared to be slipping past but then it swung left and dropped in the side door.

At last, a singles half! I had not won, but I had not lost.

'I was going to give you the half if you had got the first putt within two feet,' said Freddie, smiling widely as we shook hands warmly. In this brief unreported moment, at the heart of an intensely competitive sporting contest, I glimpsed the unique spirit of the Ryder Cup. When many would have been grimly disappointed not to have won, Fred was unmistakably delighted his opponent had not lost.

I felt as though I needed to lie down after this

drama, but there was still a Ryder Cup to be regained and I headed straight back on to the course to support my teammates. We seemed in excellent shape, leading in all four matches following me; and, even though Barry Lane was dramatically overhauled by Chip Beck, Monty, Bakes and Joakim Haeggman (the first Swede to play in a Ryder Cup) all won.

So, we led 12½–9½, and required only two more points from six matches still out on the course. It began to look promising. However, we studied the scoreboard at the 18th, saw the Americans were in control of three matches, and maybe four, and started to worry about where our points would come from.

Costantino Rocca was one-up on Davis Love and had a 15-foot putt at the 17th to win the match and secure a priceless point, but the putt slipped past. A Ryder Cup debutant, he then missed the three-foot return and lost the 18th; and another square on the scoreboard turned bright American red.

The day was agonisingly slipping away from us and, in the end, the United States team won five and halved one of the last six matches, and so retained the golden chalice by a margin of 15–13.

For once the Sunday crowds at the Belfry, so used to glory, drifted away sadly and the sombre mood was only occasionally broken by a raised, excited American voice. Glen and I drove back to Oswestry on the Monday evening and, around two in the morning, our sleep was interrupted by a raised, excited Shropshire voice.

'Eh, Woosie, you're useless!'

It had happened before. Almost everyone in our home town knew where we lived and a handful of young lads, probably no older than 12 or 13, would bother us by buzzing on the intercom at the front gate; and we would have to answer, whatever the time of day or night, and the lads would shout their nonsense and run away.

'You know something,' said Glen, wide awake as I got back into bed. 'If we ever want peace and quiet in our lives again, we're going to have to move. You know that, don't you?'

She was right. Oswestry was our home, full of close friends and family, but it had become a goldfish bowl for us; and there were times when the bowl felt too small.

Then people read about my earnings in the newspapers and money started to become a barrier. All my friends were fantastic, and treated me just as they always have done, but there were times when I would buy a round in the pub, and guys would come up to me and ask if I could buy them a drink because I could afford it. It was happening too often. I didn't enjoy that, and said so, and the atmosphere would suddenly become tense and uncomfortable.

Then, the young lads began ringing the intercom. Once or twice, I ran down to the front gate and nearly caught them, but they remained an irritation, another reason to go.

Where? Well, Jersey was obviously one option. I had always enjoyed playing in the Jersey Open, and the Channel Island obviously offered substantial tax benefits. So, early in 1993, Glen and I went to have a look around the place. We were impressed by what we saw but, when push came to shove, we decided the time was not quite right to leave our families and friends, to leave home.

Twelve months later, we faced up to the situation and decided to move. It was hard to leave behind the only part of the country that any of us had ever called home, but there has scarcely been a moment when we have regretted our decision to establish our family home in Jersey.

Soon after moving in, we received a note from our neighbours wishing us well and saying they would respect our privacy. In general, Jersey people are so accustomed to seeing well-known faces around that the novelty quickly wears off, and people like the Woosnams are generally left alone to lead quiet, untroubled lives.

Of course, we miss Shropshire and we get back as often as possible. We both miss our families, and I miss those old friends who used to call me up and suggest we meet for a game of golf, where we would play for a few pounds. That doesn't seem to happen in Jersey, but we have made good friends on the island and we feel completely settled.

Back on the Tour in 1994, I started the year in Australia and seemed to be running into form when I returned home and then flew in my own plane down to the south of France to play at the Cannes Open. It was always an enjoyable event but, by the middle of the second round, I looked like I was about to miss the halfway cut.

Sam Torrance was leading and a bogey at the ninth left me 12 shots off the pace. In fact, at three over par, it seemed most likely that I would miss the cut. As I walked down the 10th fairway, I happened to see my pilot, Robin Richards, standing behind the ropes, following my round.

'Robin!' I shouted to get his attention. Then I spread my arms like the wings of an aircraft and mimicked a flying motion. He got the message – we're going home this evening, get the plane ready, over and out – and I saw him hurry away towards the clubhouse to prepare our early departure.

Then, inexplicably, the putts began to fall. I made three birdies and an eagle over the next seven holes, finished at two-under par and easily made the cut. Back in the clubhouse, I called Robin at the airport and told him that I was sorry but, after all, we would be staying in Cannes for the weekend.

I then shot 63 on the Saturday, followed that with a round of 66 on the Sunday and finished up winning the tournament by five strokes from Monty, with

Sam a further five shots behind.

Professional golf can be a strange game, and I also emerged from down the field to win the British Masters at Woburn in September 1994. Seve was seven shots ahead of me after 36 holes, but rounds of 63 and 67 catapulted me up the leaderboard and ultimately left me as a comfortable winner by four strokes.

Two more titles and another £371,266 in prize money didn't represent a bad year's work, but I had failed to mount a serious challenge in any of the Majors and, after 11 consecutive years in the top group of European golfers, I started to sense my game was in a rut. A slump was imminent.

Some of my closest friends had left the Tour, significantly reducing the fun factor, and there were weeks when I would really miss Glen and the children, and when the unremitting treadmill of flight, hotel, golf course, hotel, golf course, on and on, week after week, would start to get me down.

It was great when I was winning, finishing in the top five Sunday after Sunday, but those days appeared to have gone. My driving was less reliable, increasing the pressure on my iron shots; and, if I wasn't getting to the greens in regulation, my head would drop because I didn't feel I had the short game to recover and keep a decent score intact. There are some players with great short games who can get away with that, but not me.

So, my 63s and 64s became rare, and my typical week on Tour seemed to be three decent rounds under par spoiled by a 74 or 75, leaving me down the field with a long flight home. This was clearly not fun and, as the sports psychologist had declared, I needed to be having fun.

Whatever was wrong, it got much worse in 1995. I suffered the indignity of missing the halfway cut in four successive tournaments on the European Tour and managed only two top 10 finishes in a year when life as a professional golfer seemed profoundly miserable. I started working with Gavin Christie during the Irish Open, but the benefits only began to appear during the following year.

By the middle of September, lying 57th on the European Order of Merit, I was resigned to the fact that I would not make the European team to contest the 1995 Ryder Cup at Oak Hill, in the state of New York.

I was disappointed. After playing my part in six successive contests, this was the first time I had needed to rely on getting one of the wild cards but, in truth, my form was poor and I could scarcely blame Bernard Gallacher, who had been retained as captain, for not naming me as one of his wild card selections.

So, a couple of days after tying for 34th place in the Lancome Trophy, I was sitting in a pub in Jersey with my friends, Stan Thomas and Gary Thompson, known affectionately as Tomo, staring at my pint and sadly contemplating what I considered to be the premature end of my Ryder Cup career. Then, my mobile phone rang.

'Hello, Woosie?'

'Yes.'

'It's Bernard Gallacher.'

'Oh, hello Bernard.'

As I said that name, I could see Stan and Tomo getting excited, so I walked away to another area of the pub, where I continued the conversation in peace. The captain was calling to say Olazabal had been forced to pull out with an injured foot, and that I was now needed to take his place at Oak Hill. I told him I was ready, and I would be pleased to join the team. Calmly, I then returned to our table.

'So what did he say?' Stan and Tomo chorused. 'What did he say?'

'Olly's out and he wanted me to play in the Ryder Cup.'

'And?'

'And what?'

'And what did you say?'

'I told him to forget it. It was too late.'

'You didn't!'

Hook, line and sinker! I let my mates wriggle on the line, earnestly trying to persuade me that this was a great opportunity, and I should never turn down a chance to play in the Ryder Cup . . . until, after half an hour or so, I put them out of their misery and told them of course I was going to play.

Together with Seve, Nick, Bernhard and Sam, I was now one of the senior members of the team, but my game was not in great shape and I tended to stand back for the youngsters.

And it was no surprise to me when I was left out of the pairs selected for the opening day. In the Ryder Cup, every player must be honest with himself and with his captain: if he's not playing well, he doesn't play. It doesn't matter if his name is Woosnam or anyone else: if he's not performing well, he doesn't play.

We drew the morning foursomes, but then lost three of the fourball matches in the afternoon and trailed 5–3 on the Friday night. Recent history suggested we needed a huge day on Saturday if we were going to fight back into the match, but the records didn't seem to count for much at Oak Hill.

Bernard told me I would be needed on the second day and he selected me with Philip Walton, of Ireland, to play a foursomes match against Loren Roberts and Peter Jacobsen. We played reasonably well, and we had chances to secure the point, but we perhaps lacked the confidence to push through and eventually lost what had been an interesting match by just one hole.

However, the other three European pairs had all won, so we were all square in the match at 6–6 with the Saturday afternoon fourballs to come; and I soon learned that I would partner Costantino Rocca against the formidable American combination of Davis Love III and Ben Crenshaw.

Costantino was in great form – his musical, expressive Italian accent accompanied by the shaking head, waving arms and the theatrical, jovial grin – because he had just made a hole-in-one at the 6th on his way to a big foursomes victory with Sam Torrance in the morning. And now he was excited about our match because he would be renewing his battle with Davis Love, the man who had defeated him in a dramatic singles match two years earlier.

We laughed together, but I respected my partner for what he had achieved in the game. From working in a factory manufacturing polystyrene boxes, he won the Italian Caddie Championship in 1978 and then slogged through seven tough years on Tour before making any decent money.

From his humble origins in Bergamo, not unlike mine in Shropshire, he reached a position where, in July 1995, he stood two shots away from winning the Open at St Andrews, but then lost to John Daly in a play-off. Now, two months later, he was in the Ryder Cup. Constantino and I enjoyed ourselves on that Saturday afternoon and holed the putts that mattered on our way to a 3 and 2 win.

Unfortunately, the news from around the course was not so positive. Encouraged and organised by their captain, Lanny Wadkins, the Americans won the other three fourball matches and secured a useful 9–7 lead to take into Sunday. That evening, as the parties started in Rochester, New York, it was difficult to find anybody who believed the European team could win from this unpromising position.

I resolved to do my bit for the team and, having been drawn to play singles against Fred Couples for the second Ryder Cup in a row, I managed to rediscover some of my best form. My driving felt steady and, again, I was pounding down the fairways, shooting at the flags, enjoying myself.

One up with three to play, I sensed the prospect of victory at the 16th when Fred's approach landed in a greenside bunker while I was on the putting surface in two. However, he splashed out and made the putt to stay in the match. He then birdied the 17th and history was repeating itself: Freddie and I lay all square as we headed down the 18th, just as we had been at the Belfry two years earlier.

The match situation had become precarious: we had won two and lost two of the singles matches already completed, and it looked as though I needed to get at least half a point if we were to have any real chance of overhauling the Americans later in the day. The pressure was now mounting.

Fred was certainly pumped up. His drive went off like a rocket, actually pitching through the dogleg and into the trees where the hole turns right. He might have been safe, or he might have been in trouble. I didn't know. I then pushed my drive into the semi-rough and, as I walked down, I just hoped I would have a reasonable lie.

I was fortunate. The lie was decent, and I managed to produce a six-iron shot that finished 25 feet left of the flag. Fred was taking his time among the trees, but he eventually did extremely well to manufacture a shot that finished in a bunker short left of the green. Even so, I seemed in good shape.

Fred hit his sand shot seven feet past the hole, which meant I had another putt to win my first Ryder Cup singles match. Bernard Gallacher and a group of European players stood at the edge of the green, willing me to hole this tough, quick putt that started straight but then broke eight feet to the right.

I struck the ball perfectly and, as the ball started to break right, I thought there is no way it was going to miss; it rolled and passed right across the front lip of the hole, but it refused to fall. Unable to believe my eyes, I fell to one knee and placed my head in my hands. I was pig-sick.

There was a still a chance I could win the point if Freddie missed his putt. But, just as I had holed bravely for the half at The Belfry in 1993, so he did now. Honours, and our contest, ended even again.

Another Ryder Cup was coming down to the wire. I wonder if any big sporting event has so consistently produced so many tight finishes: in six of the seven matches since 1983, the difference between winning and losing, between joyful delight and tearful misery, was no more than one singles match.

At Oak Hill in 1995, it was David Gilford who found himself under the spotlight. He was affectionately teased as the worst chipper on the Tour, and he seemed to have blown his chances of beating Brad Faxon at the 18th when he left one downhill chip short of the green and knocked the second chip 12 feet past the hole.

Then 'Gillie' stood up to be counted when it mattered most, and knocked the putt straight into the cup to win by one hole. We were going wild with excitement at the edge of the green.

Monty beat Crenshaw, then Nick Faldo hit a great third shot to five feet at the 18th and holed the par putt to beat Strange by one hole; Sam won, Bernhard lost and when Per-Ulrik Johansson had lost to Phil Mickelson at the 17th, the destiny of the Ryder Cup hung on Phil Walton's match with Jay Haas.

The American had been three down with three to play, but he holed a bunker shot at the 16th and won the 17th with par when the Irishman missed a five-foot putt that would have won the Ryder Cup. Now, after all the ups and downs, it came down to the last singles contest on the last hole.

In the event, as Haas made bogey five, Phil found himself needing to get down in three from a bank just short of the green. Chipping was not his favourite part of the game, but he held his nerve and left the ball ten feet from the hole, and two putts were good enough. Europe had won 7½ points in the singles, a record, won the match 14½–13½ and reclaimed the trophy surrendered at Kiawah Island.

Lanny Wadkins could hardly speak at the prize-giving, such was his devastation in defeat, but the institution of the Ryder Cup emerged far stronger from Oak Hill. The good citizens of Rochester, New York had been excited in their support of the home team, but not hostile, and sportsmanship prevailed.

My own game also emerged stronger from Oak Hill. Mentally revived, I worked hard through the winter months, using my improved performances at the Ryder Cup as a springboard that, I hoped, would catapult me back onto the leaderboards of the world in 1996. I was not even contemplating retirement from the Tour, but one more thoroughly miserable year like 1995 might have led me seriously to consider my options.

If ever I needed a strong, confident start to the season, it was in 1996; and my schedule began at the Johnnie Walker Classic in Singapore, followed by the Heineken Classic in Perth.

The excellent food and invariably friendly people ensure I have always enjoyed my trips to play in Asia; and I have generally seemed popular in that part of the world, probably because the oriental spectators like to watch the shortest man in the field taking on, and sometimes beating, the big guys.

'Come on, Oos-eee,' they shout as I walk down

the fairways of South-East Asia, and I express my appreciation by tipping the wide-rimmed hat that I occasionally wear in the stifling heat and humidity.

I played steadily in Singapore, and holed a 25-foot putt at the 72nd hole to force a play-off with Andrew Coltart, of Scotland, but then hooked my drive into the trees at the second extra hole.

Needing to thread my second shot between two branches to reach the green and keep my hopes alive, I visualised the old biscuit tin lid hanging in the cow shed at our Shropshire farm, mentally placed it between these trees in Singapore and he deliberately sliced a sweet five-iron round to the green. I then holed the 25-foot putt, collected a £100,000 winner's cheque and celebrated victory in my first tournament of the year.

The following week at the Vines Resort, in the Swan Valley winelands near Perth, I maintained my greatly improved form and, after missing several chances, finally tapped in for a birdie at the 72nd to beat Paul McGinley, of Ireland, and Jean van de Velde, of France, by one shot. The first-place cheque of £93,338 meant I had won more prize money in the opening two weeks of 1996 than in the whole of 1995.

Golf seemed fun again, and I continued to challenge week after week. In mid-July, I survived the roaring wind at Carnoustie by hitting the ball so low under the wind that it ran along the fairways. My

72-hole score of 289, one shot over par, was good enough to secure the third Scottish Open title of my career.

Then, in August, I produced rounds of 64, 63 and 65 at the German Open near Stuttgart, and, when the final day was washed out, I had claimed my fourth title of the European season. My worldwide prize money for the year had soared to £703,936 and I came second behind Monty on the Order of Merit.

Finished? Who said I was finished?

'The media,' came the reply.

Ah yes, the media: those constant companions to the leading professional golfers of the world. Swift to praise and swift to judge, they are a fact of our daily lives, to be recognised as an important part of the game, to be obliged as our connection to the public and, occasionally, to be enjoyed.

I have already mentioned Peter Alliss, of the BBC, as the finest television broadcaster in the game, raising his voice now and then, whispering, confiding, joking, musing and always staying interesting through many hours on air. I also rate Euan Murray and Ken Brown, who have moved so successfully from playing on the Tour to commentating on TV.

Of course, the production quality of golfing broadcasts has improved out of all recognition during the past decade. It is not my area of expertise, although I do watch an enormous amount of golf on satellite TV, but the cameras seem to cover almost every hole and the graphic effects are superb nowadays.

While the electronic media describe the golf as it's happening, the newspaper and magazine golf writers are expected to analyse and comment; and, throughout the early part of my career, few have fulfilled this role with more style, wit and understanding of the players than the late Peter Dobereiner.

I have also enjoyed the various writings of David Davis in the *Birmingham Post*, Bob Davis in the *Shropshire Star*, the late Frank Clough in *The Sun*, Michael McDonnell, the former golf correspondent of the *Daily Mail* and the late Michael Williams of the *Daily Telegraph*.

These have been the friendly faces. Then there are some tabloid staff writers, the guys who you don't recognise and who are employed to produce the lurid stories that prompt the largest headlines – in the end, I suppose, the stories that sell newspapers. Golf has not been a fertile hunting ground for them over the years, although I have been the focus of their attention now and then.

In 1989, I was getting ready for a practice round on the Wednesday before the Irish Open at Portmarnock when this guy approached me and handed me a letter.

'Take this,' he said. 'You should open it now.'

So I opened the envelope, and was amazed to read how a good golfing friend from my youth had sold a story to the *News of the World* telling how, back in those days, we had chased girls, gone drinking and experimented with smoking grass. I passed the letter to my manager and lawyers, and asked them to deal with it. In due course, after discussions with the newspaper, it was agreed the focus of the story would change from 'revelations' about my youth to a more general article about young lads trying alcohol and drugs.

Later in the week, I found myself being advised to take the unusual step of leaving the clubhouse by a side-entrance to avoid any further encounters with journalists.

The whole saga was bizarre. I didn't think my youth was so wild. I had got drunk a few times, and I had tried a puff of marijuana. So what? I was 20 years old at the time. I don't think my youth was anything out of the ordinary.

In any case, the incident was no big deal for me. In fact, on the day the article actually appeared in the newspaper, I produced a steady round of 70 and won the Irish Open.

Three and a half years later, the *News of the World* was on to me again, but on this occasion there was no warning before they ran the story. They had got some photographs from a party at Sun City in South Africa, and they were using them to run the Boozy Woosie theme all over again.

The organisers of the Million Dollar Challenge were renowned for the quality of the parties they arranged during the week of their event and, on the Saturday night in 1991, all the players attended an informal kind of function with music, drink and food. I wasn't feeling that well, but the atmosphere was good and it was fun.

At around midnight, John Daly was hauled onto a stage and they started playing 'Wild Thing', which had become a kind of theme song for the charismatic, big-hitting American golfer. Well, John wanted some backing support, so Steve Elkington, the Australian, and I stepped up to sing along with him.

Wild thing!

You make my heart sing!

Everyone was rocking; soon John was taking his shirt off and tossing it away; then someone was tugging at my shirt and soon, amid general disarray, the three of us were singing bare-chested.

You make everything!

Come on, wild thing!

Click. Click. Click. And the photographs of me, half-naked, singing my heart out and looking not too well appeared in Britain's largest selling Sunday newspaper the following weekend. They say photographs never lie; well, that photograph did lie because it gave the impression that I was drunk when, in fact, I was sober.

These simple realities didn't make any difference. The tag of being a 'heavy drinker' was thrown around my neck, and the nature of such widely publicised reputations is that they quickly become established as conventional wisdom.

I suppose it could have been much worse. Most people enjoy a drink now and then, and I don't think it has done me too much harm to be known as somebody who enjoys his beer. If it makes me seem just like any other ordinary guy enjoying himself in the pub, that's fine because that is exactly what I am.

Having said that, I don't particularly enjoy the 'Boozy Woosie' tag. It's not something I encourage. I have never seen any need to hide the fact that I have a drink now and then but, equally, I have never let it affect my golf and I have never been involved in any kind of trouble.

Various drink-related stories have irritated me down the years, and I did take the greatest offence to one article that alleged I was overfed and over the hill, and that I didn't care about my performance any more. It hurt my family, and it was also untrue, so I briefed lawyers and the newspaper concerned eventually settled the issue by paying a significant amount to charity.

Moving into 1997, I was keen to maintain my improved form from the previous year and three top-10 finishes in the first four events of the year suggested all was well. My annual trip to the States in April, leading up to the Masters, yielded mediocre results, but I regained my best form when I got home, coming second to Langer in the Benson and Hedges

All together – from left, Glen, Ami, me, Rebecca and Daniel; and, right, collecting my MBE at Buckingham Palace with Daniel.

A lighter moment – Ernie Els and his caddie Gary Todd sweep me off my feet.

Silhouetted at
St Andrews, 1995.

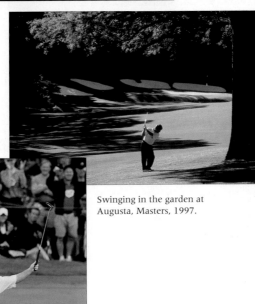

Swinging in the garden at
Augusta, Masters, 1997.

As the putt goes down, the
arms go up, Ryder Cup 1997.

The heat has sometimes got the better of me in the Far East; taking an oxygen boost in Bangkok.

Snooker has always been a favourite hobby, and having a table at home provides me with a perfect putting surface.

Payne Stewart's death in 1999 deprived the game of one of its finest gentlemen; above, playing together at the Scottish Open.

I played football as a youngster, and have been an enthusiastic competitor whenever charity matches come along.

Bernhard Langer, left, has been one of the most consistent, reliable and decent players in the game, on and off the course.

Sam Torrance has been a close friend for many years, in good times (above, winning the 1985 Ryder Cup) and hard times (helping me cure my putting problems).

I celebrate winning the afternoon fourballs with another good mate, Peter Baker, during the 1993 Ryder Cup at the Belfry.

My short game has
generally worked well…

…while the broom-handle
putter, right, restored my
confidence on the greens and
effectively saved my career.

Victory in the 1997 PGA
Championship, right, was followed
by four years without a win and it
became increasingly difficult to keep
up with the game's new superstar,
Tiger Woods, above.

Daniel, my son, plays golf now and then but, as this photograph proves, I have never pushed him into the game.

Ian Botham and I first played together in 1983, and we have become close friends.

Still balanced after all these years – on my way to victory over Padraig Harrington in the 2001 World Match Play final at Wentworth.

The 2001 World Match Play champion and my first tournament win in four years.

My improved form in 2001 was reflected at Lytham in the Open Championship, but my title challenge faltered at the second tee on the Sunday afternoon, when I took a two-shot penalty for having 15 clubs in the bag.

Small world – course design is something I enjoy, and I have recently been working on a project in China.

In 2002 the main source of frustration was my putting, as I switched back and forth from the broom handle to the short putter.

Sam Torrance proved an inspirational leader at the 34th Ryder Cup. I was thrilled to be vice-captain and to help Europe wrest back the trophy.

International at The Oxfordshire, near Thame.

The next week, the Tour headed to Wentworth for the prestigious Volvo PGA Championship and I opened with rounds of 67 and 68. I felt comfortable on the Burma Road course that I know so well, and proceeded to spend the Sunday and Bank Holiday Monday defending my lead over a high quality field.

I had to play well, and I did play well . . . and I arrived at the last hole with a two-shot lead over Nick Faldo and Ernie Els, who had both finished, and Darren Clarke, who was playing with me. As we paused on the 18th tee, Wobbly and I had one of our very rare disagreements over the choice of club.

'Take a one-iron,' he said. 'Play safe and you can win with a par five.'

I wasn't so sure. Darren was capable of making eagle, and I didn't want to get involved in a play-off. In any case, it had never been my nature to stand back when there was a title to be won, so I stayed true to the principles of my audacious youth – even at the age of 39 – and decided to attack.

'Driver, Wobs.'

Feeling the pressure, I snap-hooked the drive and almost hit it out of bounds; but fortunately for me there was no disaster, and a steady par five was enough to give me the title, and a cheque for £183,340, almost enough prize money to guarantee my place in the European Ryder Cup team at the end of the year.

Ernie Els was among the first to congratulate me in the locker room: 'I thought for a moment you were going to let us all back in at the 18th,' he laughed.

I have always got on well with the tall, laid-back South African. Quite apart from being a great player, he also recognises the importance of enjoying himself on Tour and we have shared a few beers in our time. The best was perhaps the evenings we spent together during the 1996 Johnnie Walker Super Tour, a unique event in South-East Asia where each round of the tournament was played on a different course in a different country. The sponsor had chartered a Boeing 737 to take us from venue to venue, and, for three consecutive nights, the eight players returned to a first class base that started to feel like a home from home. Some of the guys listened to music, others watched movies, but Ernie and I decided we would enjoy ourselves.

The 1997 Ryder Cup represented another leap forward in the evolution of the event, with the matches being played for the first time on the European continent. The Valderrama Golf Club at Sotogrande, Spain, was chosen as the venue and, appropriately, Ballesteros was named European captain.

Seve's style of captaincy was obviously going to be different from what we had experienced under Tony Jacklin and Bernard Gallacher, and it soon became clear that he and his vice-captain, Miguel Angel

Jimenez, would only share the details of their plans and strategies on a need-to-know basis.

That was fine. They were absolutely justified to handle the challenge as they saw fit. I would personally have preferred a more open approach with everyone knowing exactly what was going on, but Seve's flamboyant personality ensured a strong spirit within the European team and his fantastic, unquenchable enthusiasm for the Ryder Cup challenge proved utterly infectious.

I was left out on the opening day, but I enjoyed watching our guys draw the morning foursomes 2–2 and then establish a 4½–3½ lead after the afternoon foursomes. Seve seemed satisfied with the day's events and, that evening, he told me I would be playing in the next morning's fourballs with Thomas Bjorn.

The first time I came across Thomas was at an exhibition match in Denmark, when he was making his mark as an extraordinarily strong and gifted player on the Challenge Tour, and now I was pleased to be playing alongside him in his first appearance, and indeed the first by any Dane, in the Ryder Cup.

He showed amazingly few nerves, and we seemed to get along pretty well in defeating Jason Leonard and Brad Faxon by 2 and 1. Elsewhere on the course, Europeans were up in all the other matches and, although Olazabal and Ignacio Garrido eventually halved, we had moved into an 8–4 lead.

Rested again for the foursomes, I spent the Saturday afternoon out on the course, supporting our pairs as we extended our advantage to 10½–5½ with the singles to come.

Seve then placed my name at the top of his team sheet for the singles on Sunday, and I was keen to repay this expression of confidence with the first of the four points we required to win. When the draw gave me a match against Freddie Couples for the third Ryder Cup in a row, I was hopeful of success.

However, Freddie had his own plans. By the 11th hole of our match, my individual score stood around level par for the round. That was not good enough and, on a normal day, that kind of performance would generally leave you two or three holes down. On this particular day, my friend Fred was firing. His score was calculated as being eight-under par when he holed yet another long birdie putt to complete a comprehensive 8 and 7 victory. For me, it was just one of those days.

This defeat, in what may prove to be my last playing appearance in a Ryder Cup, left me with the unenviable record of having played in eight Ryder Cup singles matches, drawn two, lost six and won none. There had been so many hard luck stories, against Stadler, Beck, Strange and Couples, but I had to accept my harsh fate – that I would never taste victory on a Ryder Cup Sunday.

More often than not, personal disappointment has

paled alongside my delight at the team's success on the last day of a Ryder Cup; and so it proved at Valderrama in 1997.

Per-Ulrik Johansson beat Davis Love at the 16th green, Costantino Rocca posted a memorable 4 and 2 win over the emerging Tiger Woods and Thomas Bjorn halved with Jason Leonard. All of this left Bernhard Langer to close out Brad Faxon at the 17th green and earn the victory that carried us to the crucial 14-point mark and ensured we would retain the cup regained at Oak Hill two years previously.

It required Monty's subsequent half with Scott Hoch to ensure we actually secured an outright victory for the enthusiastic Spanish spectators, by the narrowest possible margin, 14½–13½.

This might appear to have been a low-key Ryder Cup for me, but any win over the formidable American team stands as a highlight of any European golfing career . . . and I consider myself supremely fortunate to have had the opportunity to play in eight Ryder Cups, and played a part in four wins, three defeats and one draw.

They have all been unforgettable . . . and, of course, fun.

CHAPTER TEN

Dark Tunnel

Snap-hooking drives into the rough was frustrating and missing short putts was exasperating, sliding down to 57th position on the official world rankings was demoralising, but these were not the worst effects of the poor form that frequently engulfed my game during 1998, 1999 and 2000.

'Dad, one of my friends says his Dad thinks you're over the hill.'

'Ignore him!'

'But, Dad, are you really over the hill?'

My children were being teased at school. That hurt.

I suppose it was their bad luck that their father's failures were played out not in some anonymous office, but live on television. It didn't matter how many tournaments I had won around the world, or how hard I had worked to give them a high standard of living. All they knew was that, when the bell went for break at school, it was they who were being singled out because it was their Dad who was playing badly.

'Just ignore them,' I said, without conviction.

The problem was that, more often than not through these years, I was playing badly. Some weeks would be better than others, and I might produce a decent round now and then, but consistency remained elusive and any newfound confidence would soon drain away like water through my hands.

Even though I hesitated to admit it at the time, I was suffering from the phenomenon described by Mayo Clinic Sports Science researchers in America as – and I quote – 'a psycho-neuro-muscular problem that often occurs, particularly during putting, when the golfer experiences freezing, jerking, or a tremor prior to initiating a putt; in many respects, it is an extreme response to high performance anxiety'.

On Tour, pros call it the dreaded yips.

In essence, the simple act of stroking a golf ball into a hole starts to seem like the most difficult thing in the world. You begin to shake, physically tremble at the prospect of having to attempt a putt. Your palms start to sweat as soon as they touch the grip and you effectively lose control.

There were times when I approached the green and left the putter in the bag for as long as possible because I couldn't bear the thought of touching it. There were times when just walking on to a green made me feel as though I wanted to be sick there and then. Two-foot putts terrified me.

It was a nightmare. My putting stroke became an

involuntary stab, and there were times when I would try to accommodate the problem by starting to aim right of the hole, even for a 12-inch tap-in, and somehow attempt to jerk the ball into the hole with a kind of right-hand prod.

No, not Woosie! Not the laid-back, cheerful, straightforward guy who had won so many tournaments and earned so much money! He's not the nervy, anxious type who suffers from the yips.

Yes, Woosie was.

I knew it was nonsensical. I kept telling myself the putt was the easiest shot in the game because all you had to do was stand there and move the putter a foot back and then forward. What could be so difficult about that? I couldn't understand how something so easy could suddenly seem so hard; and I would talk myself into a positive frame of mind; then I would go to a putting green and start shaking again.

Looking back, I suppose I had always been vulnerable. Ever since my earliest days as an amateur, I had tended to 'feel' my way around the greens. I never developed a mechanical, reliable, consistent stroke because it seemed so much easier and more natural to step up to the ball and rely on 'feel'. Putting represented almost half of my shots in every round, but I really didn't think too much about it.

As the weeks and years passed, I was either very good or very poor on the greens. There was no middle ground. When my putter went cold, it would be hard for me to compete at the top of the leaderboard; when it was hot, I would generally have a decent chance of winning the tournament.

From 1987 through to the end of 1993, the period when I was ranked among the top seven golfers in the world, the putter generally felt good in my hands. What I didn't appreciate back then was that I wouldn't know what to do or where to turn if, for any inexplicable reason, I ever lost that elusive 'feel'.

Of course, I was not the first golfer in history to suffer in this way. Many players have had problems on the greens when they reach their 40s, and even the celebrated legends of the game have struggled like the rest of us. Sam Snead once told how it happened to Ben Hogan.

'Ben used to say his putter would freeze just before he could move it away from the ball,' Sam said. 'He told me he had one round with seven three-putt greens and one four-putt.'

More recently, Bernhard Langer and Tom Watson have been afflicted (although Tom prefers to call them 'flinches' rather than yips), and both players courageously worked through the crisis.

My own problems were much less publicised and, through 1999 and 2000, I was left to travel through the dark tunnel, at the back of the field, out of sight and out of the headlines.

Salvation eventually arrived in the form of the broom-handle putter that Sam Torrance had been using since the end of 1996, and using with considerable success. I didn't particularly like the look of the club, but I set aside my traditionalist's misgivings and decided to give it a try.

The broom-handle putter kept me in the game.

By the middle of 2000, my putting had deteriorated to such an extent that I could not see much point in carrying on, so I started using the long putter. It immediately helped me stroke the ball better; and, as my left hand grasped the top of the putter almost under my chin, and my right hand held the middle, it stopped the shaking. Almost overnight, putts of up to four feet seemed less frightening, and I started holing a few.

However, the broom handle was more of a trade-off than a total solution because, while it did resolve the problems with shorter puts, I seemed to lose 'feel' when hitting the longer putts.

And even after two years, I still don't feel entirely at ease with a four-foot shaft. I knew that Tom Watson and Tom Kite, two great American players, had both kept faith with regular length putters while they worked out their problems on the greens, and I really admired them for their persistence.

There is no doubt the long putter has served me well, but I won't consider my putting problems are completely solved until I am once again able to use a conventional putter with real confidence – as I have been trying during the early months of 2002.

My putting may have been unreliable during these

dark, difficult years, but the rest of my game was not exactly in perfect health, and I started to rely more and more on a series of coaches to spend time with me on the driving range, making suggestions and guiding me in the right direction.

From Bob Torrance, to Gavin Christie, and on to Bill Ferguson whose assistance I sought when I saw how efficiently he was helping Colin Montgomerie with his game, I was well served by coaches who understood the game inside out, and knew precisely how to communicate their knowledge.

Professional golfers generally tend to pursue less intense relationships with their coaches than, say, the world's leading tennis players. Our need is not so much for constant emotional support through every week of the year, but rather for empathy and a moment of inspiration every now and then. This probably suits the top golf coaches, each of whom could have up to half a dozen players on their books.

In golf, the balance of responsibility also lies more heavily with the player than in other sports; and, as 1998 ran its course, I had nobody else but myself to blame for a series of frustrating performances.

At the start of February in Perth, I led the Heineken Classic after the third round, and produced a sloppy 76 on the Sunday afternoon but still only lost by one shot to Thomas Bjorn. Three weeks later in Dubai, I again played myself into contention but fell away with a 73 in the final round.

Another tantalising glimpse of form gave me the first round lead in the Standard Life Championship at Loch Lomond, one of Britain's most beautiful courses. But I followed an opening 67 with error-ridden rounds of 73 and 74 rather than the 70s that would have kept me in contention. I finished with a 66, but by then the damage had been done and another title chance slipped quietly away.

So often, one mediocre round each tournament is all that separates winners from losers and, in 1998, week in, week out, such lapses cast me as one of the journeymen on the European Tour.

I hated that. I hated not being in contention. I hated hooking drives and missing short putts. I hated to think of people saying I was finished. I hated the idea of being an ordinary pro down the field. In fact, I even started to miss being asked to speak to the press after my round every once in a while.

'Don't be so hard on yourself,' Glen would say.

She would see my disappointment and frustration, and ask why I put myself through such trauma. I had earned enough to secure our family's future, and it would have been easy to retire gracefully from the Tour and focus on other projects until I qualified to play on the Seniors Tour.

That was a perfectly reasonable option, but I kept playing because I seriously believed I could do much better. There was no doubt in my mind that I had the potential to hold my own among the talented youngsters flooding on to the Tour and I believed that, at my best, I could still win anywhere.

So, I headed to the driving range.

My approach to practice has generally been that quality is more important than quantity and, when I was playing well, it was generally enough to warm up and make my way to the first tee; when things were bad, however, I would get mad and end up spending five or six hours on the range.

Hitting hundreds of balls probably didn't improve my game, but it made me feel as though I had done something more constructive than watch TV in my hotel room. One year at the Masters, I played so poorly in a practice round that I stayed on the driving range from 2pm until the sun set over Augusta.

Yet, even this kind of commitment usually proved counter-productive because, by the late 1980s, my hours of practice were restricted by the condition of my back. An hour and a half on the driving range would leave my back so stiff the next morning that it would be difficult to swing a club.

Back pain became a fact of my life soon after my 16th birthday, and it has been my constant companion ever since. I played through the ache and discomfort for many years and, since 1987, I have only managed to control the condition by swallowing anti-inflammatory pills every morning.

In the early days, when I was working at Hill Valley, I would often wake feeling taut and sore, and my back would go into spasm, but I reckoned it was nothing more than wear and tear from playing so much golf. Everyone knew the golf swing puts huge pressure on the back as you flex and turn and, when I joined the Tour, I just accepted the stiffness as an unavoidable side effect of my profession.

At one stage, I started doing special exercises to relieve the pain. Another time, when travelling by plane seemed to make everything much worse, I learned to improve my posture during the flight by strapping myself tight into the seat and positioning my hand luggage on the floor under my feet.

These measures all helped but, eventually, in 1986, the unrelenting discomfort had become so great that I arranged to have a full examination at an orthopaedic hospital near Oswestry.

'This is not ordinary back pain, Mr Woosnam,' the doctor said, measuring his words carefully as he gave me the results. 'You have ankylosing spondylitis, in other words inflammation of the joints in your back.'

'What does that mean for me?'

'Well, the good news is that you could be able to play golf for another ten years. The bad news is that, ten years from now, you could be in a wheelchair. Spondylitis is hard to predict.'

This was not what I wanted to hear . . . but I then committed myself to a programme of regular exercise and physiotherapy and, combined with the daily doses of Voltaren, the non-steroidal anti-inflammatory drug known to all sportsmen, I have been able to avoid the doctor's worst-case scenario.

In the mid-1990s, I agreed to promote an initiative run by the Arthritis Research Campaign to promote public awareness of spondylitis and raise funds for research. The overwhelming message was that the condition is manageable, and I was happy to be put before the media as living proof.

So, towards the end of 1998, playing poorly and unable to practise too hard for fear of inflaming my back, I looked forward to the World Match Play Championship at Wentworth as an event where I could revive my fortunes and rediscover some form. Having defeated Darren Clarke in the first round, I was drawn to play a quarter-final against a 22-year-old golfing phenomenon from America.

Much has been said and written about Tiger Woods, and his impact on golf. In my opinion, he has taken the entire game to a different level in a way that nobody could have imagined.

He is by far the best player of his generation, which is all anyone can be – comparisons with Nicklaus and the greats of the past are difficult, hypothetical and don't provide an answer. He has no visible weakness in his game and, while he does hit bad shots, he has built on the rare natural talent that saw him shoot 48 over nine holes at the age of three (yes, three!) and developed truly remarkable consistency.

In many respects, he lives in a different world to

me. I have always been a normal guy who has worked hard at his game and been successful around the world, but he is a finely tuned athlete. When I step off the plane at a tournament venue, I go to the hotel and relax with friends; when Tiger steps off the plane, he goes to the treadmill and builds up the physical strength that underpins his swing.

People say Tiger spends three hours in the gym every day of his life. I'm sure I haven't spent three hours in the gym on *any* day of my life. We might operate in different worlds but we still play the same game and, at Wentworth in 1998, I relished an opportunity to play against the young superstar.

Something stirred inside this 40-year-old pro. I began to find control off the tee, and I started to drill my iron shots at the flags exactly as I did on my way to winning my first Match Play title on the same course, defeating Nick, Seve and Sandy, heroes of another age, eleven years before.

Now I was confronted by Tiger, and the Wentworth crowd seemed to enjoy the spectacle as I tried to roll back the years against the new hero. I was playing well and enjoying myself, marching purposefully down the fairways. There was not much between us during 18 holes in the morning and, by the time we reached the 34th tee in the afternoon, I was two holes up with only three to play.

We both reached the 34th green in regulation, but I knocked my first putt four foot past the hole and then missed the return. No, not now. Please, not now.

Tiger missed a 20-foot putt for eagle at the 35th, leaving me a 15-footer to save the half. I steadied myself, gritted my teeth and made the putt.

One up with one to play . . . at the 18th, we both reached the green in two. I putted up to four feet and he putted to just two feet. So, I conceded his birdie and then prepared to hole the four-footer that would give me a notable win. My right hand twitched, the putt slipped by and we were all square.

The first extra hole was a long par-four into the wind, Tiger won it and that was that. I was eliminated, left to regret the consequences of three-putting two of the last three holes.

Looking forward, people ask whether Tiger can continue to dominate the game or whether the huge demands and intense pressures will take their toll and result in burnout.

He appeared unstoppable when he won the Open at St Andrews in 2000 and the US Open at Pebble Beach by 15 shots, but other players have since picked up the challenge and raised their game. People then said Tiger had a disappointing year in 2001, but everything's relative: he still won the Masters and six events around the world, and he has maintained his prominence in 2002, winning another Masters title at Augusta.

My instinct is that he will pace himself and go from strength to strength. He is remarkably level-headed and he relates well to other players. Maybe the advice given to me by the psychologist at Gleneagles all those years ago applies to him: if Tiger can keep enjoying himself, he'll keep winning.

Into 1999, my form on Tour remained depressingly mediocre, but there was some consolation in playing reasonably well at the two biggest tournaments of the year, the Masters and the Open.

It has always been important for me to do myself justice at Augusta, and rounds of 71, 74, 71 and 72 left me respectably tied for 14th place behind Olazabal. Three months later, the Open was played in a howling wind at Carnoustie, the same conditions and course where I had won the Scottish Open three years before, and I kept the ball low again and finished a decent 24th behind Paul Lawrie.

It was respectable and creditable, but it wasn't enough. I was not prepared to sit back and accept this level of performance as the norm. I was still earning large sums of money, but I was determined not to get too comfortable in the middle of the field. After missing the cut at the US PGA Championship in Medinah, where Tiger won by a stroke from Sergio Garcia, I decided to spend a few days back in Shropshire, staying with my parents and playing golf with my Dad, my brother Gareth and some old friends, Geoff Roberts, Andy Griffiths and John Wilson.

The idea in my head was that these people who

had known me, and my game, for almost 30 years might be able to notice something technically wrong with my swing, or might be able to suggest a minor alteration that would help me regain the natural fluency that I seemed to have lost.

So, I retraced my steps on those familiar fairways at Oswestry Golf Club, and Geoff did notice a couple of things and Andy made a few points, and I worked hard, and I made progress . . . and by the end of September, I was competing strongly at the Linde German Masters, near Stuttgart.

In fact, the man who seemed to be standing between me and a first tournament win since 1997 was my close friend, Peter Baker – and he had not won on Tour since 1993. So, we were both feeling a bit desperate as he led the field into the final round, by one from me, with Garcia a further shot behind.

Bakes and I went head-to-head on that Sunday afternoon in Germany but his challenge slowly faded and I was eventually left with a straightforward four-foot putt on the 18th green to win the title. My trip home, my hard work, and my determination to improve: everything seemed to have paid off.

Then, my hands started to shake and I missed the putt. Suddenly, instead of heading to the prize-giving, I found myself hurled into a play-off against Garcia and Padraig Harrington.

'Calm down, Woosie,' I told myself. Nothing was lost yet and I seemed in good shape when, at the first extra hole, Harrington drove into the water and Garcia's tee-shot finished in the bunker. I drove down the middle, hit my approach to the edge of the green and chipped to five feet. With Harrington over the back and Garcia 25 feet from the pin in three, I thought I had the five-foot putt to win.

All seemed well. It very soon wasn't well. Within the space of perhaps three minutes, Padraig holed his chip, Sergio sank his long putt and, agonisingly, I missed the five-footer. From being poised to clinch victory, I was suddenly the one to be eliminated as the other two moved to a second extra hole.

I was stunned, almost unable to believe what had happened. Was it bad luck? Was I just not getting the breaks? Or was I finished? Was I not good enough any more? I didn't know.

Garcia proceeded to win the tournament, securing his second title in what was only his first full year on the European Tour. He is an incredibly talented player and, like so many of the top Spanish players, he has a wonderful short game. Comparisons with Seve are probably unfair, but there are similarities in the way Sergio uses his imagination to manufacture fantastic shots in unpromising situations.

He was obviously a player on the way up and, all the statistics suggested, I was going in the opposite direction. I finished in 26th place on the 1999 European Order of Merit with only one top-three finish during the year; apart from 1995, it was my worst performance since the caravanette days in 1981.

These facts were depressing, but I was certainly not depressed. Golf has always been a huge part of my life, but it has never been all of my life. It has been my passion and my means of earning a living, but it has never been my only interest, never been the only measure of confidence and self-esteem.

Thus, in November 1999, while I was disappointed to be off the pace on the European Tour, I was delighted and proud to be elected as President of the World Snooker Association.

I have enjoyed snooker since spending so many hours of my youth on the tables at the Ifton Miners Institute in my home village of St Martins; through Hill Valley and beyond, there always seemed to be a snooker table tucked away somewhere at the golf club where I was playing.

And, like many millions of people in Britain, I was gripped during the early and mid-1980s when snooker suddenly became one of the most popular television sports and a series of characters emerged as household names: Alex 'Hurricane' Higgins, Ray Reardon, Steve Davis, Jimmy White, Cliff Thorburn, Bill Werbeniuk, Terry Griffiths, Silvino Francisco, Dennis Taylor and others.

These players appealed so widely because they came across as talented, dedicated, likeable entertainers who always looked so smart in black bow ties, and they succeeded in taking snooker out of the smoky backrooms and onto the small screen as the mass appeal sport that it has become today.

As the years passed, I became increasingly aware of the close relationship that exists between golf and snooker. It is sustained by shared facilities in hundreds of clubs up and down the country and, at the highest level, by the fact that so many players of my generation on the European Tour enjoyed snooker, and so many of the world's leading snooker players were eager to play a round of golf.

This synergy spawned a series of joint celebrity events and it was at one of these enjoyable occasions, held in Milton Keynes during the British Masters at Woburn, that D.J. Russell and I played snooker against Sam Torrance and Dennis Taylor, the 1985 World Champion.

Dennis and I have been good friends ever since, and I was pleased when this impassioned Irishman was able to join me at the 2001 Masters. He broke his foot in a household accident soon after arriving in America but, even in considerable pain, he was determined to carry my bag around the nine holes of the traditional Par Three Contest at Augusta, staged on the day before the tournament starts.

At any rate, in October 1999, it was Dennis who asked me whether I would be interested in standing for election as the President of the World Snooker Association. It was a largely ceremonial position, because there is a chairman, a chief executive and office staff who conduct the day-to-day running of the organisation, but a vacancy had arisen following the resignation of author Jeffrey Archer.

'Sure,' I replied. 'Why not?'

Dennis sat on the committee and put my name forward, and I was duly elected. My main obligation – in fact, it has always been a pleasure – is to attend the final of the World Championships at the Crucible Theatre in Sheffield; and, even if I have been playing in some tournament on the same day, I have generally been able to get to the snooker in time to watch at least the evening session.

As the 2000 golf season gathered pace, I started to sense a light at the end of the dark tunnel. Whether it was the headlight of the proverbial train coming in the opposite direction or the sign of better things to come, I couldn't be sure, but my performances were certainly an improvement on 1999.

I came second in the Qatar Masters at the beginning of March and then, in the middle of June, showed signs of getting into the sort of competitive groove that characterised my best years. I tied for third with Tiger at the Deutsche Bank Tournament Players Championship of Europe in Hamburg, and a week later played well to finish seventh behind Monty in the Volvo PGA Championship at Wentworth.

Only a fortnight later, at last, everything seemed to come together when I produced an opening round of 68 in the Wales Open at the Celtic Manor resort.

The sympathetic crowds seemed to recognise how I had been struggling in recent seasons and, sensing my excited compatriots were willing me to victory, I responded with rounds of 67 and 66, and optimistically carried a one shot lead into the final day.

It wasn't enough. I wanted to please the spectators, but I suddenly seemed unable to get up and down from greenside bunkers. A bad start and three bogeys in the last ten holes carried me sadly out of contention as the Dane, Steen Tinning, came through to win his maiden title on Tour. When I drove away from Celtic Manor that night, I felt desperately disappointed to have wasted yet another chance to win again.

Perhaps it was this frustration of the Wales Open that got away that spectacularly boiled over when I was playing the 17th hole at The K Club for the Smurfit European Open a few weeks later.

With water all the way down the left of the fairway, it was clearly imperative that you drove straight from the tee and kept the ball on the fairway. Already well down the field on the second day, I confidently took my driver and nailed it perfectly, but straight left into the River Liffey, two yards from the bank.

Playing three off the tee, I took the driver again, and put the ball in the river again, almost in exactly the same place where the first drive had landed. Playing five off the tee, I stubbornly took the driver a third time, and dispatched a third ball into the water, once again to the very same spot.

Having finally managed to get my tee shot away, I walked down from the tee and decided the only appropriate course of action was to send the offending club after the balls and, with a flourish, I hurled my driver into the river as well. I subsequently learned, to my great embarrassment, that this entire performance had been broadcast on TV.

The conclusion of the story is that, about seven months later, a girl walked up to me during a golf day at Celtic Manor and told me she was now the owner of my driver. I was surprised.

'Which driver is that?' I asked.

'The one you threw in the River Liffey,' she replied.

It transpired that she had been among the crowd at The K Club and, at the end of the day, had plunged into the river, braved the current and retrieved my club from ten feet down. I suggested she should get the driver to me, so I could sign it for her. It seemed the very least I could do.

Unfortunately, ever since my wild years in the junior section at Llanymynech Golf Club, I have yielded to temptation and abused golf clubs every now and then. I once hit a putter on a tarmac path at Valderrama and split the graphite shaft. Another time, I snapped a two-iron across my knee at the Mallorca Open. Playing in the Cannes Open, I once snapped my putter against a tree and had to use a one-iron on the greens for the rest of the round. Another day, I broke a driver by slamming it back into the bag.

Of course, such flashes of temper are not right and any fleeting moment of elation as the club flies from your hands is quickly followed by a long, lingering sense of embarrassment and the often tedious task of either replacing the club or arranging for it to be repaired or reshafted.

Not surprisingly, I missed the cut by four strokes soon after my driver splashed into the River Liffey, and the remainder of the 2000 season petered away without further excitement. I languished at 24th on the Order of Merit and had now played for three and a half years without a tournament win.

This fact bothered me, troubled me and irritated me until, after competing in my last tournament of the year, the Casio World Open in Japan, I arrived home in Jersey to find our three children preparing for the Christmas holidays. When I'm with Glen and the kids, everything falls into perspective and, all of a sudden, my problems – or even successes – on the golf course don't seem to matter so much.

Daniel, our son, is a great lad, and I see in him the kind of determination that my father encouraged in me when I was young. It will be interesting to see where that takes him as he grows older.

He went to school in Jersey when we moved to the Channel Islands, but we then followed the advice of Gareth Edwards and sent him to Millfield, a public school in Somerset renowned for its sport, and Daniel has thrived in rugby and football. We have managed to get across to watch him play a few times, and have been amazed by the physical nature of schools rugby. It makes me wish I were his age again.

I have never tried to push Daniel into golf. The father–son pressure never really works, and I have always wanted him to become his own person, not an extension of me. However, he asked for his own set of clubs some time ago and, from what I once saw when we were hitting balls on the driving range, his swing looks decent even though he probably only plays a couple of times a year.

The strange fact is that Daniel and I have never played a round of golf together. He once caddied for me in the Par Three Contest at Augusta, but we have never actually played together. That hasn't been a conscious decision; it's just how it's worked out. Maybe that experience still lies ahead of us.

Rebecca, our elder daughter, suffered a setback a few years ago when she was diagnosed with diabetes while we were in Barbados, but Glen and I have been so impressed by the way she has taken responsibility for her ongoing treatment, calmly accepted it as something she has to do and got on with her life.

She loves horses, and she has had one of her own since she was five years old. Every weekend in Jersey, she takes the bus to the stables where her pony is kept, and she rides, grooms and does the chores. At school, she's keen on singing, drama and playing the piano, so we'll see where that takes her.

Ami, our youngest, seems to be the homemaker. She's always enjoyed her dolls, and she has always been keen to ask questions, and to talk to anybody about anything. Warm, friendly, likes a chat: she seems to have a lot in common with my own mother, and I'm sure she'll be a great Mum one day.

Glen and I are tremendously proud of all three of our children, and the prospect of watching them grow up and become adults, and develop their own lives seems so much more exciting and so much more important than anything I have ever known, achieved or experienced on a golf course.

Through the past decade, as parents, we have also been aware of the pitfalls that come with growing up, firstly, as a child in a relatively wealthy family, and, second, as the child of someone in the public eye.

So far as money is concerned, I was fetched up to believe that it was never to be squandered no matter how much you had in the bank, and I have tried to convey that to our children. Glen and I have wanted to give them every opportunity, but never to be extravagant or spoil them.

My father always used to say everyone must save money for a rainy day, and I have followed this advice in my largely cautious approach to financial matters. In this area, I have been assisted by my advisers at IMG, and also by Zig Wilamowsky.

I am not sure whether being recognised as the son

or daughter of a golfer has been an advantage or a disadvantage for our children. We have certainly discouraged our children from getting big heads or thinking they were special. They're ordinary kids who happen to live in a nice house and go to decent schools.

That's all, nothing more and nothing less.

And, just occasionally, hopefully not often, Daniel, Rebecca and Ami Woosnam might have to deal with somebody who picks on them and says their Dad is 'over the hill'.

My goal for the 2001 season was to provide my children with an adequate response.

CHAPTER ELEVEN

Bouncing Back

The night had dragged on since half past four. I rarely sleep well in hotels because the room never seems to be dark or quiet enough, and this night before the fourth and final round of the 130th Open Championship at Royal Lytham and St Anne's had proved no exception. My mind was racing.

There was plenty to think about. That afternoon, for only the second time in 26 years as a professional golfer, I was going to lead the field into the last day of a Major tournament. Level at six under par with David Duval, Bernhard Langer and Alex Cejka, there was clearly everything to play for.

So, I lay in my hotel bed and stared at the ceiling. After four frustrating years of indifferent form, after all the self-doubt and wondering whether I would ever get myself into this situation again, it felt so good to be back in contention for major honours, back in the headlines, back on the leaderboard.

People had said I had lost my hunger for the game,

lost length off the tee, lost touch around the greens, lost confidence and interest; people said I was in poor physical condition and out of sorts; people had said I was finished at the age of 43. That was rumour. This was fact: I was joint-leader of the Open Championship heading into the final round.

My watch ticked on to five o'clock in the morning. I started to mull over my game plan for the day. I would play patiently and within myself over the front nine, not give anything away, stay in contention; and then I would attack the course, if needed, over the closing holes. I would be aggressive. Of course, it was not going to be easy, but it did all seem so possible in my mind. The silver claret jug felt so close.

Even through the darkest moments of recent years, I had never lost faith in my ability. Even when I was three putting from twelve feet, letting myself down and wasting opportunities to win tournaments, I believed I would get through the slump and emerge on the other side, in contention again. And now it was happening at the Open Championship, at Lytham, right here on this stretch of Lancashire coastline.

Half-past five. I began to think about Pete Cowen, and his role in my revival. He had worked as my coach since the windswept Open at Carnoustie two years before and, not for the first time in my life, I had responded well to the blunt, clear-cut direction of a straight-talking Yorkshireman.

Pete was a decent touring pro when we first played together at Hill Valley, back in 1974, and he had left the Tour and learned his stuff. Then, he reappeared one day at the Forest of Arden, standing behind me on the driving range, telling me this and that, adopting a forceful tone with me. I wondered who on earth this guy thought he was. I didn't need anyone talking to me like that.

Or maybe I did. Several months later, in a moment of despair, I found his number and phoned him. Well, I wanted to see what he had to say for himself. Everybody knew Pete had done really well with Lee Westwood and Darren Clarke, so perhaps he could do something for me. It was worth a try. He said I should come to his place in Sheffield, and he would have a look at me and we would take it from there.

That week before the Open in July 1999, I did exactly that, and we started working together. I liked him from the beginning. He turned up to most of the tournaments, and we would typically spend 15 or 20 minutes together at the start of the week, longer if I was having any problems; and he would stand at the back of the driving range while I hit balls, telling me this and that.

'Ten years ago, you had one of the best swings in the world,' he would say, candidly. 'I have no idea why you tried to change it, but now we need to focus on getting it back.'

So, we worked. There was never going to be an

instant solution but, week after week, Pete helped me to rediscover my old swing, to regain the natural shape, the draw and rhythm. I didn't immediately start jumping up leaderboards but, without doubt, we were moving in the right direction.

We worked at the golf course during tournaments and, at other times, we used the very latest technology to close the distance between my place in Jersey and his house in Sheffield. I had installed an A-Star system in a garage at home, which enabled me to send him video footage of my swing. Pete would look at it, and phone me to discuss what looked right and what was wrong.

The system involves two cameras – one behind you and one square on – and a computer, and enables you to record, check and then measure any aspect of the swing. Most pros use similar versions of this system nowadays because it enables any player to work with any coach anywhere in the world, at any time.

It was still only a quarter to six. I looked out of the window, to check whether the wind was still coming off the Irish Sea: it was. That was good. That meant it would generally be blowing across Royal Lytham, and that suited me because I wanted to avoid having to drive into the teeth of the wind on some holes.

My strategy during the 2001 Open had been to use my old one-iron off the tee as often as possible and make certain of keeping my ball on the fairways, and it had worked well through the first three days because, with a crosswind, I had only needed to use my driver on four or five of Lytham's 18 holes.

And yet, each morning I had woken and anxiously checked the blustery weather because, if the wind did change direction and start to blow straight into and down the seaside links course, I would probably have to use a driver on ten or eleven of the holes, and obviously increase the risk of losing control from the tee.

Five past six. I tried to visualise images and scenes of the day ahead: crowds pouring across the course, cheering the British challenger, urging him to win the Open title that would put such a perfect seal on his long, distinguished career; thunderous applause rolling down from the vast scaffolding stands at the 18th; members standing at the windows of the ivy-clad clubhouse; an engraver hard at work on the base of the claret jug; my name in black letters, block by block on the huge yellow scoreboard overlooking the 18th green.

It was exciting. The previous evening, I had called a couple of friends back home in Shropshire, and they said everyone at Oswestry and Llanymynech was excited; and I knew how much it would mean to people in Wales, from Anglesey to the Severn Bridge, to see one of their own win the Open.

It all seemed so close, and I had always believed

it could happen . . . and yet, to be honest, my form in the first five months of 2001 had scarcely suggested any great days ahead.

I had played well at the Dubai Desert Classic in March, but all the good work of 23 birdies was undone by a series of bogeys on the closing holes and I tied for fourth in an event I might have won.

In April, I was deeply disappointed to miss the halfway cut at the Masters for the first time since making my debut at Augusta back in 1988; and I had only fallen short after scoring a freakish 77 on the Friday, included a back nine comprising one par, six birdies and two 8's.

Two weeks before Lytham, I had got myself into contention in the Smurfit European Open at The K Club in Ireland, but suddenly got nervous with my driver, missed too many fairways and finished joint second.

I glanced at my watch again: half-past six. For a moment, I allowed myself to wonder how much better I would be feeling if only my driving was less erratic. The broom-handle putter had solved most of my problems on the greens, and my hard work with Pete Cowen had restored much of the old confidence and rhythm to my swing, but I was still inconsistent off the tee . . . and then I banished the negative sentiment and urged myself to focus on the positive. 'This is going to be your day,' I muttered. 'Your day.'

In any case, the wind was fine, so I would use the

one-iron. This club had assumed the status of an old friend. I had bought it in 1983, and used it on and off ever since, depending on the course and its set-up. Then, rummaging around at home before setting off for Lytham, I had impulsively decided to put it in my bag because I thought it would be ideal for keeping the ball beneath the wind, hitting shots that sometimes never rise higher than 15 feet off the ground.

And so it had proved.

The one-iron went well in practice, and it had been fundamental to the steady success of my opening two rounds. Tee to fairway, fairway to green, putt it close, tap in for par. Over and again, over and again. I had not tried to attack and embark upon any dramatic birdie rush. I had set myself a target to hang in there, stay solid and produce two steady rounds to leave me tucked in behind the leaders, quietly in contention.

In a sense, simply the avoidance of spectacular disasters like double bogeys or four-putts served to boost my confidence and prompt the belief that I could actually win the Open.

Ever since my earliest days, I had felt fragile and vulnerable on seaside links golf courses where it always seemed tough to control the ball on the greens. That meant I would so often be confronted by huge putts of 40 feet or more, and these would be followed by nervous four-to-five-footers; and I would miss too many of those, and so the pressure and uncertainty would spread through my entire game.

I would feel it was doubly important to put my drive on the fairway, because it was doubly important that I put my approach as close to the flag as possible, so I would be sure of a two-putt, at worst; or small seeds of doubt would be sown in my mind, and too many of these would grow into bogeys on my card. My challenge would falter, and I would get frustrated, and start yearning for an inland course like Wentworth where the ball was easier to control on the greens, and where you could hit a shot down the fairway and be certain it would not bounce off a bump in the fairway and scuttle into the rough.

Success on a seaside links course requires patience and an ability to accept the rough with the smooth, and then a bit more of the rough, and neither of these qualities were my strongest suits. Through most of my career, I had preferred to find my rhythm, pound the fairways and shoot at the flags, but a bold, aggressive approach more often than not ended in disappointment at the seaside.

It had so far been different at Royal Lytham in 2001 because the one-iron had maintained direction and discipline off the tee, and the broom-handle putter kept me solid on the greens.

I had started with a birdie at the first hole but faltered late on the opening day stalling with three bogeys in five holes and finished the day with a mediocre 71. My game was much better than that score suggested and I repaired most of the damage

327

with an improved 68 on the Friday, and then produced my best form in the third round on Saturday, shooting three birdies and an eagle, with one bogey, for a 68. This left me at six under par, tied for the lead at the front of a congested, competitive field.

Just before seven o'clock, I finally climbed out of bed. My back felt good and I took a couple of swings in the full-length mirror. Everything felt right. Maybe this was going to be my day.

Over breakfast, I found myself dwelling on the disappointing news of the previous evening when it had been confirmed I would play in the penultimate pair on the last day. I have always thought it was easier to play in the last pair on the Sunday because you get the advantage of knowing exactly what you need to do over the closing holes. If you're ahead, you play safe. If you're behind, you take a risk.

In a situation where more than two players share the lead going into the final day, I had assumed the pairings would be determined by the order in which players' cards were submitted after their third rounds; and I had handed in my card before Langer when we finished on Saturday.

However, I had then phoned the Championship office to confirm the situation and they informed me that, since I had played with Langer in the third round, the fact he had teed off first on the Saturday meant he was deemed to have holed out first, and it followed that I would go before him on Sunday. I had never heard of this ruling, but had to accept the rules had fallen in favour of my rivals. There was nothing I could do about the draw. Cejka and I would tee off at 14.15, with Langer and Duval playing as the last pair, starting right behind us at 14.25.

After spending most of the morning watching on television as the early starters began their final rounds, and gladly noting confirmation of the breeze coming off the sea, I ate a light lunch and made my way across to the course, arriving at Royal Lytham and St Anne's not long after one o'clock.

Everything felt right. I chatted with a few friends standing near the locker room, and was surprised by the number of guys who wished me luck. There is obviously a lot of competition around the Tour, but there is also a strong sense of solidarity between the pros. These people knew I had been battling for the last few years; they had seen me miss the putts and cuts, and now they were wishing me well.

I waited to meet my caddie, Miles Byrne.

He had been working for me for almost 10 weeks, ever since I parted from Wobbly, and this quiet, gentle Irishman, 33, from the village of Bray, south of Dublin had done well. In fact, I had known him for some time because he came from a well-known caddieing family – two of his brothers were also working as caddies on the European Tour – and he had previously been employed by Peter Baker.

Miles had not had a bag for 18 months when I contacted him in Dublin, where he had gone to work in the construction business, and he enthusiastically agreed to work for me. A bright, intelligent guy, he had numerous qualifications and used to have no trouble racing through the cryptic crosswords in both *The Times* and the *Daily Telegraph*, but golf and caddying were his passions. That's what he wanted to do.

He arrived before long, and we prepared to warm up at the driving range.

'Woosie, did you want this?'

It was Malcolm Clark, a guy representing a shaft company on Tour, and he was holding forward a driver with a steel shaft. I suddenly recalled my conversation with Robert Allenby at an IMG dinner the previous night. I had been telling him about my inconsistency with the driver, and the Australian mentioned this new steel-shafted driver, and suggested I should have a look at it. Since he was due to start his final round at 09.55, he had said he would leave the club with Malcolm.

'Robert said you might want to try this out before your round,' Malcolm said.

'Thanks,' I replied, taking the club and handing it to Miles.

Even now, an hour before one of the most important rounds of my life, my search for a driver that felt right in my hands was continuing because, despite the fact my one-iron was going well, there were still those four holes at Lytham where I needed the big-headed club to get enough distance. I had used a Japanese graphite-shafted driver during the first two rounds, but then switched to another graphite-shafted driver for the third round.

The latter club had felt all right, but it wasn't perfect and now Robert Allenby's steel-shafted driver had entered the equation. Pete Cowen was already waiting for us at the driving range, and I explained to him that I had to decide which of these two drivers I would use for the final round.

I started hitting balls at the driving range and immediately felt right. I was in the groove. Some days, you just feel good, you just feel as if things are going your way. You can't plan it, and you can't predict it. It just seems to happen, and it felt as though it could happen to me on Sunday 22 July 2001.

After loosening up with some iron shots, I tried out the steel-shafted driver. It was decent club and it kept the ball down in the wind, so I made the decision to use it for the final round, and resolved the issue.

'Have you seen the way David Beckham curls the ball at free-kicks?' Miles asked.

'What?' I said.

'Have you seen the way Beckham hits the ball? It's like a golf swing.'

'What do you mean?'

'You know, the way he approaches it from the inside.'

I caught Pete Cowen's eye, and he glanced at me quizzically . . . as if to say what on earth is Miles talking about. I had absolutely no idea, and tried to keep concentrating on my swing, which was still going well. Miles did seem nervous, perhaps even jittery but, if this was a huge day for me, it was also a big day for him, so it was only to be expected that he should seem a bit more jumpy than usual.

However, Pete seemed concerned. 'Well, we've got the pro right,' he said a few moments later, with an obvious edge to his voice. 'Now we just have to get the caddie right.'

'No, no, no, I'm fine,' Miles insisted. 'Don't worry about me. I'm fine.'

'I hope so,' Pete said.

It had been an uneasy, unusual exchange, but I didn't take much notice. I was hitting the ball well, our tee-off time was drawing near and I still sensed this could be my day.

'Miles, please take the graphite-shafted driver and put it back in the locker,' I said, with Pete walking beside me, as I left to practise chipping in an area between the range and the putting green.

Not more than 10 minutes later, we were together on the putting green. Miles was picking up the balls and rolling them back to me. The broom-handle was feeling good; everything was rolling nicely. Bernhard Langer was there as well, preparing to bid for what he hoped would be his first Open title.

'What time are you off?' I asked casually.

'Half-past,' Bernhard replied, 'but it's nearly quarter past now. You should go.'

I looked across at Miles. He nodded.

That struck me as odd as well. Surely Miles would have been keeping an eye on his watch to make sure we reached the first tee at our appointed time. I didn't say anything, and we walked briskly across to arrive at the first tee maybe a minute before our time. Some people said that was cutting things tight but, in fact, it was perfect. I don't like hanging around on the tee. We weren't late. We didn't have to rush.

Alex Cejka and his caddie were already there, so I greeted them and then reached towards the section of my bag that contained the middle irons. The first hole at Lytham is a par-three and, with a breeze coming from right to left, I knew I was not going to need any more than a firm six-iron. The Czech-born German played first, and knocked his tee-shot into the bunker. I stepped up, and hit the six-iron as sweetly as I could ever have wished. The ball flew towards the green, on line for the flag, pitched at the front of the green and rolled forward, coming to rest no more than four inches from the hole – it was that close to being the first hole-in-one at the first hole of the final round in the history of the Open

I was up and running. One confident tap of the broom-handle putter later, my birdie two at the opening hole was confirmed. And all around the golf

course, students working at the temporary scoreboards leaped into action, moving the blue magnetic
metal strips reading 'Duval', 'Langer' and 'Cejka'
down one position, creating room to fit the strip
marked 'Woosnam' at the top of the board. Niclas
Fasth, the Swede, had made progress on the course,
but now I was level with him, sharing the lead at
seven under par.

It had been a great start, a clear statement of intent.
All right, I might have slipped way down the world
rankings over the past few years. All right, I might
have endured a bad run. But I was here now, a
Welshman with his game together when it mattered,
sharing the lead at the Open Championship with only
17 holes left to play. Anyone could see I was fit and
ready to launch a concerted bid for the title.

Arriving at the second tee, I bent forward to tee
up the ball, stood back to visualise exactly how I
wanted to hit the tee-shot, and turned to take the
one-iron from my caddie.

'You're going to go ballistic.'

I looked up. Miles was walking towards me, across
the tee, hands raised, palms upwards.

'What do you mean? Go ballistic?' I asked.

'I've got two drivers in the bag.'

I was amazed, dumbfounded. I didn't know what
to do or say, didn't know what to think. Five seconds
passed like five minutes, but I showed no outward
emotion while I tried to work out how I should react

to this scarcely imaginable situation.

Miles had not taken the graphite-shafted driver back to our locker, as I had asked him to do. That meant we had 15 clubs in the bag, and I would incur a two-shot penalty. If the 15th club had not been noticed at the second, the penalty would have multiplied with each hole to a maximum of four shots.

'I give you one job to do,' I said to him, 'and you can't even do that.'

He said nothing at all. My first instinct had been to sack him there and then, but that would have solved nothing. Instead, I flung my cap on the ground, walked to the bag, took out the graphite-shafted driver and moved towards the back of the tee, where John Paramor, the respected, experienced match referee, was standing.

'John, two drivers in the bag,' I said, knowing what would happen. 'What's the situation?'

'That's a two-shot penalty,' he confirmed.

With those words, my birdie two at the first was scratched from my card and replaced with a bogey four. One step forward became two steps backwards. An ideal start became a poor start.

I took the driver and, in anger, threw it on a grass bank at the back of the tee.

The immediate effect of this incident was that the honour switched to Alex, so I bent down, picked up my ball and tee peg, and stood back for him to drive. I stared straight ahead. I felt as though I had been kicked in the teeth, and anger and frustration started to flood through my senses.

How could he have missed the second driver? Since I don't carry a three-wood, there was only ever one big, furry club head cover sticking out of my bag. How could he have not noticed two?

It would have been bad enough to start the monthly medal with 15 clubs in the bag. This was the fourth round of the Open Championship, and I had been joint leader! As I stood on that tee, desperately trying to control my emotions, I couldn't bring myself to look at Miles, let alone talk to him.

My mind was in a blur when I finally stepped forward to hit my tee-shot at the second but the one-iron, at least, didn't let me down and I was on my way, releasing some of my pent-up energy and fury as I stormed down the second fairway. I kept asking myself how that could have happened.

Curtis Strange had been commentating for American television at the time and, as soon as he recognised what was happening on the second tee, he apparently declared that, if he had found himself in my situation, he would have fired his caddie on the spot and found someone else to carry the bag.

Jack Nicklaus later took a different view, saying he thought it was the player's responsibility to check the number of clubs in his bag. I understood Jack's theory, but the practical reality on Tour is that very few players take time to count their clubs. It is universally regarded as the caddie's job. In fact, for many years at the Open, it was the official starter on the first tee who asked the caddies to check the players' clubs in each bag. That practice was scrapped because the caddies complained the starter's role implied they couldn't do their job properly.

It was also correctly pointed out that these events could only ever have happened in an Open at Lytham, where you start with a par-three. Every other course on the Open rotation starts with a par-four, where you generally take a wood off the tee. In reaching for my driver, I would certainly have noticed the extra driver in the bag and been able to remove it before I teed off and therefore avoid any penalty.

'Come on, Woosie, put it behind you!'

'Keep going, mate.'

It was amazing how quickly news of my 15-club fiasco spread around the course. I suppose many of the spectators would have been listening to the radio coverage through ear-pieces, or maybe it was just word of mouth. In any case, by the time I had drilled my second shot onto the second green, it seemed as if everybody knew exactly what had taken place back on the tee. And the crowd's support was deafening.

'Get this putt, Woos, and you'll be on your way.'

'Don't give up!'

In normal circumstances at a major tournament, the crowd tends to blur into multi-coloured scenery that reflects the action by the noise it makes: applause, cheers, sighs or silence. But this was now a very abnormal situation, and I felt as though somebody had altered the focus on my eyes.

Instead of being remotely aware of a patchwork of people, perhaps seven or eight deep along the fairway and around the green, I started to notice rows and rows of individual faces, apparently every bit as angry and upset as me. An elderly man on his shooting stick, a middle-aged woman, a group of lads standing at the top of a steep sand hill . . . and they were all looking at me, shouting encouragement, urging me to put the two-shot penalty behind me, imploring me to go on and win the thing.

If Hans Christian Andersen had been writing the script for the 2001 Open Championship, I would have instantly forgotten about what had happened, sunk my putt for birdie at the second and gloriously advanced to become the 'Champion Golfer for the Year', as they always describe the winner at the prize-giving.

That would have been fun, but real life is not so easy. With my mind in turmoil, just getting down in two putts for par at the second seemed like a major achievement. I had started this day with such high hopes that I found it incredibly difficult to accept what had happened, and just move on.

It hurt. I hooked my tee-shot at the third, and dropped a shot; then my good-looking approach to the fourth plugged right under the lip of a bunker, and this piece of bad luck cost me another bogey. Within 40 chaotic minutes of regaining what I had thought was the lead at seven under, I had fallen back to three under and slipped off the leaderboard. I then saw Duval hole a birdie putt at the third, and, suddenly, I was four shots off the pace. I felt sick. This was meant to be my day, but everything was going against me. In a brief, low moment, I felt like packing it all in and walking back to the clubhouse.

Then, the cheers swelled again, and I became aware of people shouting encouragement, and I realised I couldn't let them down. The day had become a battle and I started to fight.

After making a par at the par-three 5th hole, I whacked a big drive down the par-five sixth fairway and then powered my second shot to just 20 feet from the pin. The crowd gathered around the green roared as if I had won the tournament, and they bellowed again when I holed the putt for eagle.

I had got back to five under but Duval kept edging further away, advancing to make birdies at the sixth and seventh to reach nine under par. The American was on form, but he was challenging for his first Major win and I sensed he might wobble if I could just get close enough to apply pressure.

Miles and I had not spoken one word to each other for a few holes after the second but, as the afternoon wore on, we had gradually restored a professional relationship and, when I chipped in from off the green for a birdie at the 11th, I dared contemplate the slightest prospect of a miracle.

I was playing without restraint and starting to enjoy myself, and another birdie at the 13th took me to seven under par. Within a few moments, our gallery was buzzing with the news that, having birdied the par-five 11th, the previously unflappable Duval had dropped a shot at the par-three 12th.

Suddenly, I found myself studying the scoreboard beside the 14th green: Duval stood at nine under par, with me still battling at seven under par. I was only two shots behind. Two shots! I was desperately trying to stay positive, but I couldn't shake the penalty out of my mind. I couldn't look at a scoreboard and resist working out where I would have been placed if I had not sacrificed those two precious strokes.

'Keep it together,' I muttered to myself. 'Keep fighting.'

There was to be no miracle. I bogeyed the 15th, birdied the 16th and then bogeyed the 17th when I tried to draw the ball in to the green, but nailed the shot without any draw and hit it over the back right of the green. Some people reckoned Miles had given me the wrong line, but that was not true. To be fair, he had pulled himself together since the second hole, and we walked up the 18th fairway with our heads held high at six under par.

A par-four at the last would give me 71 for the round and, although it was by now clear Duval would win the Open, I reckoned this was a decent performance after our setback at the second tee.

The crowds packed in the enormous scaffolding grandstands either side of the fairway seemed to agree. Over the years, I have always deemed myself fortunate in receiving a generous reception at the Open, but nothing had prepared me for the ovation that began as I walked up the fairway.

The cheers grew louder and louder as people rose to their feet. Maybe it was sympathy; maybe it was appreciation for the way I had held my challenge together. Whatever the reason, I found tears welling in my eyes. I was touched and moved, and I will never forget this reception at Lytham.

Fifteen minutes later, Duval was accepting the applause as the new champion. He finished at ten under par with Fasth second on his own at seven under, and Ernie Els, Billy Mayfair, Darren Clarke, Miguel Jimenez, Bernhard Langer and me tied together in third position, at six under par.

In the press interviews that followed, I brushed off the saga as 'just one of those things' and told the journalists that I was definitely not going to sack Miles. 'He's probably made the biggest mistake of his life,' I said, 'so the chances are good that he's not going to do the same thing again.'

Simple statistics suggest the two-shot penalty only cost me second place on my own, but it is impossible to know what might have happened if I had not suffered the two-shot penalty, impossible to know how Duval would have reacted if I had been breathing down his neck on the closing holes.

It doesn't matter now. He won; I lost. That's the fact. I have accepted what took place, and moved on. It's not something I'm going to dwell on and debate for the rest of my life.

Several months later, someone removed from golf asked me whether I could have disposed of the 15th club in a way that nobody would have noticed. 'Couldn't Miles have gone to one of the portable toilets on the course,' he asked, 'and "accidentally" left the second driver in a bush?'

This option never crossed my mind. In golf, people often say, you can be anything except a cheat. The game has always relied on players to police themselves and, as soon as Miles told me about the 15th club, I was always going to tell the referee.

That's golf. It's supposed to be a gentleman's sport, and I believe in that.

One occasion many years earlier, playing at Fulford, I hit a shot into the deep rough and we couldn't find the ball. Then my caddie, a guy who I had hired, declared: 'I've got it!'

I hacked the ball out, saved my par and then birdied two of the next four holes, but I wasn't comfortable with something and, at the eighth tee, I told my playing partners, one of whom was Sam Torrance, that I was going to disqualify myself. 'I'm sorry,' I said. 'I just don't think this is my ball.'

Back at the clubhouse, I eventually got the caddie to admit he had dropped the ball he claimed to have found, through a hole in his pocket, down his trouser leg and into the rough.

I'm not claiming any medals for being honest on the second tee at Lytham. I'm certain any professional golfer would have done exactly the same thing. You have to respect the game.

Somebody else said Miles might have got through the round without even telling me about the 15th club, but I don't even want to imagine what would have happened, or how I would have felt, if I had won the Open and then discovered I had been carrying more than 14 clubs. In any case, a professional caddie should always own up to his mistakes and, in that respect at least, he couldn't be faulted.

Life moved on. Two hours after the Open had finished, we were flying to Norway to take part in the SAS Invitational match between an International team and a Scandinavian team. Miles was obviously quiet on the flight, and I tried to be sympathetic. I was angry and disappointed with him, but I had told him anybody could make a mistake and, as I said to the media, I had decided not to sack him.

'Look, Miles,' I said. 'Are you sure you want to carry on?'

'Yes, I do.'

'Fine.'

'Thanks.'

So, we did carry on. I took the next week off, but returned to action at the Scandinavian Masters where I narrowly made the cut. Miles seemed fine but, soon after our third round, there was an incident when a couple of players, who he had known for a long time, walked up to him in the clubhouse and began to tear a strip off him for what had happened at Lytham. He just sat there, and took the criticism.

We had an early tee-off time on the Sunday morning, so we arranged to meet at the locker room one hour before the final round. I arrived on time, but there was no sign of Miles.

Ten minutes passed, and still nothing. Miles had taken the key to our small locker, so I wasn't even able to get hold of my shoes. I asked the guy running the locker room if he had a spare key, but all he could do was hand me a whole bunch of keys, adding hopefully: 'It must be one of those.'

So, I began trying key after key, without success. Time was racing by and, now, less than half an hour remained until my tee-off time, so I got hold of someone to keep trying the keys in the locker and I left to buy a new pair of shoes at the pro shop.

By the time I returned, they had got my locker open, but there was still no sign of Miles. So, I quickly put on my original shoes, grabbed my clubs and rushed out to the first tee. The caddie master at the course had seen what was going on and he volunteered to carry my clubs for the round.

I managed to complete the round, and had just borrowed some cash to pay the caddie master, when I looked up to see Miles standing there. He said he had overslept and arrived late.

'I'm sorry,' he added. 'I tried to phone you on your mobile.'

'Look,' I said, firmly. 'You know what the answer is. You've messed things up again. I'm really sorry, but I can't have that happening twice. That's it. I have to let you go.'

'Fair enough,' he replied.

And we haven't spoken since. I don't know why he didn't turn up on time that Sunday. My guess is that he had been affected by all the criticism, and he just wanted to get out of the situation. I understood that, but I feel no anger towards him now. We can't change what happened. It's all in the past. I have asked his brother how he's getting on back in Ireland, and I was pleased when he said Miles is fine.

Suddenly in search of a new caddie, I asked Nick Hooper, a physiotherapist who had been assisting me with my back and a friend of ours from Jersey, whether he could help me out until the end of the season. Nick is a reasonable golfer in his own right, and I was pleased when he agreed.

As the weeks passed, my improved form was not reflected in an average series of results, but I was still in a positive frame of mind when I flew to America to play at the American Express Championship in St Louis, Missouri. On the morning of Tuesday 11 September, I was preparing to start a practice round when rumours of what was happening in New York started to circulate around the putting green.

I went back into the clubhouse and joined a whole group of pros watching television, like many millions of other people around in the world, open-mouthed in disbelief as we watched the aftermath of the attacks on the Twin Towers of the World Trade Center and the Pentagon in Washington.

Initially, we were told that only the first round would be cancelled, and that we would play on Friday and Saturday, and then complete two rounds on the Sunday. However, when the scale of the events became clear, it was formally announced that the entire tournament would be cancelled.

America was in a state of shock. We were all in shock and the Europeans in the field were eager to get back home as soon as possible. After a few days, when air travel in the USA was closed down, Guy Kinnings, of IMG, managed to get hold of the plane used by the Phoenix Suns basketball team, and approximately 50 of us were flown back to London on the Friday following the attacks.

Within a week, it was announced that the 2001 Ryder Cup matches, scheduled to be played at The Belfry in the last week of September, would be postponed by one year. I had not qualified to play but

Sam Torrance, the European captain, had asked me to join the team as his vice-captain.

Then, when it became clear that most American players were not prepared to travel across the Atlantic, I was contacted by IMG, the organisers of the 2001 Cisco World Match Play Championship at Wentworth, and asked if I could join the 12-man field as a late replacement. I had not been invited to take part in the event for the last two years, so I eagerly accepted the opportunity to prove myself once again.

I arrived to find the Burma Road course in prime condition, and was hitting the ball reasonably well in practice. However, I sensed most people thought I wouldn't be hanging around for the weekend when I was drawn to play Retief Goosen in the first round.

The South African had enjoyed a fantastic year, winning the US Open and leading the European Order of Merit, and he looked as though he had the appetite for another piece of silverware, but he putted poorly on the day, and I played solid golf throughout and emerged with a comfortable 4 and 3 victory.

'Are you feeling tired, Woosie?' asked one golf writer.

'I'm 43, not 83,' I replied.

As I prepared for a quarter-final against Colin Montgomerie, I found I was being treated with the kind of warm reverence accorded to veterans returning to the scene of former triumphs. I was flattered, but also a bit irritated, because this was not a nostalgia trip for me. I wanted to win.

Monty seemed to be struggling with his distances, but I was just starting to enjoy myself. I stoked up my round with an eagle at the fourth when I drilled a five-iron to the green and rammed the 22-foot putt into the back of the hole, and was four up by the 14th hole. He soon pulled one hole back, but I steadied in the afternoon's 18 holes, and won 4 and 3.

'Are you tired, Woosie?'

'Well, I'll have a massage tonight,' I sighed, 'and I'll be fine tomorrow.'

Suddenly, out of nowhere, I was in the semi-finals. Nobody had expected me to get far in the event, so I had played without pressure and, now, people were starting to discuss whether I could become the oldest man to win the title, and the first to win the event in three separate decades.

Some people had suggested the absence of the Americans had diminished the quality of the field, but I can't say I was noticing any weakness in my half of the draw. I had beaten the US Open champion and 2001 European Order of Merit leader in the first round, then the seven-time European Order of Merit winner in the quarter-final, and my opponent in the semi-final was Lee Westwood, winner of the European Order of Merit in 2000 and the defending World Match Play champion.

Free of the burden of expectation, I was starting to believe my game was going as well as it did during those exciting surges of form during the summers of the late 1980s. This was fun.

I led from the first hole of the morning against Lee and, when he won his first hole of the day at the 11th, my response was to play a wedge to two feet from the flag at the 12th and to hit a seven-iron to four feet from the hole at the 13th. The No.5 in the world may have been 15 years younger than me, but I was seven up after 18 holes in the morning, and I advanced further after lunch to win the match 10 and 9.

Sam Torrance had been enjoying an equally successful week, but he lost the other semi-final to Padraig Harrington, and the popular, gifted Irishman became my opponent in the final.

'Do you think you can win, Woosie?'

At least, the question had changed.

'Why not?' I replied, smiling. Strangely, although I was pleased to finish my semi-final at only the 27th hole, my legs seemed to be getting stronger the more I played. I had felt weary during my match with Retief, but as many as 36 holes a day for four days in a row seemed to be doing me a lot of good.

On Sunday 14 October 2001, at Wentworth, only twelve weeks after my eventful bid to win the Open, I managed to produce one of the best performances of my entire career.

Statistics don't always tell the whole story in golf but, in overcast conditions, playing on a renowned and difficult course, I lost the first hole and then proceeded to birdie the next seven holes in a row. My iron shots were of such quality and accuracy that, even though I single-putted six of these seven holes, no putt needed to be longer than 16 feet. I had attacked the flags again and again, hole after hole.

I completed the front nine in only 28 shots, a record for the competition . . . but, on a genuinely remarkable day, Padraig had gone out in only 31 shots, and I was only three up when we reached the 10th.

We had both played incredible, almost error-free golf; and the crowd's emotions had swung from stunned disbelief as we started trading shot for shot, through roaring delight as the birdies kept coming, and on to pure pleasure that they had been present to watch two golfers at the top of their game.

Padraig then staged a dazzling recovery, playing the back nine in only 30 shots, posting the lowest round in the 36-year history of the tournament, an outstanding 61. I got home with 64 and, under the circumstances, was relieved to be no more than two holes down after the morning's round.

We had made 20 birdies between us, playing a better ball round of 56, and my drive into the trees at the 17th hole was probably the only time anyone could say either of us hit a bad shot.

The afternoon's play was probably an anti-climax in terms of the quality of golf – indeed, anything would have seemed an anti-climax – but the level of entertainment remained high as the lead swung back and forth. Padraig moved three up at the fifth, but I won the seventh when he hit his drive into a ditch, and then clinched the ninth as he drove into the trees and called a penalty on himself after his ball moved.

I sensed the tide turning in my favour, and pressed home the psychological advantage, winning the 11th by holing a 16-foot birdie putt, winning the 12th with another birdie and making it three in a row when Padraig missed a putt for par at the 13th. Now, I was two up with only five to play.

We both had chances over the next three holes, but all were halved and I approached the 17th tee at two up with two to play. I was eager to end the match at this 17th hole, because he was driving the ball an average 20 yards further than me and I knew that would be an advantage at the last.

'Come on, Woosie, come on!'

For the first time in the week, I was feeling nervous. I had not won any professional title since the 1997 Volvo PGA Championship, played on this same course at Wentworth four and a half years before and, suddenly, I was struck by the reality that I was now on the brink of victory once again.

Padraig followed a great drive with a fantastic five-wood that finished 18 feet from the flag. Meanwhile, I had pushed my drive into some light rough on the right, hit a decent approach and chipped up to 12 feet from the pin. So here he lay: he had played two, while I had already played three.

The Irishman putted first, but left his putt short and right, leaving me my 12-footer to halve the hole in fours and win the World Match Play title by the margin of 2 and 1.

There had been a couple of showers during the afternoon, and my clothes felt slightly damp as I studied my putt. The 17th green had always been a difficult green to read ever since I first played at Wentworth in 1977; from one side, it looked like it would swing from left to right; from the other side, it looked as though it would swing from right to left. Growing anxious, I decided to hit the ball dead straight.

And it fell into the hole. My immediate reaction was to stand still, momentarily frozen in disbelief, knees slightly bent, both arms raised and both fists clenched, as if I was waiting for confirmation from some greater power that, after all these tough years, I had actually managed to win again.

I walked across to congratulate Padraig on his performance, and I could see the deep disappointment in his eyes. He had finished second 15 times in three years, and he was runner-up again, but he is a massively talented golfer and there is no doubt in my mind that his time will come.

For my part, I felt a very real and powerful sense of joy. I had been written off so many times, and had started the week as an afterthought, a rank outsider who some people had said should not have been invited to play at all, but I had managed to emerge in triumph, a champion once again.

Glen was watching, cheering and weeping beside the green. More than anybody else, my wife knew the real significance of my surprise victory at the 2001 World Match Play Championship.

It showed that, after all, 'Dad' was not over the hill.

He had bounced back.

Now, at last, my children could answer back.

CHAPTER TWELVE

Still Believing

After 26 years spent travelling around the world as a pro golfer, I am content with what I have achieved in the game. That is not to say I am smug or self-satisfied in any way, but I am content because I have worked hard to make the very most of my ability, managed to win 44 professional tournaments, including the Masters, played in eight Ryder Cups and been ranked as the No.1 player in the world for 50 weeks.

Some people will probably say I could have done more, could have worked even harder and won more than one Major championship. I don't agree. If you could have offered my career in golf to the excited seven-year-old who was so uncertain of what to expect when his parents drove him and his brother and sister to the Llanymynech Golf Club for the first time, then I am certain he would have grabbed it with both hands.

Of course, there have been days when I wish things could have turned out differently, for example when

I wish there had only been 14 clubs in my bag, or when I was disappointed with my form, but I do consider myself incredibly fortunate to have been granted such a full, rewarding and fun life in golf.

And it isn't over yet. I might have scaled down the number of tournaments I play each year to around 25, but the truth is that I only continue to compete in tournaments all over the world because I still genuinely believe I can win.

Hale Irwin won the US Open at the age of 45, Jack Nicklaus won the Masters at the age of 46, and Ray Floyd was 47 when he reached a play-off at the 1990 Masters. If I can repeat the form I showed during the four days of the 2001 World Match Play Championship in the right place at the right time, there's no reason why I can't win a big tournament in my mid-40s.

Only time will tell if my confidence is justified or not, but my performances at Lytham and Wentworth in 2001 encouraged me to work hard in preparation for the following year.

As usual, after spending January in Barbados, I joined up with the European Tour in the Far East, missing the cut at the Singapore Masters but hitting the ball pretty well to finish 13 under par and tied for sixth place at the Malaysian Open. The weather was sweltering in Kuala Lumpur, so phenomenally hot that I developed painful blisters on the soles of my feet.

My game remained reasonably solid in Dubai and Qatar and, by the time I arrived at Augusta to compete at The Masters, I had managed to shoot below 70 in seven of my 14 tournament rounds so far in the season. I wasn't exactly dominating the headlines, but I was competing well and I felt good.

The Masters, the first major of the year, is always important to me. Former champions are revered at Augusta and, in return for the outstanding hospitality, I like to play well. Unfortunately, 2002 was not my year. I was well rested after spending a week with friends in Fort Lauderdale, but my back was sore, the weather was poor and I was disappointed to miss the cut with rounds of 77 and 78.

Tiger Woods claimed another green jacket and the new-look Masters, played on the revamped and lengthened course, was generally regarded as a success. Advances in technology made the changes necessary, but the result was a tournament that suited the game of players who were longer off the tee. While the younger, stronger, longer hitters could typically clear the hills and banks at 275 yards and then attack the flag with a six-iron or a seven-iron into the green, anyone (like me) who struggled to carry their drive more than 275 yards invariably had trouble with their second shots. They were generally left with a three-iron or four-iron and this made it difficult to stop the ball on the greens.

I understand that more modifications are planned,

and it will be interesting to see how The Masters evolves. From what I know of the people at Augusta, when it comes to course design and keeping pace with modern technology, they won't be left behind.

It was important for my self-confidence to regain some form quickly and, two weeks later, a third round of 66 put me in contention at the French Open. I eventually tied for third and prize money of just over €103,000 suggested my game was back on track.

My approach was straightforward: if I was going to be chugging along down the field, then I could not see much point staying on the Tour and going through the motions. I had to be competing. I had to believe, deep down inside, that I could win every tournament that I entered. There could be no other reason to play.

And, with the help of my coach, Pete Cowen, and the support of my caddie, Lee Adelly, I worked hard. My driving seemed more accurate and consistent than it had been for several years, probably due to the fact that I had switched to use a more stable graphite shaft, with less torque.

There was not much wrong with my irons either, although I did struggle to get the soft draw shot that I have always preferred. This problem was only resolved towards the end of the season, when I adjusted the loft of my iron clubs.

In 2002, the main source of frustration was my putting, and the endlessly recurring question of whether I should use a normal, short putter or rely on the broom handle.

The bottom line was my continuing conviction that I *ought* to use the short putter because I somehow felt it was the proper club, and I wanted to play the game properly. The broom handle had helped me through some of the most difficult periods of my career, indeed had kept me in the game, but there was always a nagging voice at the back of my mind reminding me that this innovation didn't only look like a crutch: it *was* a crutch for players who had lost confidence on the greens.

Major winners used short putters. I wanted to compete at that level, so I was determined to use a short putter.

This sincere intent paid dividends at the start of the year, but then I missed a few putts, lost some confidence and switched back to the broom handle. After a while, I felt better, and turned back to the short putter again . . . and so it continued throughout the year, as I switched back and forth, back and forth.

Sometimes I changed putters after a few weeks. On other occasions, I switched after only one tournament. More than once, I used a short putter in the pro-am event, but then reverted to the broom handle when the tournament began. And, yes, in one or two cases, I did change my putter between rounds.

Tinkering with my game has never given me a problem. Far from being unsettled by changing this or that, I see the process as part of an ongoing quest for perfection; and the extensive range of putters on the market presented me with plenty of choices in my search for consistency on the greens. Aside from the standard short putter, and the broom handle, I also tried the belly putter, and other types. Every option felt great at some stage, every option felt wrong at some stage, and the question burned all year.

My form was respectable, but not much more. I tied for sixth at the Tournament Players Championship of Europe, missed the cut at the Volvo PGA Championship, played better to finish level par but well down the field at the British Masters, and was content to finish below par and in the middle of the pack at the Irish Open, the European Open and the Scottish Open.

I was hitting the ball really well, maybe better than my scores suggested but, round after round, my card seemed to be spoiled by a couple of stupid mistakes and the odd bad hole.

It was incredibly frustrating.

The margin between finishing somewhere between 20th and 50th, as I was, and getting on the leaderboard was small. Making one more putt in every round – improving your tournament total by only four strokes – was the difference between staying down the field and challenging at the top of the Order of Merit.

At the end of the year, somebody pointed out to

me that my overall average round was just over a stroke worse than Padraig Harrington, but the talented Irishman finished second on the Order of Merit, and I eventually ended in 34th place.

Perhaps because of what had happened at Lytham in 2001, there seemed to be a widespread belief that I would mount a strong challenge for the Open Championship at Muirfield in 2002. I arrived in North Berwick on the east coast of Scotland and found people wanting to rake over the whole 15th club saga, speculating whether the penalty had cost me the title. My form was decent and, as my name started to appear as a contender in the newspapers, I began to get excited about my chances.

In the event, it turned out to be another of those weeks when everything felt right but nothing seemed to happen. I didn't do too much wrong, but I just didn't get the breaks.

The course was brilliant, set up with severe rough down each side of fairways that got narrower and narrower towards the driving landing areas. So, you could take a driver if you wanted, but it was a big risk because anything in the rough could easily result in a double bogey. Most of the guys opted to play for position and hit irons off the tee, with the result that the tournament seemed more even and competitive.

That was my strategy: play safe. The one-iron served me well again, as it had at Lytham the previous year, and I seemed to be reaching the greens in regulation but I just wasn't sinking the putts, making birdies and getting any real momentum.

I started with a couple of one-over-par 72s and had an excellent opportunity on the Saturday when I played my third round before the weather took a dramatic turn for the worse. If I could have put a 68 or a 69 together, with the leaders then slipping back, I could have pushed myself right into contention. Instead, I posted a frustrating 73 and, even with a 68 on the Sunday, had to settle for a share of 37th place.

Ernie Els won the claret jug after a tense play-off, but the tournament will also be remembered for Tiger Woods' extraordinary 81 during the storm on the Saturday afternoon. It might have been the highest round of his professional career, but the American emerged with great credit when he faced the media afterwards, and answered their questions. He didn't run away from what had happened, and he didn't look for any excuses. Even in humbling adversity, Tiger conducted himself like a champion and explained that he had tried his hardest on every shot.

There was a danger that my year would fade away after the Open at Muirfield. I didn't make an impact at the Wales Open, and I missed the halfway cut both at the US PGA Championship and, back in Europe, at the BMW International Open. It wasn't good enough and I headed to the Linde German Masters at the Gut Larchenhof club, near Cologne, determined to get back on top of my game and start competing again.

Suddenly, the putts started to drop and a second round of 64, just a stroke outside the course record, gave me the halfway lead. 'That was probably my best round since the final of the World Match Play last year,' I told the media guys afterwards. I was smiling, and enthusiastic. It felt good to be back in the shake up on Sunday, and even better to be in a position to secure my 30th tournament win on the European Tour, my first stroke-play victory in more than five years.

In the end, I fell a couple of putts short. A respectable 68 on the Saturday left me three strokes behind the leader going into the final round. There was not much wrong with my game from tee to green, but I missed a couple of short putts on the home straight and had to be content with third place, on 20 under par, only two behind the winner, Australian Stephen Leaney.

Another solid performance at the Trophee Lancome, where I tied for 13th place, maintained the momentum approaching my bid to defend the World Match Play title at Wentworth; and, after a bye in the first round, I came up against Michael Campbell, the talented New Zealander who looked in excellent form.

I would obviously have to play well, and the standard of play was pretty high by the time we completed the 28th hole all square; then, using the broom handled putter, I hit a putt on the 29th green that horseshoed the cup 360 degrees and stayed out.

Michael won the hole, edged ahead, and took the match 3 & 2.

It was disappointing but, even with a handful of bogeys, my score was seven under par after 29 holes. Sometimes in match play, you have to hold up your hands and accept your opponent played better. It was a hard-fought competition and, once again, the event produced a series of amazing scores, probably because the format allows players to play aggressive golf and take risks.

Another decent performance, tying 13th at the Volvo Masters in Andalucia, established me in 34th place on the final Order of Merit in 2002, with annual earnings in excess of £380,000.

I suppose there were some people who might have looked at me and seen an ageing pro drifting gracefully towards the sunset of his career, biding his time until he qualified to play on the Seniors Tour, but this was certainly not my understanding of the situation. I was playing to win tournaments. That had been ambition as a youngster driving a VW Dormobile around the continent, and it remained my source of motivation a quarter of a century later.

Of course, that is easy to say, and of course my financial situation has become much more comfortable as I have got older, but my basic demeanour and commitment on the course have not changed at all. I still want to win, desperately; and I still believe I can win at the highest level.

It comes down to respect. I believe every elite sportsman or sportswoman wants, more than anything, to be respected by their peers. Part of that is being respected for what you have achieved in your career, but maybe the most important thing is being respected for what you are and continue to be in the game. And, for as long as you stay on Tour, the only way to earn that respect is to be competing on the leaderboard. It's easier when you retire; then you can trade on the past because that's all there is and people are more inclined to be kind. But, until then, you must compete. Respect is not something that can be stored away; it must be earned and re-earned week after week.

In my mind, 2002 had been a decent year, but it did feel a little bit like the one that got away. I felt as though I had been just a handful of strokes away from an outstanding year, and that fact left me feeling frustrated, and even more determined to work harder, get back on the European Tour in 2003 and convert some winning positions into tournament victories.

There have been many times when the hassles around the game – the travelling, the long weeks spent away from home, the monotony of airport, hotel, golf course, airport, hotel, golf course – get me down, but perhaps the saving grace is that I still enjoy getting on the course and playing golf. I know that will sound trite and unlikely, but it is true. My passion

for getting together with a group of mates and playing for a few pounds on the match, and a press here
and there, is as strong as ever.

A couple of close friends, D.J. Russell and Gary
Thompson, spent some time with us in Barbados not
long ago, and we had a fantastic time, joking and
laughing around Royal Westmoreland. It says something about golf's enduring appeal that it can be your
job week in, week out for 26 years, and yet you can
still have as much fun as I did that week with D.J.
and Tommo.

Outside of the regular Tour events, I also enjoy
taking part in the various special events organised in
recent years with the aim of gathering those players
who dominated the game in the late 1980s and early
1990s. There were a lot of great characters around at
that time, and it seems as if sponsors and spectators
are keen to get us together in a competitive, friendly
environment.

The Warburg Cup, for over-40s, where an
International team captained by Gary Player plays an
American team led by Arnold Palmer, is one such
event. The inaugural match proved a fantastic occasion at Kiawah Island in November 2001 and, despite
some bad luck with the weather on the Sunday, the
2002 match at Sea Island, Georgia was also successful, and a lot of fun.

Both sides are keen to win, but both events have
been played in a wonderful, sporting atmosphere, in

a spirit that was illustrated by one incident during my singles match against Mark Calcavecchia on the concluding day of the match in 2001.

'Calcs' and I were all square when we reached the 17th hole on the Ocean Course at Kiawah Island, exactly the same par-three 17th where he hit three tee-shots in the water during his infamous match against Colin Montgomerie on the Sunday of the 1991 Ryder Cup. That was when he had been four up with four to play, but then lost the 15th, 16th, 17th and 18th, and, distraught and disbelieving, ended up with a half. That experience left a scar and, as we stepped on to the tee in the Warburg Cup, both of us were mindful of what had happened ten years before. He was being tested again.

I hit my tee-shot into a bunker front left of the green, then Calcs stepped up and hit a scorching three-iron straight at the flag, coming to rest no more than 12 feet from the hole.

It looked as though I would need to hole my sand shot to keep the match alive. With Gary Player standing on the edge of the bunker, urging me on, I managed to splash the ball out, and send it running down towards the hole. Two more rolls, and it would have gone in, but it stayed out. The crowd were enjoying the drama and Gary was beside himself. He couldn't believe it.

Calcs then slammed his 12-foot putt in for a two, going one up. It was a big moment for him and, as we walked off the 17th green, I looked across and said: 'Great two, Calcs. That answers a few people's questions.'

He smiled. Nobody had mentioned the events of 1991, but he obviously knew exactly what I was talking about, and it was a great moment for him. The spectators were going mad. It was just a fantastic moment. After a pair of par 4s, he closed out the match at the 18th, winning by one hole.

From my perspective, it didn't escape my notice that I had just lost another singles match, but I managed to exorcise some of those ghosts at the Warburg Cup in 2002. I was drawn to play Tom Kite in the singles on the Sunday and, to my delight, I managed to come out on top, securing the full point from a singles match in either a Ryder Cup or Warburg Cup for the first time.

Before long, I will become eligible to join the Seniors Tour and, by then, I wouldn't be at all surprised if there hasn't been heavy investment in the European Seniors Tour either by a large corporate sponsor or perhaps even a major broadcaster.

The thought is appealing: players like Seve Ballesteros, Nick Faldo, Sandy Lyle, Bernhard Langer and I will all be reaching 50 around 2007–08, and I anticipate this group will promote the same kind of growth in the European Seniors Tour that they inspired on the regular Tour during the late 1980s.

Recent experience in America has shown Seniors

golf relies heavily on charismatic personalities to capture the public's imagination. The US Seniors Tour boomed when Palmer, Nicklaus, Player and Trevino reached 50 and started playing the tournaments, but recent spectator figures seem to indicate interest has waned as these legends have reduced their appearances.

I think European spectators will be excited by the prospect of seeing their old favourites, the heroes of those historic Ryder Cup matches of the 1980s, renew their rivalry in the Seniors arena. To my mind, this simultaneous maturing of vintage golfers represents a huge commercial gap for some company and, as I say, I expect some company to seize that opportunity.

Their investment will work because the standard of play will be excellent. Playing on courses of around 6,800 yards, these guys will be hitting the ball just as far when they are 50 as they used to when they were 25 because modern golf club technology will have replaced whatever advancing years have removed.

With a bit of luck, I will still be playing, still enjoying myself, still working hard on the practice tee, still fancying my chances of winning every tournament I play . . . still believing.

CHAPTER THIRTEEN

Restoring the Ryder Cup

The underdog European team won the 34th Ryder Cup for many of the same reasons that lay behind their celebrated, spirited victories in four of the previous eight matches.

In 2002, in eight words . . . we were a *team* playing against 12 individuals. It didn't make any difference that those 12 individuals were ranked higher in the world, or had earned more money, or even seemed to be in better form. It mattered only that, through three intense and exhilarating days at The Belfry, the European guys worked together. We were an authentic team; at times, we were even more than that . . . we were a family.

The Ryder Cup remains the most prestigious team event in an emphatically individual sport and, throughout the past two decades, successive European teams have worked hard to develop genuine team spirit among the players and their management. Such shared resolve translates into a thousand tiny gestures, most of which pass unnoticed but all of which contribute to the whole: a happy, determined group pulling in the same direction.

In foursomes, European players are actively encouraged to offer their opinion when their partner is lining up a putt. In fourball matches, they are invariably to be found walking down the fairways together, discussing the next shot. In the singles matches, as soon as a European completes his match, win, halve or lose, he goes back on the course to support his teammates.

Many of the Americans do many of the same things but the overall impression remains that, by and large, they approach the Ryder Cup as if it was an ordinary stroke play tournament. It's their nature. Week in, week out on the professional Tour, golfers exist in their own cocoons, each individual focusing on his own game, his own circumstances, his own problems. In Europe, the Ryder Cup is completely different. The 'I's become 'we's.

I am certainly not suggesting one approach is superior to the other. However, in assessing the nature of the contest, I think it is worthwhile to draw the distinction: in general, the Americans fight their own battles and tally up the scores while the Europeans relish the idea of mucking in and battling as a team.

At the 2001 Ryder Cup (postponed after the terrorist attacks on 11 September, played 12 months later, but still officially known as the 2001 Ryder Cup), the catalyst and central personality in the European 'team' campaign was a shrewd, strong-minded and widely liked Scotsman from Largs . . . our captain.

Sam Torrance proved an exceptional leader before, during and after the event, above all because he fetched so much emotion and passion into the job. He had been positively associated with the Ryder Cup ever since he holed the winning putt in 1985, and wept with joy at the 18th green, and he remained a symbol of everything that was good in the matches. Maybe more effectively than anyone else, he has managed to marry a burning desire to win with sincere respect both for his opponents and for the event.

Younger players looked up to him as someone who had been there and done it, the senior players listened to him with affection and respect, and everyone admired him for his direct approach. Sam never wanted to offend anyone but, if something needed sorting out within the team, it didn't make any difference to him if someone was going to get upset. He would say and do whatever he thought was necessary to keep his team on track.

The captain knew exactly what he wanted and, in his honest, quiet, lugubrious, dry manner, he showed the way. He eagerly wanted to win but, virtually from the day of his appointment, Sam had repeatedly declared his determination to restore civility to the Ryder Cup. He had been vice-captain to Mark James at Brookline in 1999, and knew as well as anyone how the hostility that surrounded and followed those matches had seriously damaged the reputation of the event. In some respects, it seemed as though Sam felt some kind of historic obligation to set a calmer and more respectful tone at The Belfry.

He publicly addressed the issue over and over again.

'Of course, the contest may be close,' he would state, with every justification: four of the previous five Ryder Cups had been won by the narrowest possible margin of 14½–13½.

He would continue: 'Of course, emotions will run high during the three days of competition, but this only makes it all the more important that everybody involved recognises their obligation to keep things under control. There is no future for the kind of scenes that we saw at Brookline.'

The players listened well and followed his lead. The tone was set and, in turn, the best traditions of sportsmanship were upheld by the tens of thousands of excited spectators who flooded across the course throughout the week. In years to come, long after the results of the 2001 Ryder Cup have faded into the history books, it should not surprise anyone if Sam Torrance is remembered as the man who brought decency back to the Ryder Cup.

Sam and I have been close friends for more than 20 years, sharing many great times, and a few pints here and there, since we played that first fourball at

West Palm Beach in the 1983 Ryder Cup, but, when he telephoned me early in February 2000, I couldn't think of any obvious reason for his call.

'Woos, it's Sam. How are you?'

'Fine. No problem. You?'

'OK. Listen, will you be vice-captain at The Belfry?'

'You mean you don't want me to play,' I replied, pretending to be disappointed. Sam knew all about my continuing ambition to perform well enough on Tour and earn a place in the team, but he also knew the reality of my current form; so did I.

He laughed softly.

'Of course, I will,' I replied. 'I would love to help.' In truth, I was delighted by the prospect of being involved.

When we eventually met to discuss his plans, Sam explained how he wanted me, as vice-captain, to combine with Mark James and Joakim Haeggman in a management team that would focus on two main areas. First, we would be his extra eyes and ears out on the course, helping to assess who was playing well and who should play with who on the first two days; second, we would mix with the players, offering advice, building team spirit.

It made sense. I understood what he expected. It would be a new experience, charging around the golf course on a buggy with a walkie-talkie pressed to my ear, but I loved the Ryder Cup, and I was confident of doing a decent job.

'Does all that sound OK, Woos?'.

'No problem, Sam.'

Not everyone agreed. We live in a time when people are far quicker to criticise than to praise, and it was not long before certain pundits were questioning the size of the European management team. There were certainly more of us than there had been at any previous Ryder Cup. Mark James had needed only a vice-captain, Sam, at Brookline, and it was also the case that, on the American side, Curtis Strange was bringing only one assistant to help him at The Belfry, but the muttering about gravy trains and jobs for the boys was ridiculous. Sam was simply trying to build a winning structure, and, of course, when we did manage to win the thing, the pundits suddenly weren't questioning anything at all!

As a management quartet, we were able to spread ourselves through the team on practice days, keeping an eye on everything, gathering information for Sam to make an accurate assessment of who was playing well, and who should partner who.

And on the Friday and Saturday, during the foursomes and fourballs, with four matches in each session, we were able to follow one match each, from practice tee to the last putt.

As assistants, we were restricted insofar as Ryder Cup rules stated that only the team captain is entitled to offer specific advice to players during play, so anything like that had to be relayed to the players concerned via Sam, but there were no regulations to stop us offering vocal encouragement and support.

The system worked, and we managed to avoid any frenzied dashing between matches, where the team captain usually tries to watch everything and ends up seeing nothing.

We kept in contact by radio, updating each other on the state of the match we were following, sharing information about how this or that hole was playing, what club so-and-so had used off the tee, even passing on players' requests for more sandwiches or bananas. Our communication system needed to be perfect and we generally managed to stay on the same wavelength.

Mark, Joakim and I worked pretty hard off the course as well, making ourselves available to the players. In the team room, at breakfast, lunch and dinner, on the practice ground, on the putting green, we were ready to share our own experiences of the Ryder Cup, tell the guys what to expect on the first tee, advise them how to cope with nerves and perform under pressure.

We were a resource, supplied to help the mix, available if and when required, and it didn't take long for people to find each other and settle down. Looking back, I think I spent a fair amount of time chatting to Phil Price, of Wales, and the Irish guys. It just worked out like that. Joakim was obviously close to the Scandinavians, and he provided them with an easy route to Sam.

All in all, we managed to overcome the language and cultural barriers, ensuring nobody was left out. You could say we emerged as an excellent advertisement of pan-European harmony.

Sam had taken great care in designing his ideal management machine and, by general consent, it purred.

His planning had begun early in 2000, and everything was in place by the second week of September 2001. Then, the Al Qaeda attacks on New York, Pennsylvania and Washington DC stunned the world, and the Ryder Cup was postponed for a year.

I know there were some people who thought the event should have gone ahead as planned, sending a message of defiance to the terrorists, but all of us agreed with the decision. To be fair, there was no way the Americans could have been expected to fly across the Atlantic at that time of mourning, trauma and uncertainty.

We refocused, confirmed our team would remain as selected, irrespective of the players' form during the intervening 12 months, and looked ahead to the new date in September 2002.

Sam came up with idea of organising a series of team dinners during the year, as a way of keeping everything on the boil, and we got together once before the Benson and Hedges tournament at The Belfry, then again during the week of the Irish Open, and for a third time shortly before the BMW tournament in Munich. Each time, we discussed the match ahead, listened to the players' opinions, kept in touch with each other and cultivated team spirit.

'We must be a family,' the captain declared at one of these occasions. 'That's our best hope. They will bring a strong team but, if we can be a family, we have a real chance.'

Whenever Sam and I had a chance to sit down and chat, our conversation invariably turned to the difficult task of settling upon our strongest combinations for the foursomes and fourballs. In search of clues, we distributed forms to each of the players, asking them to indicate, in confidence, who they would like to partner. The results were helpful and, step by step, we edged towards what we hoped would prove the most effective blend.

June passed, July rushed by and August gathered pace. Some people were fretting that some members of our team were not playing well on Tour, but Sam and I were unconcerned. Clearly, we would have preferred to see the guys winning tournaments, but we always believed they would perform as a team.

That was the point. We never considered them as a bunch of individuals. In our mind, the players were cogs in a wheel and, with the right support and encouragement, we remained convinced that they would perform well at The Belfry. The ebb and flow of form on Tour was essentially irrelevant to our challenge.

Focusing firmly on our preparations, we turned our attention to the state of the Brabazon course. It was our right, as the home team, to ensure the golf course was prepared in exactly the way we wanted. There was nothing underhand in this, the Americans had been doing precisely the same for years, and we were determined to make the very most of this advantage.

We had two particular requests: the first was that the rough beside the fairways between 280 and 300 yards from the tee should be particularly severe and punishing. Everyone knew that certain American players would be longer off the tee than our guys, so we tried to discourage them from using drivers. If thick rough around the landing areas sowed doubt in their minds, they would come back to three-woods or long irons.

Second, we asked for the aprons around the greens to be cut nice and short, and extended to six or seven yards wide. This would assist the kind of bump-and-run shots that our guys liked to play on the European Tour, and it would give the Americans something else to think about because they were used to playing on courses where the grass is long and fluffy around the greens.

It's difficult to say whether these adjustments made too much difference and the unpredictable weather, which often makes course preparation seem more of an art than a science, played its part. As it turned out, the preparation of the greens was hampered by some kind of fungus; then persistent rain in the first week of September meant the rough grew so thick that, two days before the matches, we asked for an inch to be trimmed off the top.

All of which meant we were doubly delighted to discover the course in almost exactly the condition we wanted. We owed a great deal to those professionals at The Belfry who had worked so hard. Maybe the most accurate reflection of their achievement was to be found in Curtis Strange's remarks on the Thursday afternoon. Asked what his players needed to do to win, the US captain said they would have to stay on the fairways. 'You won't advance the ball far out of the rough,' he continued. 'We'll have to play safe.'

Sam's planning was paying dividends.

Our players assembled at The Belfry and quickly felt at home. Looking as though they were enjoying every minute, they smiled and joked their way through the necessary series of official functions and approached their practice rounds with the right blend of serious purpose and light-hearted pleasure. Amid the bets and presses, the high spirits and practical jokes, the mood was right.

Pierre Fulke was playing in his first Ryder Cup and, on his first day in the hotel, the Swede caused a stir when he told the captain he had a major problem. Sam looked aghast, until Pierre solemnly explained he needed help with his tie. This was promising: even the debutants were cracking bad jokes.

It wasn't all plain sailing. When Sam outlined his ideas for the foursomes and fourballs, it wasn't long before the grapevine buzzed with rumour that one of the players was not happy. Apparently, he was saying he didn't think his proposed partnership would gel.

That seemed pretty childish and petty, so I suggested to Sam that I would have a chat with this player and ask him to explain his problem. It would obviously be better for everyone if any rumblings of discontent were confronted and quickly resolved.

'You've just got to communicate,' I told him.

'We don't seem to be on the save wavelength,' he replied.

'OK, hold on,' I said, trying to be calm and practical. 'If you just talk to him, things will improve. During the practice round, don't go off and do your own thing. Ask him what club he is using, read each other's putts and get more involved in each other's games. On the course, congratulate him on his good shots and make sure you always walk together on the fairways. Keep talking and share your thoughts. If you support him, he will support you and you'll be a team.'

The guy seemed to be listening and, to be fair, he got on with the job. They did communicate and they soon began to realise that, in fact, they could get along. In the end, that particular partnership worked out well.

Sam held court at the regular team meetings, keeping things moving along with his relaxed blend of straight speaking and dry humour. He tried to ease the pressure by telling the guys they had nothing to lose because they were playing against many of the best players in the world and, on one memorable occasion, he made his point by telling the story of David and Goliath.

The captain also produced two rousing video tapes, where images of our players winning tournaments and playing great shots were edited with footage of great moments in previous European Ryder Cup triumphs, and these pictures were set to breast-beating rock anthems like 'Hero' and 'We are the Champions'.

It was great stuff and we had some fantastic meetings. Sam would run through the schedule for the following day and take any questions. He would speak for a while and finish by playing one of his videos. All eyes would focus on the screen as thumping music filled the room, and everyone would walk away feeling upbeat and positive, bursting to get out there and perform.

The Americans were preparing in their own way and, from what we saw of them at the various dinners and functions, and on the practice days, they looked serious and motivated. There was no tension between the teams, and all the players greeted each other easily, sharing jokes and enjoying the occasion.

Perhaps the pressure did start to show on the course. On one of the days, some of their big names began their practice round so early in the morning that they were already on the back nine before the gates were open, and that didn't seem fair to the paying public. Another time, a group of American players briskly cut in front of our guys, suggesting we were playing too slowly.

There was no hostility, but there was obviously an edge. This was the Ryder Cup. It mattered. Everyone was polite, but everyone wanted to win, and that was how it should be.

In fact, several times, Sam and I remarked to each other that things were going eerily well. By the Thursday evening, the tone of the newspapers and people around the hotel suggested the burden of expectation now rested firmly on the United States team because almost everybody expected them to win. And yet, within the privacy of our team room, we felt positive. As quietly confident underdogs, our psychological condition seemed ideal. 'We're ready and we just can't wait to get going,' Sam told the media.

Friday, 27 September 2002, dawned overcast and still over Sutton Coldfield. At last, the matches could begin.

As the home team, we were entitled to choose

whether the match would start with fourball matches in the morning, and then foursomes in the afternoon, or vice versa. Aware of our success in the fourball format in the past, we reckoned that starting with them gave us the best chance of making a fast start.

Darren Clarke and Thomas Bjorn had been chosen to launch our challenge in the first of the Friday morning fourballs, and they rose to the occasion against Tiger Woods and Paul Azinger. Where the Americans might have anticipated a simple point, they found a gutsy European pair eager to fight for every hole.

The quality of golf was phenomenal. Darren opened up with three birdies, but Tiger countered with a couple of his own. Thomas then moved into overdrive, making birdies at the 10th, 12th, 15th and the 16th. Incredibly, our guys were two up with two to play. Tiger responded to the situation by winning the 17th with a birdie, and it seemed as though we would have to settle for a half when Azinger hit his approach a foot from the hole at the last.

There was one more twist. Thomas was left with an awkward 15–foot putt for a birdie that would halve the last and win the match by one hole. The Great Dane, as we called him, held his nerve and, to our delight, gave us the best possible start. Woods and Azinger looked astonished: they had posted an excellent 63, and yet still lost to a 62.

'We need a fast start,' Sam had said that morning.

Now we had one, and the momentum was sustained when first the Lee Westwood and Sergio Garcia combination, and then Colin Montgomerie and Bernhard Langer produced brilliant 4 & 3 victories. The United States did take the concluding match of the morning, but we enjoyed lunch with a 3–1 lead.

Calm confidence is one thing, but points on the board is quite another. Confidence flowed amid the cold meat and salad. We were in contention, equal to the challenge. A handful of experts had said the Americans would prove too strong, and coast to an easy victory. It had not taken long for them to be proved completely wrong. Yet again, the Ryder Cup was heading for a close finish.

We breathed deep, took stock and moved on. Throughout our planning, Sam and I had talked about the importance of winning the foursomes and fourballs on the first two days. Recent history proved the American strength in the singles matches, and it was always our goal to take some kind of lead into the Sunday. Now we had moved ahead, the new challenge was to stay ahead.

Our strategy almost seemed too obvious, but we decided to keep intact our three winning pairs from the morning and put them back out on the course to play foursomes in the afternoon. It would have been foolish to try and hold them back. They were right in the groove, and bursting to get back into the fray.

In the event, Thomas and Darren lost when they

might easily have won. Lee and Sergio played magnificently once again, beating Mark Calcavecchia and Tiger Woods 2 & 1, inflicting a second defeat of the day on the World No.1. It was proving a tough afternoon but Bernhard and Monty dug deep for a half, and we reached the end of the first day with a precious 4½–3½ advantage.

I was pleased . . . and exhausted. The relentless pressure and constant activity had blown away any notion I might have had that management would not be too demanding. As a player, you only have to focus on your own game, but as a vice-captain, you worry about everybody in the team, from the first to last.

My mind was buzzing that night, full of what had happened and our options for the next day. It was stimulating, and a few of us spent time chatting into the night. Sam was also in the group and, to some people's surprise, he confirmed his objective that every member of the European team would be given the opportunity to play at least once in the first two days. Some people doubted this policy, but he was very determined.

'Our whole strategy is based on team spirit,' the captain said, 'and we must give everyone a chance to feel part of what we are doing here. It's not fair to leave anybody out for two days and then throw them into a singles match on Sunday.'

You couldn't argue with the logic and, given that we were not going to meddle with our established combinations – Westwood and Garcia, Clarke and Bjorn, Langer and Montgomerie – our remaining pairs quickly fell into pace. It was decided that Phil Price and Pierre Fulke, both savouring their first Ryder Cups, would play together in the opening match on Saturday. It was going to be tough, because the Americans had been stung by falling behind, but Sam was keen to show the rookies he trusted them to do well.

In such situations, the human instinct is to take either a pace forward or a pace backwards: you either meet the challenge or you retreat. Drawn to play foursomes against the formidable US pair of Mickelson and Toms, our rookies took a bold step forward and, not for the first time in the Ryder Cup, nor the last, the apparent gulf in pedigree was compensated by pure determination.

Against every prediction, Price and Fulke were two holes up at the tenth. Updates of their heroics were relayed on scoreboards around the course, delighting their team-mates following on behind but, unfortunately, this particular Cinderella did not get to the Ball. The Americans rallied to win the match 2 & 1.

Westwood and Garcia restored our advantage. Never behind against Stewart Cink and Jim Furyk, this pumped-up pairing moved ahead at the fourth, sustained that form throughout and celebrated their third win in three matches. Lee had ripped up the formbook and been a revelation, and Sergio had emerged as the rightful heir to the proud Ryder Cup legacy of Seve and Olazabal. They clicked, bounced off each other and played phenomenal golf.

We looked to Monty and Bernhard for another point, but they had become embroiled in a tight struggle with the American Scotts, Hoch and Verplank. Two up at the tenth, our guys were hauled back to all square at the 15th. Everything had seemed to be going so well for Europe, but the temperature was rising and we needed our most experienced combination to 'hang tough' and produce the results in what now started to look like a pivotal match.

As we wondered if we could withstand the pressure, Bernhard and Monty came through on cue, like the cavalry.

Bernhard played an approach into the 17th green that was ranked by many as one of the finest shots of the week; then, Monty stepped forward and rammed the testing five-foot putt into the cup, making the birdie and winning the hole. All guts and concentration, they closed out the match with a cast-iron par at the 18th, banking a crucial point. Big hearts had won a big moment.

In the last match of the morning, Darren and Thomas had won the opening hole against Tiger Woods and his third partner in the space of 30 hours, Davis Love III, but the greatest player in the world began to find his best form and, ominously, his birdie at the 15th helped to secure an emphatic 2 & 1 win for the visitors.

You could almost see the Americans take heart. 'Europeans have great spirit,' they seemed to be saying, 'but if we play to the best of our ability, there's nothing they can do.'

From our perspective, we had fought hard through an intense morning, won two and lost two, and successfully clung to a narrow 6½–5½ lead. The Americans had clearly raised their game, but we had responded in kind and held firm. Yes, it was tough, but it was also energizing. We were up for the battle.

Sam, Mark, Joakim and I set to work in the team room during that lunch break on the Saturday, talking to the guys, encouraging them, offering advice where it was required. We had smiled our way through the dinners and enjoyed an excellent first day, but this was crunch time. We were going to stand or fall.

In choosing our pairs for the afternoon fourballs, we decided to lead with the all-Swedish partnership of Niclas Fasth and Jesper Parnevik. With Bernhard saying he was weary, we drafted Padraig Harrington in to partner Monty. Sergio and Lee would follow them, and, when Thomas Bjorn also asked for a rest, we called upon Paul McGinley to join Darren in the concluding match.

There was no grumbling or second thoughts. Every individual was submerged within the team goal, and we were ready to get out there and play. The pairings looked strong and, proving as good as his word,

Sam had given all 12 guys a chance to play.

We bravely charged at the trenches that Saturday afternoon, and emerged with one and a half points out of four. The Americans played well, and the margins between victory and defeat were tiny but, for once, we found ourselves falling short.

Niclas and Jesper played well in the opening match, but lost by one hole. We hit back through Monty, who continued his magical form, and Padraig, who beat Mickelson and Toms 2 & 1.

The crucial contest of the afternoon seemed to be Garcia and Westwood's match against Tiger and Davis Love. Our pair had not been driving the ball especially well, but they dovetailed neatly and managed to get around the golf course so effectively that they held a one hole lead with only two to play.

Now, within touching distance of taking a perfect four points from their four matches in the first two days, Sergio and Lee finally faltered. Three putts on the 17th green and an exasperating bogey at the last left the door ajar, and the Americans gratefully skipped through to snatch a dramatic one-hole victory.

Meanwhile, Darren Clarke and Paul McGinley were walking up the 18th, still all square with Hoch and Furyk. The two Irishmen had combined efficiently, with Darren shooting birdies and Paul churning out steady pars, and they bravely halved the last. At the end of a massively demanding day, our lead had gone and there was nothing between the teams, now locked together at 8–8.

We were all disappointed, and there was no point denying the fact. Everybody was aware how we had set our minds on carrying a lead into the singles matches on Sunday and it was very frustrating to have held an advantage from the first morning and lost it. It was hard not to sit and consider that if only Lee and Sergio had held on, we would be leading 9–7 and looking strong . . .

'Forget all that,' Sam announced firmly when everyone was back in the team room. 'That's gone now. It's in the past. We have a job to do tomorrow, so let's concentrate on that.'

At a time when the tide of the match seemed to be turning against us, at a time when many might have panicked, our captain remained absolutely clear and positive. He had been working hard and he proceeded to outline a brave, audacious strategy for the 12 singles matches on Sunday, whereby we were going to put almost all our strongest players at the top of our order.

This was unusual.

A few of our experienced players seemed surprised. 'This is one hell of a gamble,' somebody muttered.

The conventional approach, established by generations of Ryder Cup captains on both sides of the Atlantic, was to spread the available talent evenly through the list, and, if the state of the match was relatively even, they would generally take care to start and finish the day as strongly as possible.

Curtis Strange seemed to be following this tried and trusted policy when he named his two best ranked players, Mickelson and Woods, in 11th and 12th places respectively on his list. The US captain had discussed the issue with his team and a clear consensus emerged that, since another tight finish seemed almost inevitable, it would be much better to have the team's biggest guns firing in the likely do-or-die matches at the back of the field.

It was Sam who dared to be different. In card playing terms, he was throwing down his trumps from the very first hand, and this had changed the entire nature of the competition.

Some said his tactic was inspired.

Others reckoned it was doomed to failure.

The announcement of the two team lists and publication of Sunday's order of play sent a buzz through the Press Room. When our players saw who they were playing the next day, they seemed encouraged and excited. Nobody was taking anything for granted, but our task suddenly seemed less daunting.

The first six matches read as follows: Montgomerie v. Hoch, Garcia v. Toms, Clarke v. Duval, Langer v. Sutton, Harrington v. Calcavecchia and Bjorn v. Cink. Every match looked tough, but every match also looked undeniably winnable.

People were talking, discussing the prospects,

speculating on what could happen, and most people reached the same conclusion. If Europe could dominate the early matches, Woods and Mickelson could find themselves playing dead matches with the Cup already lost; on the other hand, if Europe failed to get ahead, it would be hard for them to fight back later in the afternoon.

All that lay in the future. What was beyond dispute was that, at the end of a day when the Americans appeared to have captured the momentum, we were still setting the agenda.

The captains held separate Press conferences on this eventful Saturday evening and, while Sam looked positive and upbeat, many people thought Curtis appeared surprised and uncertain.

'We have planned carefully,' Sam concluded, 'and we realize we have to get blue on the board from the start.' This became the European mantra as Sunday dawned over The Belfry.

'Let's get blue on the board.' It was seemingly the only thing anyone said at breakfast. We were referring to the huge scoreboard beside the 18th green, which indicated the scores of matches where Europe was winning, or indeed had won, in blue numbers. This was our simple mission now: get blue on the board.

Monty led the way.

Overcoming any doubts about his fitness, Colin was thriving and at the peak of his game. He had looked happy and relaxed all week, joking with the galleries, at one point inviting a spectator to play a stroke during a practice round, relishing his role as a senior player, making birdie after birdie, reaping point after point.

He was in fantastic form and, in my view, was the right man to lead our challenge in the singles. Sam agreed, and we put him at the top of our order of play, effectively nominating him as Europe's No.1, our standard-bearer on this decisive day. Monty responded by doing everything we could have expected.

First and foremost, he played more phenomenal golf. Playing against Scott Hoch, he quickly turned the top line of the scoreboard blue and he made absolutely certain that it stayed blue. News of his success in the opening match was constantly posted all around the course, and it not only encouraged our other players but it whipped up the spectators and got them behind the team.

Monty blazed this trail of glory, and the rest of the European team followed in his path. As he completed his 5 & 4 victory over Hoch, he provided the crucial first push of the stone and effectively challenged our guys to keep it rolling. Bernhard Langer was equal to the task. So steady under tremendous pressure, he clinically took control of the match against Hal Sutton, his fellow 44-year-old, and efficiently closed out an emphatic 4 & 3 win.

Two rows of the scoreboard had turned blue and,

with cheers erupting around the course, the news got better.

Padraig Harrington moved one hole up on Calcavecchia, then another, and another. Our top-loaded tactics seemed to be working like a dream. The Irishman eventually won his match 5 & 4 and, in a blur, we had sprinted into an 11–8 lead.

Sergio looked ready to add another point when he raced to a two-hole lead over Toms, and we were just starting to contemplate the total vindication of Sam's strategy. However, the American kept calm, was only one hole down with two to play, then pulled level at the 17th, won the 18th and walked away with the win.

'Garcia lost,' somebody told me out on the course.

'You're joking,' I replied.

This result placed a big red mark on the score-board, and it seemed to be flashing danger for us. Darren Clarke emerged with a valuable half from a tough duel with David Duval, but our lead had been cut to an edgy 11½–9½, and we were just starting to wonder, just a little anxiously, just a little nervously where we were going to find the three points we still needed for victory.

Everything was happening so fast.

I was rushing around the course, jumping from one match to the next, keeping Sam, Mark and Joakim up to date with what I was watching and taking in whatever they were saying. We were making suggestions to each other, plotting and planning, all the while trying to keep our balance on an emotional rollercoaster.

One moment, we were up; the next moment, we were down. One of our guys would win a hole, and we would be sitting pretty; then an American would sink a putt, and things would start to look dodgy again. It was exhausting – and invigorating.

Amid this frantic activity, Thomas Bjorn continued serenely on his way. The Dane took the lead against Stewart Cink with a birdie at the fifth, held his advantage and secured the win by 2 & 1. When he had been hugged by his team-mates at the 17th green, we turned to the scoreboard and looked for two more points.

Where were they?

Four and a half points was a decent return from the first six matches of the day, but the Ryder Cup was still in the balance, and we needed two or three guys playing down the order to emerge as the match-winning heroes. It seemed a tall order.

Westwood was trailing, Fasth was one up, McGinley was one down, Fulke was battling, Price was level with Mickelson, and Tiger was leading Parnevik. Out of the six matches still on the course, we were up in one, all square in one and down in four.

We needed two more points.

Lee Westwood fought hard but, when he lost to

Verplank, our attention switched to what was becoming an extraordinary contest between Phil Mickelson, the widely admired world No.2, and Phillip Price, then ranked 119th in the world. Leading up to the event, there had been some unfair press speculation that the Welshman should step down because of his relatively poor form. That was ridiculous, and, when it really mattered, he proved his worth.

It was early in the afternoon when we noticed that Pricey had gone one up against the American superstar. We were pleased, but dared not contemplate the lead would last. Then, the underdog won another hole, and moved two ahead. The man from Pontypridd had picked a great day to play the round of his life.

I was following the match in a buggy and became aware of more and more spectators joining the galleries. By the time we all reached the 16th tee, there were thousands lining the fairway and Phil, heroically, was two holes up with three to play.

As courage overcame nerves, he pounded another fine drive down another fairway, and then sent another fantastic iron into the heart of the green. Mickelson made his par, and left the Welshman standing over a 25-foot putt for birdie, and the match.

Against certain people's predictions, Pricey sank the putt and posted a sensational 3 & 2 victory. Out of the blue, he had put his match into blue. Running across to congratulate him, I could not have been happier for my fellow Welshman: his success seemed to embody the best battling qualities of European golf and it was no more than many years of hard work deserved.

Phil's success took us to 13½ points, just one point away from winning the Ryder Cup and, amid gathering delirium, a group of us rushed from the 16th green forward to the 18th fairway where Niclas Fasth was one up with one to play against Azinger.

The match seemed to be hurtling towards a conclusion. Within barely 15 minutes, our emotions had swung from genuine anxiety to the brink of glorious celebration. I joined Sam at the 18th green, and said we were nearly there. He didn't reply. We were both so full of feeling and excitement, words seemed useless.

Niclas only had to halve the last and, when Azinger hooked his approach into a greenside bunker with the Swede already on the green for two, we were virtually popping corks from the bottles of champagne that had been discreetly brought to hand. Everyone had assembled behind the 18th: players and their wives, members of the European management team, gathered on a grass bank, sitting and kneeling, crouching and squatting, all of us together, buzzing.

This was the moment!

Then, silence, followed by ecstatic American cheers.

Not for the first time on the last hole of an event, Azinger had holed his bunker shot. Renowned for such heroics, he emerged from the sand, punching the air, his face contorted with delight and defiance in equal measure. The Americans had looked dead and buried, but now a great escape seemed possible.

Niclas had to be content with a half, which took us to a total of 14 points and meant we couldn't lose the match, but our aim had always been to win the Cup and a 14–14 draw would enable the US team to retain the trophy. We needed just another half from any of the three matches on the course but, after Azinger's miracle bunker shot, we were not taking anything for granted.

On cue, the stocky figure of Paul McGinley came into sight on the 18th fairway. He had just birdied the 17th and, after trailing Jim Furyk for most of the round, pulled level with one to play. Now, he needed a half at the last to secure our triumph.

Nobody should have been remotely surprised to find a smiling Irishman on hand to win the Ryder Cup for Europe. Thirteen years before, on this same 18th green at The Belfry, Christy O'Connor had launched the trend, and those of us who could remember the 1989 match reckoned the pin placing was almost identical; then, in 1997, Philip Walton achieved the same feat at Oakhill.

Now, history beckoned McGinley.

It would not be easy. The Ryder Cup still hung in the balance, several thousand spectators were packed around the 18th green and many hundreds of millions were watching on television. Under such pressure, nothing was going to be straightforward.

He managed a steady drive, then hooked his approach to the left of the green. Everything came down to this. All the planning, organising and effort led to this equation: with Furyk in the same bunker that Azinger had been in moments earlier, Paul would cover himself in glory and win the day for Europe if he could simply secure a half.

The Irishman's chip ran and bobbled down the hill, but came up short an agonising 11 feet from the hole, leaving him with an awkward left-to-right putt. Furyk needed to hole his bunker shot, just like Azinger, to win the hole, and he nearly did. The ball hit the hole and came to rest stone dead for a par.

Paul was just one putt away from covering the team in glory, and yet the match was so close that the consequences of missing could have been calamitous. Nobody could assist him. Paul had to sink that putt and, to his eternal credit, he made a smooth stroke and he did sink the putt.

In an instant, our kneeling, crouching group rose to their feet, arms outstretched, shouting. We had won.

All the pent-up tension and strain of three years' planning and three days of competition was unleashed in joy. Sergio skipped and danced, Sam Torrance softly wept beside the same green where he had softly wept 17 years before, and I felt fantastically happy for a team of which so little had been expected and yet, through courage and determination, had now achieved so much.

'Hold on, guys,' somebody said. 'Calm down.'

It was a great moment but, remembering how we had been so upset by US celebrations at Brookline, we had to show discipline and self-control. There were two matches to finish.

Pierre Fulke and Davis Love swiftly shook hands on a half, but it soon became obvious that Tiger Woods and Jesper Parnevik would play through to the end of their game. There followed a strange sort of hiatus: we had just won the Ryder Cup, but it was the world No.1 who moved uncomfortably into the spotlight.

Even in defeat, Tiger rightly wanted to conclude his match in a proper, professional manner but, when he took time over his putt at the 18th, there was giggling among the spectators. On the US Tour, the culmination of his final round invariably represented the triumphant climax of the week, but here, in a team contest that was already decided, it suddenly seemed irrelevant.

And as Tiger prepared to stroke his putt, a few ducks started to waddle up the hill from the water, and the crowd's giggling broke into laughter. The situation was just unfortunate.

Some people saw symmetry in these scenes because, only the week before, the greatest player in the world had seemed to cut the Ryder Cup down to size. After firing 65 in the first round of the $1m American Express

Championships at Mount Juliet in Ireland, he had said he could 'think of a million reasons' why that Amex tournament was more important than the famous team event.

These comments provoked criticism, much of it unfair because Tiger felt obliged to protect the interests of one of his sponsors, Amex. However, his subsequent suggestion that the team concept and the functions made it difficult for him to prepare in the way he did for an individual tournament further created the impression that he was not especially comfortable at The Belfry.

There was more: there were rumours that he seemed unhappy with the team clothing, using rubber bands to hitch up his sleeves and sometimes playing in different outfits to his team-mates. People started saying he was too 'big', too important to function within a team.

I don't agree at all. Great success and wealth makes Tiger an easy target, and perhaps he does prefer to do things his way rather than follow a captain's directions, but I have always been impressed by his attitude on and off the course. He may not have enjoyed the taste of defeat at The Belfry in 2002, but he will surely be smiling at the end of many Ryder Cups in the years ahead.

And all said and done, it should not be forgotten that, as proof of his class and quality, Tiger concluded his match with Jesper by conceding a testing four-footer for the hole and settling for a halved match.

Even when things were not going his way, he emerged with dignity.

The final margin of victory was 15½–12½ but, once again, the match had hung on a knife-edge and we were just relieved that fate had come down on our side. Curtis Strange and his players couldn't have been more sporting and, as the two groups of players walked to the closing ceremony, side by side, it was clear that the aura and reputation of the Ryder Cup had been restored.

Personally, I was knackered. My back was sore at the end of a week spent sitting on a buggy, and I appeared to have damaged my shoulder in all the punching the air with delight. So, feeling fragile, I cautiously joined the celebrations in the team room.

A few beers soon put me right, and the guys enjoyed the rest of the night. The spirit between the teams was outstanding, and we were pleased when Hal Sutton, the United States captain for 2004, came with Paul Azinger and David Duval to join our party. This was not an obligation; it was an outstanding gesture.

In fact, it was some time after two in the morning in our team room when David accurately summed up everybody's feelings. 'This Ryder Cup has revived my love for the game,' he said. We all knew what he meant. The competition had been fierce and serious, but it had been conducted with honour and integrity.

The players and management involved in the next

Ryder Cup, to be contested at the Oakland Hills Country Club, Michigan in 2004, have a hard act to follow. At the time of writing, I really don't know what role, if any, I will play in those matches.

I don't believe there is any greater thrill than actually playing in the matches, but the truth is I thoroughly enjoyed being involved in the Europe team management at The Belfry and, if asked, would not hesitate to accept a similar position again.

The European Ryder Cup Committee, the body charged with the responsibility of appointing the captain, have obviously done a great job in recent years: from Tony Jacklin, through Bernard Gallacher, Seve Ballesteros, Mark James and Sam, the last six captains have all won the respect of the players and been a success.

My experience, as a player eight times and as vice-captain in 2002, leads me to make a few observations.

The first is that, above all, the Ryder Cup captain must be an outstanding listener. This is not a situation where anyone, however gifted and inspired, can walk in and lay down the law. The team is invariably a blend of eager rookies and senior players, and the key for the captain is to draw on the experienced guys.

He should talk to them constantly, asking them how they feel, discussing strategy with them, listening to their views and making them feel they have a proper stake in the team. Then, so long as he has listened well, the players will happily accept his decision.

Sam perfected this art. He always appeared approachable and relaxed, talking to everyone as individuals, and he was firm enough to draw it all together and show the way forward.

Successive European teams have relied heavily on team spirit, and it is invariably the captain who must become the central pole in that tent. Simply put, he'll do this by drawing senior players around him, and he will do that by listening to them.

Second, in terms of making appointments, I reckon there is significant benefit in a policy of continuity, whereby the vice-captain succeeds the incumbent as captain. That might be an obvious thing for me to say, but the evidence is there.

Sam Torrance believes his experience of being vice-captain at Brookline in 1999 proved the perfect preparation for taking over the captaincy at The Belfry. The involvement with the team gave him a chance to get to know the players, understand what made them tick and generally get into the swing of things.

So, when he eventually took over as captain, he was able to develop his strategy on a firm foundation of knowledge. He was not a stranger in any sense, and he settled quickly.

By and large, such smooth, signposted transitions of authority have proved successful in every walk of life and, barring situations where things have gone so seriously wrong that a completely fresh start is required, continuity is desirable. This theory would appear particularly appropriate at an event such as the Ryder Cup where top players often hang around for a decade or more.

There is also something to be said for the idea that captains should step aside after one Ryder Cup. Sam resisted considerable pressure to stay on after winning at The Belfry, and said he thought somebody else should do the job at Oakland Hills.

His point was that a new man at the top brings new ideas and new emphasis, and keeps the team fresh. He also said that, with an increasing number of people who are obviously qualified and willing to accept the task, the honour should move around.

Lastly, most past and prospective captains would probably agree the system of selecting the European Ryder Cup team should be updated and reformed. At present, it is the top ten professionals on the European Ryder Cup Team Rankings, calculated on results in 12 months of events from the previous September, plus two wild cards nominated by the captain, who make up the 12-man team.

The flaw in this system is that a player who chooses to live in the US and play on the US Tour, rather than in Europe, or who mixes his time between the two, must rely on being a wild card to participate in the Ryder Cup, It seems wrong that such players, like Parnevik, should be penalised.

It has been suggested that future teams should be drawn first from the top five of a ranking system based on the European Order of Merit, then the next five highest Europeans on the Official World Golf Rankings plus two wild cards. This would appear a more equitable method of selection.

However, I would personally favour the introduction of a new, separate ranking table for the European Ryder Cup (ERC) team with points being earned at events played all over the world.

Such a league could either be run over a two-year period from the end of one Ryder Cup until the time of selection for the next, to ensure that the most consistently strong players make the team, or it could be run from September 2003 to August 2004.

ERC points would be calculated in the same way as points are allocated for the official world rankings, with every performance on every professional tour worldwide being weighted and valued. There would have to be a few adjustments – right now, a player performing reasonably well in every European event might just finish outside the points – but something like this structure can be a fair means of selection.

It could also provide a new revenue stream because there are certainly companies who would be keen to buy the naming rights to such a high-profile, potentially exciting league.

Whatever happens, the 35th Ryder Cup matches will be played at Oakland Hills in September 2004 and, even now, you can be sure the contest will be tense and close-fought. Happily, the future of European golf seems to be in safe hands. We have already seen youngsters like Justin Rose, Ian Poulter, Bradley Dredge, Paul Casey, Luke Donald, Nick Dougherty and others making a mark on Tour and, all being well, they should provide the foundation of a competitive team for years to come.

The 2006 Ryder Cup matches are to be played in Ireland, and it goes without saying that the locals will provide outstanding support and exceptional hospitality. The *craic* will be amazing, and not only if another Irishman holes the winning putt.

Naturally, I was delighted by the decision that the 2010 Ryder Cup will be staged in Wales, played on the Wentwood Hills course at the Celtic Manor resort, near Newport. I appeared in an exhibition match against Mark James to mark the opening of the par-72 course in May 1999, but my connections with Celtic Manor extend right back to the early 1990s when I took a position as the touring professional attached to the club.

The parkland course, designed by Robert Trent Jones junior, will be revamped for the Ryder Cup, with five new holes being added and two more being redesigned to create a superb venue for match-play competition. I'm sure the prestigious event will provide an enormous, sustained boost to golf in Wales.

In fact, I am certain the Ryder Cup, as a whole,

will continue to stimulate interest and growth in the game of golf throughout Europe and the rest of the world. Its public image was restored by events at The Belfry in 2002, and the event is now widely recognised as one of the world's premier sports events. Personally, I am privileged to have played a role, and I am excited by the prospect of somehow being involved again.

CHAPTER FOURTEEN

A Game for Life

Growing crowds, increasing revenue, and escalating prize money: by any measure, professional golf is in excellent health. However, the greatest challenge facing the professional game is the introduction of new technology, and we need to find a solution.

The problem is simple: most of the world's top golf courses were designed and set up for players driving between 250 and 280 yards, but recent advances in club and ball design, combined with improved levels of physical fitness, mean many of the top pros are now regularly hitting the ball between 290 and 320 yards.

In many ways, it has become a different game.

Bunkers originally created to make players think twice about hitting drivers off the tee are now being comfortably cleared with three-wood shots. The crucial balance between the demands of the course and the ability of the players – the essence of the game – is being lost as, all around the globe, classic courses are being made to look much too easy because so many of their long-established hazards and obstacles are being taken out of play.

Even at Augusta National, tees have been pushed back and bunkers repositioned to maintain the Masters as a true challenge for the top players and their newfangled equipment; other Committees are also having to spend many millions revamping their golf courses to present a relevant test in the modern game.

Many believe universal regulations should be introduced, restricting the composition and design of all equipment, something like the rules that regulate the design of cars in Formula One motor racing. I believe we have reached a point where this has become necessary. Restrictions could be imposed on equipment used by the pros, and they need not apply to amateur players.

The only alternative is for golf courses to be adjusted, and it seems inevitable that such alterations would be bad news for older players, who are no longer physically equipped to hit the ball as far as the younger guys. The danger is that the game will become a beauty contest for big-hitters, with older players being taken out of the equation as easily as the old bunkers.

My view is that it remains possible to produce courses that present a fair, entertaining test to every type of golfer, and I have been able to convert these ideas into reality through my increasing involvement in the business of golf course design. This has proved an enjoyable challenge for me and I have found there is nothing quite so invigorating as being challenged to conceive and create a new course out of an undeveloped piece of land.

To date, I have designed two courses, one in East Sussex and one in China, with others in Ireland and Asia in progress. In each of these projects, my guiding principle has been to produce something that challenges players of all abilities and ages, and holds the golfer's interest from the first tee through to the 18th green.

The Woosnam designed course at Dale Hill, in Ticehurst, was opened in September 1997, and appears to have been very well received. The par-four ninth is perhaps typical: a sharp dogleg to the right with a stream running in front of an elevated green but, to give everyone a chance, the back of the green is tiered into a grassed amphitheatre. So, a low handicapper has a tough shot to get close to the pin, but the weekend golfer can still have fun too.

Whatever happens, no tinkering with the regulations or with the course will reduce the mental examination. Nobody is going to win a Major tournament unless they can manage the psychological pressures, unless they can learn to avoid choking when they're ahead, unless they can remain unruffled by a mistake and much more. New technology may have a big effect on golf, but it can't control what happens in a golfer's head.

The game is indeed seriously threatened by the introduction of new technology, but the danger is not fatal.

More generally, golf grows from strength to strength, clearly delighting millions of spectators week after week, and providing a decent career to those who play the game for a living and succeed at the top level. However, nothing is perfect in this world, and there are areas of the game's structure that need reform.

Four Major championships – the Masters, US Open, the Open Championship and US PGA – continue to thrive as the four premier events in the game, each with its own atmosphere and history; and, whatever the marketing men say, however much money is offered elsewhere, these four will remain pre-eminent.

The Open Championship, often known as the British Open, is an extremely special week in the calendar, set apart for many pros by its unique mood and a sense of continuing history.

Every player dreams of seeing his own name engraved on the base of the famous claret jug, along-side many of the great players of the past . . . Vardon, Braid, Hagen, Jones, Locke, Thomson, Player, Palmer, Nicklaus, Trevino, Watson, Ballesteros, Faldo and Woods. It remains perhaps the most coveted prize in our game.

However, I strongly believe the aura and standing of the Open Championship would be enhanced if the Royal and Ancient Golf Club created a permanent home for this much-loved event.

Ever since Prestwick staged the first 12 championships in the years between 1860 and 1872, the Open has moved on a strict rota around leading British golf courses, a sporting gypsy, forever on the road. Tennis has Wimbledon; football had, and will soon have again, Wembley; rugby has Twickenham; golf has a rota.

The effect is that the leading players in the world arrive at the Open every year uncertain of what they are going to find; and, as time has passed, constantly changing conditions for the event have resulted in a constantly changing reputation.

For example, many thought Carnoustie was set up too tough for the 1999 Open, but then many said St Andrews played relatively easy at the 2000 Open. Weather always plays a huge role, but the rota system does not promote consistent quality.

In contrast, every April, the golf world descends on Augusta, Georgia, where so much of the Masters' magic is wrapped up in the course on which it has been played since 1934.

While the Open endlessly packs up and moves on, the Masters gracefully resides in its own home. It is decorated with plants and flowers, embroidered with traditions... the Champions dinner on the Tuesday night, the Par Three tournament on Wednesday afternoon, the amateurs staying in the Crow's Nest at the top of the clubhouse, the presentation of the green jacket in the Butler Cabin.

And the players, the spectators and television audiences know what to expect; as the years pass, they become familiar with the 18 holes at Augusta, see how to read the greens and brace themselves as they approach Amen Corner. Every Masters champion has faced, and passed, almost exactly the same examination.

With this in mind, I would love to see the Royal and Ancient embrace the vision of a lasting home for the oldest championship in golf, a place where former champions can be honoured, a place that can live and breathe the venerable spirit of the Open, a place where time can stand still, in the very best sense.

Many people will propose the Old Course, St Andrews, as the outstanding candidate to become a permanent home. However, while this ancient seaside links will always be revered as the Home of Golf, there are many who point out the impracticality of keeping enormous crowds on the outside of a course.

My own view is that the Open deserves a brand new course of its own, specially designed to challenge the superstars of the 21st century (and their equipment), rather than a course that was set up to test the finest players of the 18th or 19th centuries. The prospect is tremendous: a course that properly honours legends of the past and is equipped to challenge the legends of the future.

Of course, there will be many traditionalists who regard these suggestions as heresy, but I believe they are absolutely consistent with the spirit and ideals of the 22 original members of the society, who assembled in 1754 to advance the standing of their game and eventually evolved into the Royal and Ancient.

Perhaps the 250th anniversary would be an ideal opportunity for the R&A to make the decision that its cherished Open Championship will have a beautiful and permanent home of its own.

As for my own future, I can't see myself ever straying too far from golf. With a growing number of special age-group events, the Seniors Tour, the Ryder Cup and various course design projects, the game will remain central to my life for many years to come.

The day when I eventually decide to stop competing on the European Tour will be sad, insofar as I will be saying goodbye to a routine that has been so much of my life for so long. The upside is that I will suddenly be free to enjoy all those things I have missed during my professional career, and to start repaying one enormous debt that has stacked up over the years.

What have I missed? Glen and the children, obviously; my friends, home life, Glen's Shepherd's Pie, Welsh Spring lamb served as a Sunday roast with all the trimmings etc.

And the debt to be paid? That is to Glen, for looking after our children while I've been away playing golf, being at home for them, taking them everywhere, for understanding the demands of my job and supporting me in my ambitions. She has received great support from many friends, most particularly from my sister-in-law, Magretta Clarke, who lived with us for many years and has loyally helped me as my administrative secretary in Oswestry.

Since we have had to spend so much time apart, Glen and I have so much to do together. We want to travel, perhaps to spend time at game parks in Africa and certainly to tour around Australia, a country we both enjoy. I have played golf all over the world, but have never had time to see beyond the hotel and course, so it will be fun to discover new places, travelling with Glen.

In due course, it must be for others to assess my career and judge my performance. For my part, I hope history will be able to reflect kindly upon somebody who wasn't changed by fame, who always tried his best, who was always up for a laugh, who smiled often, who proved a loyal friend, a caring, respectful son, a loving husband, a devoted father . . . and someone who could hit a one-iron.

Career Statistics

Tournament victories (European Tour)

	Year
Cisco World Match Play Championship	2001
Volvo PGA Championship	1997
Volvo German Open	1996
Scottish Open	1996
Heineken Classic	1996
Johnnie Walker Classic	1996
Dunhill British Masters	1994
Air France Cannes Open	1994
Trophee Lancome	1993
Murphy's English Open	1993
European Monte Carlo Open	1992
Torres Monte Carlo Golf Open	1991
Fujitsu Mediterranean Open	1991
Epson Grand Prix of Europe	1990
Suntory World Match Play Championship	1990
Bell's Scottish Open	1990
Torres Monte Carlo Open	1990
Amex Mediterranean Open	1990
Carrolls Irish Open	1989
Panasonic European Open	1988
Carrolls Irish Open	1988
Volvo PGA Championship	1988
Suntory World Match Play Championship	1987
Trophee Lancome	1987
Bell's Scottish Open	1987
Cespa Madrid Open	1987
Jersey Open	1987
Lawrence Batley International TPC	1986
Scandinavian Enterprise Open	1984
Silk Cut Masters	1983
Ebel Swiss Open	1982

Prize Money	Round Scores				Final Score
£250,000	n/a	n/a	n/a	n/a	n/a
£183,340	67	68	70	70	-13
£116,660	64	64	65	n/a	-20
£80,000	70	74	70	75	+1
£93,339	69	71	65	72	-11
£100,000	69	68	69	66	-16
£108,330	71	70	63	67	-17
£50,000	72	70	63	66	-17
£91,500	64	70	68	65	-13
£100,000	71	67	65	66	-19
£73,475	66	65	66	64	-15
£68,928	67	66	61	67	-15
£66,600	70	71	71	67	-5
£66,660	65	67	67	72	-13
£100,000	n/a	n/a	n/a	n/a	n/a
£66,660	72	62	67	68	-15
£59,158	66	67	65	60	-18
£66,660	68	68	74	n/a	-6
£43,783	70	67	71	70	-10
£50,000	65	66	64	65	-20
£38,690	68	70	70	70	-10
£50,000	67	70	70	67	-14
£75,000	n/a	n/a	n/a	n/a	n/a
£50,000	65	64	69	66	-24
£33,330	65	65	66	68	-20
£27,500	67	67	69	66	-19
£16,160	68	67	72	72	-9
£21,660	71	71	66	69	-11
£22,779	71	70	69	70	-4
£16,660	68	69	67	65	-15
£10,085	68	68	66	70	-16

Tournament victories (other)

1997 Hyundai Motor Masters (S.Korea)

1991 USF&G Classic (USA), Masters Tournament (USA), PGA Grand Slam of Golf (USA)

1988 Million Dollar Challenge (Sun City), Welsh Pro Championship

1987 Hong Kong Open

1986 '555' Kenya Open

1985 Zambian Open

1982 Cacharel Under-25 Championship

1979 *News of the World* Under-23 Match Play Championship

European Order of Merit

	Total earnings	Official earnings	Final position
2002	£560,847	£381,812	34
2001	£773,427	£520,915	18
2000	£430,263	£330,670	24
1999	£270,830	£269,367	26
1998	£282,853	£237,571	20
1997	£601,851	£503,563	5
1996	£703,936	£650,424	2
1995	£127,045	£90,107	65
1994	£371,266	£273,265	12
1993	£583,900	£501,353	3
1992	£447,573	£281,407	11
1991	£421,453	£257,434	8
1990	£737,978	£574,166	1
1989	£303,969	£210,101	6

	Total earnings	Official earnings	Final position
1988	£270,674	£234,991	4
1987	£439,075	£253,717	1
1986	£148,467	£111,799	4
1985	£153,605	£82,235	4
1984	£68,126	£62,080	6
1983	£48,164	£43,000	9
1982	£48,794	£38,820	8
1981	£1,884	£1,599	104
1980	£3,481	£2,198	87
1979	£1,049	£934	122

Teams

Ryder Cup 1983, 85 (winners), 87 (winners), 89, 91, 93, 95 (winners), 97 (winners)

Alfred Dunhill Cup 1985, 86, 88, 89, 90, 91, 93, 95, 2000

World Cup 1980, 82, 83, 84, 85, 87 (individual winner & team winner), 90, 91 (individual winner), 92, 93, 94, 96, 97, 98, 2000, 2002

Four Tours World Championship 1985, 86, 87, 89, 90

Hennessy Cognac Cup 1982 (winners), 84

The Seve Trophy 2000, 2002 (winners)

Warburg Cup 2001, 2002

Miscellaneous
Low rounds and course records

60 (-9) Monte Carlo Open 1990

62 (-10) Benson and Hedges International 1985

62 (-10) Mercedes German Masters 1990
63 (-9) Dunhill British Masters 1994
65 (-7) Panasonic European Open 1987

Holes in One
European Tour – 2
Total – 11

Lowest 72-hole total on European Tour
258 (-18) Monte Carlo Open 1990

Most birdies in succession during European Tour event
8 – Benson and Hedges International, Fulford, 1985

Index